Mutual Funds
for the
Utterly Confused

Mutual Funds
for the
Utterly Confused

Paul Petillo

New York   Chicago   San Francisco   Lisbon   London
Madrid   Mexico City   Milan   New Delhi   San Juan
Seoul   Singapore   Sydney   Toronto

1 2 3 4 5 6 7 8 9 0   DOC/DOC   0 1 0 9 8

ISBN: 978–0–07–160018–7
MHID: 0–07–160018–3

This publication is designed to provide accurate and authoritative information in regard to the subject matter covered. It is sold with the understanding that the publisher is not engaged in rendering legal, accounting, or other professional service. If legal advice or other expert assistance is required, the services of a competent professional person should be sought.

> —*From a declaration of principles jointly adopted by a committee of the American Bar Association and a committee of publishers*

McGraw-Hill books are available at special quantity discounts to use as premiums and sales promotions, or for use in corporate training programs. To contact a representative please visit the Contact Us pages at www.mhprofessional.com.

To Bon,

The woman who taught me how to be content.

And special thanks to Knox, Pattie, and Alice. Without their help, this book would not be possible.

Contents

Introduction

◆◆◆◆◆◆◆◆◆◆◆◆◆◆◆◆◆◆◆◆◆◆◆◆◆◆◆◆◆◆◆◆◆◆◆◆◆

I Am a Fan

I am a fan of mutual funds. Ever since Bill Griffeth hosted *Mutual Fund Investor* on the old Financial News Network (now CNBC), I have been fascinated by the concept. Large groups of like-minded investors gathering together behind a like-minded manager, who was hired to bring us into the fold of Wall Street investing. I have been a fan of mutual funds since the days before the Internet, when the only information you had on who was who came from the newspaper, the quarterly reports that were published in the *Wall Street Journal*, or someone who knew someone who . . . you get the idea. Before the information age put fund information at your fingertips, you had to do your homework.

If you didn't have a broker, you had to call the fund family directly at its 800 numbers and wait for it to send the investment information in the mail. Imagine having to wait weeks before the prospectus arrived. And once it did, you were left to your own devices. These information-packed booklets were hard to read and difficult to comprehend; in addition, they were, at best, a look at where a fund had been, not where it was now.

That was the heyday of mutual funds. The field was much narrower, and the best stood out. People like Peter Lynch (who managed the Fidelity Magellan Fund from 1977 to 1990, during which time the fund's assets grew from $20 million to $14 billion), Sam Islay (managing partner of Orbimed Advisers), David Dreman (chairman of Dreman Value Management), J. Mark Mobius (emerging-markets guru and fund manager for Templeton Worldwide), William Gross (manager of Pacific Investment Management's Total Return fund, the world's largest bond fund and fifth largest mutual fund), John Bogle (founder of the Vanguard Group), Jeff Vinik (Vinik Asset Management), Kenneth Heebner (cofounder of Capital Growth Management), and Bill Berger (deceased founder of Berger Associates), some of whom are still around and some of whom have since retired, were investment rock stars.

Many of the firms they worked for are no longer around: Dean Witter, Scudder, and Smith Barney have all been absorbed into larger fund families. Mr. Griffeth wrote a book called *Mutual Fund Masters* that profiled these and other fund managers who, at the top of their game, created wealth for everyday investors who knew only a fraction of what these money titans knew. And that was why they were hired.

I am still a fan of mutual funds all these years later. However, I will warn you right at the onset that at some places in this book, that hero worship may seem to have worn somewhat thin. There was a time when mutual funds and the people behind them were not at all like us. They were cool and calculating, informed and smart, willing to take risks based on the individual fund's focus. They made decisions based on the long term even if they were in the business of making short-term moves. In other words, they were true investors. And this is why they succeeded. Some of them failed at times, but hindsight and history have elevated each of them to hall of fame status.

Then, and it is difficult to say exactly when this happened, mutual fund managers became more like us. They began to worry as the field grew, with new funds offering more specific investment objectives. New fund families began to spring up everywhere, with these new entrants apparently believing that if they could imitate those past successes, they could also attract millions of new investors and their dollars. It all seemed to happen very quickly.

In that earlier period, I was a fan of mutual funds because they provided five basic concepts to investors: diversification (the ability to buy large baskets of stocks and/or bonds), professional management (which could be a person, a group of individuals, or a computer running an algorithm designed to invest based on strategy), clarity (the investors knew what the fund was focused on and thus, more or less, what they were buying), efficiency (because these funds had access to vast amounts of information, they could make clear and unemotional decisions based on certain criteria and do so in the most profitable manner for the shareholder), and convenience (these investments were easy to buy and easy to track, and, most important of all, they saved the individual investor the time it takes to sift through vast amounts of research material to make a single investment).

But how could you convince the average Main Street investor that this was a good idea, that this sort of group investment was the best of all possible worlds? What would convince someone like you or me to get involved in our investment futures and embrace the culture of mutual investing? Change the tax code.

When the Employee Retirement Income Security Act of 1974 (ERISA) was enacted, everything seemed to change. Although that piece of legislation was the turning point, the process was actually begun in 1961 by President Kennedy, who was concerned about the fate of the autoworkers at the Studebaker Corporation.

Until then, it had been widely assumed that when an employee worked for a company, his retirement was fully funded in return for years of loyalty. Employees provided human capital in the early years of their employment, and the company would provide them with retirement capital when they were older. However, when Studebaker closed its doors, it disclosed that it had not fully funded its pension plan, and as a result, more than two-thirds of the employees received a fraction of what they expected or, worse, nothing at all.

By 1975, the first individual retirement account was created. It allowed workers to safeguard their own futures by permitting them to put money away for their retirement and deduct the amount of that investment from their gross income. This had the net effect of lowering their tax bill and, by giving them the opportunity to invest in their future, took some of the pressure off the pension plans run by companies.

There were restrictions on these new IRAs. At first, only employees without pensions were eligible to contribute. Those annual contributions were limited to 15 percent of pay or a maximum of $1,500. Several years later, the program was expanded to allow for increased eligibility and contributions.

In August 1976, the Vanguard 500 Index Fund was created. This "benchmark" index, which attempted to purchase all of the stocks tracked by the Standard & Poors 500 Index, a list of the largest companies trading on the U.S. exchanges, gave this new breed of investors a very low-cost, incredibly easy-to-understand investment strategy.

Then the most significant change took place: Subsection (k) of Section 401 of the Internal Revenue Code was added. It was originally intended to allow executives to participate in profit sharing at the companies they worked for, but, thanks to the diligence of Ted Benna, who worked at an employee benefits company in Philadelphia, it created a new wrinkle in retirement savings. It also signaled the death knell for the pension plan, giving employees more control over their retirement savings.

The real beneficiary of these changes in the tax code was the mutual fund. It became the backbone of the retirement industry, opening doors for investors that had not been easy to access before.

The competition for those retirement dollars was fierce. The mutual fund industry grew exponentially, and with this growth came confusion. The five basic principles behind the mutual fund became blurred. Diversification now could be much narrower as new funds came to market, taking away a perceived level of safety; professional management was now focused on luring more and more investors, with the goal of outperforming other funds more for rankings than for the fiduciary responsibility; and in the process, some of the clarity was sacrificed. Efficiency, which also includes how the fund was taxed, seemed to go by the wayside as fund managers sought investor dollars. The only thing that actually improved was convenience. Now funds were easier to buy than ever. You simply enrolled in your company's retirement plan and you were set.

Only, that isn't the whole story. Mutual funds are a complicated investment tool that offers great opportunities to investors who understand what they are and how they function. As we go through the book, we will break down each of these components.

I also understand that many folks, when they pick up a book like this one, tend to turn directly to the topic that they are most interested in. But that would be unwise, for two reasons. First, we begin the book by discussing the markets in which funds invest. Then we progress from the safest types of funds to the more risky investments, some of which are relatively new, to indexes, and then to exchange-traded funds. And second, as we proceed, we will uncover certain points of interest and break them down, describing those important nuances. Although bond funds are different from equity funds, they share some common traits, and each one of those traits will be discussed as it is uncovered.

When we are finished with that dissection of the mutual fund, we will offer some solid suggestions on how to use these funds to your best benefit. This section might surprise some of you and will enlighten others.

As I said, I am a fan, and I want you to be one as well. If you can be a better-educated participant, you will be a better investor. This book will not only help you choose where to put your money, but give you some new insights that will make you less likely to overreact, less likely to be blindsided, and far more likely to be profitable.

Mutual Funds
for the
Utterly Confused

CHAPTER 1
The Great Investor Equalizer

◆◆◆◆◆◆◆◆◆◆◆◆◆◆◆◆◆◆◆◆◆◆◆◆◆◆◆◆

A s I type the first words of this book in 2008, the investment sky around me is falling. Huge pieces are coming down on the unsuspecting, of whom many are investors, some are mortgage holders, and more than a few are the very people who should have seen the problem coming: bankers. People don't know whether to run or to stay in one place. It's like dodging raindrops. You know you will get wet, but will you get less wet if you run?

Writing a financial book when Wall Street, the economy, and the stock market seem to be imploding is actually an excellent opportunity that I would be remiss to pass on. It's June 20, and although you won't have this book in your hands for quite a while, by which time the downturn will have already taken hold (and perhaps will still be going on), the situation gives someone like me the unique opportunity to look at two mindsets in the same frame.

It is extremely difficult to talk about bear markets when things are good. Bull markets tend to dull the senses. That can't be changed; it's human nature. Bull markets make us believe that anything is possible, and if that is the case, risk can basically be left out of the equation. The slow fall from the top begins long before the bull market reaches its all-time highs. Once the idea that every investment is a win-win situation takes hold and the thinking becomes that you can do no wrong, the market is always expanding upward, and the risk of riding it to the end is now negligible, the stage is set for yet another bubble.

But that period of time when your hopes and dreams are pinned to something, whether it is the stock market or your house, is a truly wonderful time. It becomes a memorable moment that gives you a sort of aphasia. You know the words to the song, but you don't hear the meaning.

So, at this point in time, we can all conclude that our portfolio, if we have one, has taken a hit. Because we are fragmented investors, we probably own a mutual fund in one place or another. Even if you personally have somehow managed to avoid the embracing atmosphere of mutual fund investing, you are in all likelihood only once removed from a mutual fund investor.

If you participate in a retirement plan where you work, you have funds working toward that magical day in the near or distant future. You may have been enticed into opening an individual retirement account (IRA) when you were younger, perhaps prompted by a well-meaning relative who understood better than you did the importance of investing young. Or maybe you use them to park money in between investment strategies, during times of sudden windfalls, or simply because you heard somewhere that having a mutual fund was a good thing—easier than the stock market because all of the stock market's angst is tempered.

The Bubble . . . Again

The truth about bubbles was uncovered by Italian physicist Carlo Marangoni and is largely based on the work of American theoretical physicist Joshua Willard Gibbs. By discovering the effect of surface tension on the outside layer of a bubble, he was able to tell which additions to a liquid made the bubble stronger or weaker. Soap, he found out, actually stabilized the surface tension rather than strengthening it, which was the common assumption before he published his paper on the subject in 1865.

The first days of 2008 were not good for the markets. In the first 12 trading days, the stock market lost ground on 7 out of 12 trading days, and 5 of them had triple-digit drops. On Martin Luther King's birthday, the overseas markets realized what was happening in the United States. If the consumer was removed from the equation by a recession, then who, if anyone, would buy the goods that so many overseas companies had for sale? Those markets plummeted.

And, as can be expected in these kinds of volatile times, those sudden drops were immediately followed by equally—sometimes unexplainable—sudden surges.

The Dow Jones Industrial Average, which between you and me doesn't really mean anything to a mutual fund investor, had lost nearly 7 percent as of January 25! The S&P 500, which, as many of you know, has been the index of choice since John Bogle successfully marketed the first of his index funds, had fallen 7.75 percent over the same period, while the Nasdaq [also offered as an index fund with ticker symbol QQQQ and sold as an exchange-traded fund (ETF) on the American Stock Exchange] had lost much more, nearly 11 percent of its value, which was already depleted after a slide at the end of 2007. Those numbers may mean little in the coming days, weeks, months, or even years. They are simply an illustration of what can happen and how quickly it can transpire.

Meanwhile, the economy was beginning to feel the pressure from housing foreclosures, past, present, and yet to come. People stopped spending, and businesses began to falter. New orders for goods failed to materialize, and the unemployment rate began to climb. Things slowed down. By the time this book is published and for quite a while afterward, people will talk about why these things happened, whether what was used to fix them worked as well as it should have, and what can we do to prevent them from happening again. And then we will forget about it.

There is some pleasure even in words, when they bring forgetfulness of present miseries.

Sophocles

People are like that, which is why the conversation about the reasons for this particular economic hiccup in 2008 will be timeless. It is a lesson in risk.

Because we live in a global marketplace, the actions of other global economies exert a certain force as well. There was a time when the force was largely an American birthright. No longer.

The way the global marketplace has worked in this century so far does not bode well. Countries sell goods and service to other countries. When one country sells more than it imports, a surplus is created. The excess money that the country receives will need to go somewhere. Some countries give it back to their people in the form of new development projects, lower taxes, improved working conditions, and better services. But that can only last so long. Too many handouts can have a reverse effect on an economy as well.

Learning from the
World's Mistakes

So the excess cash is invested. Smart investors look for the best return with the least amount of risk, and countries with boatloads of money are no different.

Consider what happened in Mexico in 1994. According to Francisco Gil-Diaz, general director of Avantel, S.A., and former vice governor of the Bank of Mexico, "Several factors contributed to facilitate the abundance of credit: (1) improved economic expectations; (2) a substantial reduction in the public debt; (3) a phenomenal international availability of securitized debt; (4) a boom in real estate and in the stock market; and (5) a strong private-investment response." Sound familiar?

He continued, "Poor borrower screening, credit-volume excesses, and the slowdown of economic growth in 1993 turned the debt of many into an excessive burden. Nonperforming loans started to increase rapidly."

How do I survive an economic downturn?

The Small Business Administration answered this question more than 20 years ago. It offered a 14-point checklist, and many of these points apply to your own household economy as well. It suggested that the first things the owner of a small business should do are "1. Watch your inventories carefully" and "2. Monitor your cash flow." These actions are contrary to what the economy as a whole needs if it is to recover, and this is why the response to many downturns is sudden relief packages such as cash handouts, much like those offered by President George W. Bush in 2001. Statistics prove that most people do spend the money, but there is little evidence that the additional money drives the economy any faster than if it had not been distributed at all.

The SBA also suggests

> 3. Separate the "nice to do" from the "have to do," and eliminate nonessential expenses as much as possible. Ask yourself, is that activity necessary? If not, don't do it.

> Also consider cutting personal spending.

On a personal level, where economic upheavals are very real, this is good advice, but once again, saving money never got any economy moving again.

But in survival of the fittest, we look inward at how we are doing, not really trusting that, even if prompted, the other guy will begin spending as well. The fourth point on the list addresses this thinking: Reduce or stretch out debt, and build up your capital reserves.

(The SBA's advice, especially if you have or are thinking about starting a small business, is timeless and can be found at http://www.sba.gov/gopher/Business-Development/Success-Series/Vol4/tips.txt.)

What happened in Brazil in 1999 was a bit different. This time, instead of global investors lending money to facilitate economic growth, as they did in Mexico, they instead bought the Brazilian currency, the real. Currency speculation, a topic for another place and time, is influenced by global sentiment. If people suspect that there is value with limited risk, the money piles in.

Satya Gabriel wrote the following on January 14, 1999:

> The world's attention has now turned to the eighth largest economy in the world. Brazil's economy generates twice the value of products and services as Russia, accounts for over half of Latin American output (whose consumers and firms buy 20 percent of U.S. exports, totally about 115 billion dollars), and has the potential to do significant damage to the earnings of many American firms, if the current crisis results in a collapse in corporate and household spending in Brazil.

What happened in Argentina is also worth noting. Argentina's problem is the result of its highly literate populace, wealthy agricultural base, numerous natural resources, and continuing inability to live within its means. Beginning in 1945 and continuing until the early 1970s, when it borrowed heavily from banks and private institutions, the Argentine government fought inflation, a phenomenon of rising prices that begins with rising costs of manufacturing. At first, the government simply issued money to cover its growing deficits and then, turning to overseas creditors, borrowed money.

This surge of huge amounts of capital from one hot country to another made its way through several emerging markets, including Thailand and Indonesia.

Fast-forward to the American economic landscape of 2008, where global investors had been helping banks by buying loans the banks had made that were, for lack of a better phrase, not worth the paper they were printed on. Once the problems with those loans were recognized, the investors that were holding them and that had bought them as bundled baskets of nearly risk-free profit had to write them down.

But American consumers had spent the money that was given to them through mortgages with great abandon. Everywhere, American dollars were flowing into overseas coffers. And then these smart investors loaned it right back to us. Until we could no longer pay the bill. Pop!

The vulnerability of the over-extended American consumer can hardly be taken lightly. That could well be a big problem for the rest of a U.S.-centric global economy.

Stephen Roach

Although less like a bubble and more like a balloon circling the room after you untied the knot, the air rushed out of what had been, just months before, a bullish economy that could see no worries on the horizon.

Out of the Line of Fire

Mutual funds do not provide a safe haven from events of this kind. They provide a *safer* haven. By their nature, they invest broadly, whether they are actively managed or indexed, and because of that "spreading of risk," they represent something that is hard to pass on. Call it a buddy system. Call it strength in numbers. The mutual approach to investing, often in places that are fraught with risk and just as often in places that are not, should appeal to all levels of investors.

In the next several chapters, we will discuss the different types of mutual funds. Because of the opportunity to discuss them in parallel—what is good during a bear market and what is good during a bull market—we will not try to pinpoint an exact moment in time. Doing that would serve the advertising and marketing arm of the industry, as every ad touts how well a particular fund did. Instead, for each type of fund discussed, we will list some of the best, some of the worst, and some that are immune to what is happening at any given moment. This sounds like a tall order—and it is.

CHAPTER 2
A Safe Haven(?)

◆◆

The average person faces several problems when she tries to wrap herself around physics. One of these is superposition. This odd event suggests that, at the subatomic level, a particle can be in several different places at the same time, and that as long as you don't check to see if this is true, it will stay that way. Is it possible for your money to have the same principles applied to it?

As we begin the discussion of money market funds, we have to consider the impact of the financial events that burst to the surface at the end of 2007 and well into 2008. In short, once the Federal Reserve's plan to focus on inflation by using its power to adjust short-term interest rates was undermined by the fallout from the mortgage-backed securities market, money market mutual funds suddenly became a piece of overcrowded real estate.

Okay, so maybe the whole mess can't be explained "in short." It was a very complicated situation with so many backroom dealings that even people with a very close association with the industry were amazed not only by the depth of the eventual fallout, but mostly by the fact that they were caught unaware.

When you buy a house or refinance the one you are currently in, you can "buy" your loan from any number of sources—banks, home financing companies, credit unions, and so on. But because these institutions need to continue to lend money in order to make money, they sell your loan, bundled with other similar loans, to investors. Essentially, this creates liquidity, giving the bank the funds to continue to lend money. Things didn't always happen this way. There was once a time when your neighborhood bank continued to hold your mortgage, but this limited the amount of money that the bank could lend.

This type of debt was once considered to be a relatively safe investment. However, because laws in the United States allow mortgage holders to pay off their loans early, the actual income that an investor in a mortgage-backed security (hundreds of loans bundled together and sold with some handsome guarantees) might earn is unknown. In other words, this "safe" investment had some built-in risk. That risk was graded and blessed by credit rating agencies (which we will discuss throughout the book), but these agencies did not factor in the quality of the underlying loans or the possibility that large numbers of them might default—a much nicer word than *foreclose*.

Mortgage-backed securities seemed to be in a superposition. They seemed to be everywhere at once, and it was not until they were measured that they seemed to collapse before our very eyes. Once the Federal Reserve began raising short-term interest rates, an action that affects overnight loans to the largest banks, alarm bells concerning mortgages that had been bought with adjustable rates begin to ring. Not only were many adjustable-rate mortgages about to reach an adjustment point, but the cost of refinancing those loans was about to jump as well.

Adjustable-rate mortgages, or ARMs, as they are often called, have a fixed rate for a period that depends on how the contract is written. The rate is fixed for a certain period of time (three, five, seven, and sometimes even ten years), after which the rate is adjusted by an amount stated in the contract, but not exceeding an agreed-upon cap. The cap is a set rate; for the sake of our example here, we will use 12 percent as the highest rate to which the adjustable-rate loan can adjust. Sometimes only the interest on these loans was due during the first years of the contract, with payments of the principal being deferred. This is only an example of two of the most common and often most easily understood types of ARMs. Beyond this, ARMs are limited only by the creativity of the lender and the gullibility of the borrower.

	Fixed-Rate Mortgage	ARM	ARM, Interest only
Mortgage	$300,000	$300,000	$300,000
Interest	6%	5%	5%
Interest rate cap	—	12%	12%
Monthly payment	$1,798.65	$1,610.46	$1,250.00

Once interest rates rose and the credit markets began to tighten their requirements (making it harder for borrowers to refinance), more and more borrowers using these types of loans found that they were unable to pay their mortgages. Foreclosures began. Lenders stopped lending. Write-downs (a fancy word that means lowering the value of an asset on your books to what it is really worth, not what you had assumed it was worth) and write-offs started to dominate the headlines. Talking heads analyzed the situation end-lessly, not only on the investment channels (where investors had been enjoy-ing a robust bull market built on some financial assumptions about the consumer), but on the national news (which wondered if consumers would understand the breadth and depth of the problem) and the local news (which began reporting on homes in local neighborhoods that had, until recently, been selling at a record pace). And, because of all this, the yields on money market funds fell.

How did that happen? How did this relatively safe investment find itself worth less to its investors because somewhere out there, someone couldn't make his mortgage payment?

Superposition. While the net asset value of a money market fund is always a dollar, the yield, sometimes referred to as the interest, can rise and fall depend-ing upon the credit markets. If the credit markets falter, which usually means that the stock market will take a tumble as well, investors look for safe havens to park their cash.

Money market funds get flooded with new investors who are "sitting on the sidelines," and when that happens, the effect resembles a fat man in a bathtub: it just doesn't take that much water to stay wet. So the yield goes down, paying investors less.

It is as if your almost completely risk-free investment is almost income-free as well. But that happens.

There are basically two types of money market funds: taxable and nontax-able. People often confuse these funds with money market accounts and money market instruments. They are different not only in whom they appeal to and how they operate, but in what they invest in as well.

What's the difference between a money market fund, a money market instrument, and a money market account?

A money market account is issued by a financial institution and is insured by the Federal Deposit Insurance Corporation (FDIC). It may have certain rules that you must follow, such as a minimum balance or deposit, and often, restrictions on transactions. Commonly, the financial institution that issues the account gives you checks that you can use to draw from the account, but it usually does not allow you to write more than three checks a month. You can make physical withdrawals from the account, but there are often limits on them as well. A money market instrument acts like a money market fund, but it is usually priced out of the range of the average investor. It invests in high-quality credit and short-term debt. This debt can be in a variety of currencies, and the investment quality of the instrument depends on the rating the debt receives—the lower the rating, the higher the risk and, sometimes, the greater the reward. Money market instruments look for only the best available securities and are used by wealthy investors as a safe place to park their money. Investors who use brokerage-issued money market funds seek to do the same thing, but at a much lower entry point. Money market funds are low-risk investments that have a constant net asset value of $1.00; what changes is the yield. But risk is not completely absent and that NAV can fall if the fund does poorly. These funds invest in government securities, CDs (certificates of deposit), and other liquid (easily sold) investments.

Let's take a brief look at a money market instrument (DMIXX) managed by the Dreyfus Funds. (Information on a wide variety of mutual funds is given throughout the book, but this will be only snapshots of where these funds have been. It is not be intended as a sales tool for any fund, since neither I nor my publisher has any affiliation with these funds, except perhaps as a personal investment. If I have any such investment, I'll disclose it, and I promise to go out of my way to avoid any investment interest I might have.)

Dreyfus has been managing this money market instrument since April 28, 2005. It is full of the sort of short-term investments that such a fund might own, with what it bills as an effective maturity date of 68 days (based on information as of year-end 2007). The $1.7 billion under management has an average annual rate of return of 2.63 percent over a five-year period. The cumulative return was much higher. (The difference is discussed later in this chapter.) Let me finish explaining what Dreyfus does with this investment.

According to the Dreyfus Web site,

[The] Money Market Series invests in a diversified portfolio of high-quality, short-term debt securities, including:

- securities issued or guaranteed by the U.S. government or its agencies or instrumentalities

- certificates of deposit, time deposits, bankers' acceptances and other short-term securities issued by domestic or foreign banks, or their subsidiaries or branches

- repurchase agreements, including tri-party repurchase agreements

- asset-backed securities

- domestic and dollar-denominated foreign commercial paper and other short-term corporate obligations, including those with floating or variable rates of interest

- dollar-denominated obligations issued or guaranteed by one or more foreign governments or any of their political subdivisions or agencies

Normally, the Money Market Series invests at least 25 percent of its total assets in domestic or dollar-denominated foreign bank obligations. The Government Securities Series invests only in short-term securities issued or guaranteed as to principal and interest by the U.S. government and repurchase agreements, including tri-party repurchase agreements.

This fund also has an average expense ratio of 0.74 percent, which is about normal for this type of fund. But there are risks, and this is why money market instruments are usually used only by the very largest investors. Not only is there share price volatility, but the underlying assets could have different rates of interest payments. Although the base value of the share is $1.00, a lot of factors can cause an investor's money to gain ground or, in some cases, lose.

Once again, the Web site offers these warnings:

While each series has maintained a constant share price since inception, and will continue to try to do so, the following factors could reduce the series' income level and/or share price:

- interest rates could rise sharply, causing the value of the series' investments, and its share price, to drop

- interest rates could drop, thereby reducing the series' yield

- as to the Money Market Series, any of the series' holdings could have its credit rating downgraded or could default

- as to the Money Market Series, the risks generally associated with concentrating investments in the banking industry, such as interest rate risk, credit risk and regulatory developments relating to the banking industry

- as to the Money Market Series, the risks generally associated with dollar-denominated foreign investments, such as economic and political developments, seizure or nationalization of deposits, imposition of taxes or other restrictions on the payment of principal and interest

- a security backed by the U.S. Treasury or the full faith and credit of the United States is guaranteed only as to the timely payment of interest and principal when held to maturity; the current market prices for such securities are not guaranteed and will fluctuate

- the risk that a counterparty in a repurchase agreement could fail to honor the terms of its agreement

That's a lot of information, and most people don't get much beyond the first three bullet points. "Interest rates could rise sharply" and "interest rates could drop" refer to a phenomenon that we will discuss at length when we get to the bonds part of the book, but it works like this: if the price of a bond rises, the yield that the bond pays drops.

Picture an analytical balance scale, the kind with two trays that, when empty, are balanced evenly. When the bond price rises, the bond, which is always seeking to maintain equal or what is sometimes known as par value, gives some of itself to the yield side, weighing it down. When investors put money in, the bond price rises, so the yield that it needs to pay in order to keep things even needs to go down. When investors take money out, the yield rises. As I said, more on that a couple of chapters further on.

Because rating agencies are so heavily relied on to determine a security's creditworthiness, the third point, "any of the series' holdings could have its credit rating downgraded or could default," is looked at closely when an investment like this considers what to hold.

Does a money market instrument invest differently from a money market fund?

Essentially no. But there are some differences that are worth noting. Looking at what Dreyfus bills as its Basic Money Market Account (DBMXX), the only difference between the two investments, once again, according to the site, is that the money market fund does not invest in "dollar-denominated foreign bank obligations." The five-year average annual yield is 2.85 percent.

Measuring Performance

I promised you a description of average versus cumulative, and this is as good a place as any to give it. Determining your true return is often done, at least in the case of the mutual fund, once.

Performance is a measurable quantity. And while we will discuss performance throughout the book, we should look at some of the different ways to measure it.

We all like to see our investments grow. This is called *capital appreciation*. When we can put in a dollar—so to speak—and get more than that out of our investment, we consider that investment to have appreciated in value. A dollar invested that returns a 50 percent profit shows a capital appreciation of 50 cents. Our account is now worth $1.50. How that additional money got there is not important. It can come from a number of different sources, but the fact of the matter is, we made money. We had a return on our investment.

Sometimes the underlying investments in our funds, whether they are money market funds, bond funds, or equity funds, pay dividends or make interest payments.

But on the flip side, there are taxes. Taxes are a fact of life, and your invest-ments will always hold certain taxable obligations. When a stock that the fund owns is sold at a profit, this creates a taxable situation, and this is passed on to you. Then, when you sell the shares, you are taxed again. (This sounds worse than it is, and we will talk about it a little later on.)

So how do you calculate how well you are doing relative to how the fund says it did? While there are numerous references to average and cumulative returns, especially when a mutual fund makes its performance claims as part of its marketing material, these terms have totally different meanings.

To understand the benefits of owning an investment—in this chapter, a money market fund—it is important to understand which measurement is a better judge of future income and which is really just so much hype.

 The creative person is both more primitive and more cultivated, more destructive, a lot madder and a lot saner, than the average person.

Frank Barron, author

We have been looking at the funds in the Dreyfus family, so we will continue to its BASIC Fund for the sake of illustration.

Dreyfus BASIC Money Market Fund, Inc. (DBAXX)				
1 Year	3 Year	5 Year	10 Year	Since Inception
The Average Annual Total Return				
4.99	4.16	2.85	3.64	4.04
The Cumulative Total Return				
4.99	13.02	15.07	42.98	85.88

The difference between average and cumulative, it turns out, is not really the issue. Instead, why each one is important depends on why you are look-ing at it. When you look at the average annual return, you are curious about how your money would have done if you had invested in the fund for only a year.

The average calculated this way is often called the arithmetic average. Take the average returns for a given number of years, add them together, and divide them by the number of years. The fund discussed here had a one-year return of 4.99 percent. In that one year, your investment would have returned almost $5 on your initial investment.

But what would have happened if you had held the fund for a longer period? Once again, the fund had a one-year return of 4.99 percent. Let's use that year as year 1. In year 2, let's say the fund runs into a bit of trouble and has a negative yield of -1.01 percent, just to make it more interesting. (This posted loss is just for the sake of our example; we know that the net asset value of a money market fund almost never falls below $1, but there is the possibility that the underlying investments have done so poorly that they did not actually give the investor a positive yield.)

The math required to determine the average is really very simple. First, you need to take the return for any given year and convert it into a fraction. As a fraction, 4.99 percent would be 0.0499. The next year saw a loss of 1.01 percent. That fraction would be 0.0101.

When we get to the math part, we simply add that fraction to 1 or, in the case of our example, subtract the loss from 1.

First year: $1 + 0.0499 = 1.0499$

Second year: $1 - 0.0101 = 0.9899$

Now add the two numbers together:

$1.0499 + 0.9899 = 2.0398$

Now divide that number by the number of years, in this case, 2:

$1.0499 + 0.9899 = 2.0398 \div 2 \text{ years} = 1.0199$

To get the return expressed as a percentage, subtract 1 and multiply the result by the share price, which in our case is $1.00, times 100:

$$1.0499 + 0.9899 = 2.0398 \div 2 \text{ years} = 1.0199 - 1$$
$$= 0.0199 \times 100 = 1.99\%$$

If the two returns for those two years were instead multiplied together, the answer would be far different. From a cumulative standpoint, your investment would have been up 3.92 percent.

Let me explain, because this is a point of comparison that is really important only to investors who were actually *in* the fund in question. Nonetheless, if you were to take a cumulative number, you could find out what effect compounding has had on your investments.

I don't believe that anyone has written more words about mutual funds than John Bogle. He has written numerous books on the subject, many of which suggest that indexing is the be-all and end-all in the world of mutual fund investment. (My thoughts on that later.) Mr. Bogle, in a book published in 1993, simply titled *Bogle on Mutual Funds: New Perspectives for the Intelligent Investor*, wonders, "What is too often ignored in fund comparisons is how much total return is derived from capital appreciation and how much is derived from dividend income." Because all funds are essentially different in how they perform for the investor and why the investor holds them, it is important to be able to measure why they do things differently. The underlying investments in equity mutual funds are stocks, which, despite bumps in the road (which optimistic traders refer to as corrections) are always moving upward. How funds use that upward momentum is what makes one better than the other. That volatility can be either good or bad, positive or negative, based mostly on capital appreciation. A fund can be made less risky by adding more conservative investments—balanced funds can add bonds to equities, and bond funds can add higher-rated bonds to the portfolio to eliminate volatility. Money market accounts, because their net asset value does not change, have none of this to worry about. But when the return on the fund depends on income, as that on money market funds does, the volatility of the funds suddenly shifts. If you base performance on total return alone, equities will do better. But if you are basing your investment choice on return minus volatility, your choice might be totally different.

The first year's return of 1.0499 is then multiplied by the second year's return of 0.9899 to receive a total of 1.039236:

$$1.0499 \times 0.9899 = 1.039236$$

which when multiplied by a minimum investment of $100 would leave you with a rough estimate of how your money would have grown:

$$1.0499 \times 0.9899 = 1.039236 \times \$100 = \$103.92.$$

In this case, it would have grown to $104, or roughly 4 percent.

We now have a number that we can use to reach a total return. Your $100 purchase price did not change, but the value of your investment did. [In bond and equity funds, the share price (net asset value) changes as a result of capital appreciation and dividends or interest reinvested, so to determine how well you did, we need to do some fancier math.] Remember, this is purely illustrative. Most of this is figured out for you; it is just important for you to understand what it means. So hang in there for another minute or so.

 Appreciation is a wonderful thing. It makes what is excellent in others belong to us as well.

Voltaire

The equation to break down how much an investment held for a certain period earned involves a couple more steps and looks something like this: [($104 × 1.039236) − $100] ÷ $100 =, and works this way:

Let's take our fund's worth of $104 after two years and multiply it by our cumulative rate of return, or 1.039236:

$$(104 \times 1.039236)$$

then subtract the $100 or the share initial investment (in an equity fund, this would include reinvested dividends):

$$(104 \times 1.039236) - \$100 = 108.0804 - \$100$$
$$= 8.0804$$

Now divide that by 100:

$$[(\$104 \times 1.039236) - \$100] \div \$100 = 108.0804 - \$100 \div 100$$
$$= 8.0804 \div \$100$$
$$= 8.08\%$$

Which looks better: the annual rate of return of 1.99 percent or the cumulative rate of return of 8.08 percent?

In a money market fund, the capital does not change, but the return does. This becomes much more important to equity and bond investors when we discuss how to best allocate a portfolio toward the end of the book.

Taxable versus Nontaxable

At the top of every money market fund manager's list is the preservation of share price. Because the funds lack FDIC protection, giving investors a safe place to park their money, either while they wait for other opportunities to come their way or simply for short-term safekeeping, maintaining the nominal share value of a dollar is the cornerstone of their efforts.

 The surest route to breeding jealousy is to compare. Since jealousy comes from feeling less than another, comparisons only fan the fires.

Dorothy Corkville Briggs

Generally, the debt that a money market fund holds is short-term—so brief, in fact, that the underlying investments are often referred to as cash. But there are different types of money market funds, and they have different tax implications.

Government money market funds invest in securities issued by the U.S. Treasury or other agencies of the federal government. In many cases, the securities they invest in are limited to 90 days, but in the case of the American Beacon US Government Money Market Fund (AAUXX), much of the debt matures within 7 days.

According to the company, its investment style "utilizes a top-down approach, analyzing macroeconomic data to anticipate economic momentum shifts, inflationary trends, the shape of the yield curve and Federal Reserve policy."

When the company refers to macroeconomic data, it is focusing on the economy from a broad perspective rather than drilling down to look at specific events, such as how the price of oil affects the overall economic performance. Much like the Federal Reserve, the advisors for the fund are sensitive to much of the data that scroll across the business news reports. Inflation numbers are closely watched, mostly because of their effect on how short-term bond traders react. Briefly, because we will discuss this in more detail in the coming chapters, folks who invest in bonds and bond funds usually do so in anticipation of a steady stream of income over a specific time. If the outlook is grim, they want to lock in a certain yield, and bonds often give an indication of this kind of sentiment.

 While money market funds are not FDIC insured, they are regulated by the Federal Reserve using Regulation D. It states, "The Federal Reserve Act, as amended by the Monetary Control Act of 1980 (title I of Pub. L. 96–221) imposes Federal Reserve requirements on transaction accounts and non-personal time deposits held by depository institutions." (The full text of the regulation can be found at http://www.federalreserve.gov/Regulations/#d.)

The shape of the yield curve (discussed in Chapter 7) is also an indication of future income and is largely a comparative tool. Federal Reserve policy is also closely monitored. Words and phrases are parsed; markets discuss and project future interest-rate moves and listen for indications of interest-rate moves. While most of America fails to fully grasp the newsworthiness of the final decisions of these economic academics, money market fund managers do. They pay close attention to each Fed move and key in the information in hopes of providing the best possible return for their investors—all the while preserving the share value. The rest of us believe that all this has a direct effect on our mortgage and credit card rates.

This fund also focuses on increasing "returns by actively managing the duration and quality of the portfolio, consistent with historical relationships between economic growth, inflation and the direction of interest rates."

It does this by investing

in high-quality, U.S. dollar-denominated, short-term obligations with minimal credit risk, as determined by American Beacon. The Fund invests exclusively in obligations issued or guaranteed by the U.S. Government, its agencies or instrumentalities, repurchase agreements that are collateralized by such obligations and other investment companies that limit their investments to the foregoing securities. The average dollar-weighted portfolio maturity of the Fund will not exceed 90 days.

Whom does the federal government borrow from?

The federal government borrows by issuing Treasury bills (T-bills) and federal agency notes (Ginnie Mae or Freddie Mac). This differs from the way corporations borrow. Many corporations get short-term financing through IOUs, often called commercial paper, and banks, which in turn issue large certificates of deposit (CDs) and make agreements to repurchase government securities.

General-purpose or corporate money market funds also create a taxable event. These are the funds you will find inside your brokerage accounts, inside your defined-contribution plans at work, and as an offering of your mutual fund family.

Before we move on to tax-free money market funds, let's answer the question of which type is better. First, you need to determine the comparative yield, or what some call the taxable equivalent. The higher your tax bracket, the lower your taxable equivalent yield.

Because tax-free money market funds generally compensate for the tax factor in taxable money market accounts, it is important to determine which would better serve your short-term purposes.

Using the fund from American Beacon that we just discussed, which has, as of the time of this writing, a seven-day yield of 3.65 percent (and a thirty-day yield of 3.84 percent), and assuming that you have a tax bracket of 28 percent, we can come relatively close to determining the value of the fund.

The first part of the equation requires you to subtract your tax bracket from 100:

$$100 - 28 = 72 \text{ or } 0.72$$

The next step is to multiply that number by the yield:

$$0.72 \times 3.65 = 2.68\%$$

Now, suppose you parked a couple of thousand dollars in the fund for a couple of months. Before we even account for the fees charged by the fund's management—yes, someone has to pay for those managers hunting around for the investments with the best possible yield—was the taxable account a good place for your money for two months? Not likely.

Inflation, or the annual decline in the buying power of your money, is hovering around the 2.7 percent mark. This is what is known as the core inflation number, or the consumer price index excluding food and energy, which are considered too volatile from month to month to be measurable with any degree of accuracy. (The inflation rate including food and energy, as of year-end 2007, was 4.1 percent.) You can find updated information on the inflation rate at http://bls.gov.

Using the after-tax yield that we just calculated, you would have actually broken just slightly to the downside:

$$2.68\% - 2.70\% = -0.02\% \text{ (before fees)}$$

Money market funds have their purpose. They keep your money available (liquid), and they provide a safe haven during turbulent times or when you are indecisive about exactly where you plan on putting your investment dollars. But as an investment, they are not considered the best place for your cash. Some brokerages have a banking side, which, if it is online, often offers better interest rates than its brick-and-mortar brethren. But if you believe that the money will remain unneeded for more than a month or two, a certificate of deposit is by far the best way to go. Even though the rates are constantly changing, if you had invested in a CD at the time of this writing, you would have done far better—and without the fees. Here is a sample list of banks, their shortest CD offerings, minimum deposits, and the yield on those investments as they appeared on bankrate.com, by far the best aggregator of this type of information online. As you can see, you would have done far better in the short term investing in these instruments. But your money would have been tied up (illiquid) for the duration of the CD.

	Length of Term	Minimum Deposit	Annual Percentage Yield
GMAC	6 months	$500.00	3.76%
E-Loan	6 months	$10,000.00	3.76%
H&R Block Bank	6 months	$10,000.00	3.75%
Zion Bank	6 months	$1,000.00	3.64%
Element Financial	6 months	$50,000.00	3.55%

Note: These rates change daily; the above quotes were gathered on August 8, 2008.

Municipal money market funds offer the advantage of tax-free investing. There are actually three types of tax-free offerings. Those that gather debt securities from numerous municipalities across the country are exempt from federal taxes. Some funds focus on the municipalities of a particular state, making them exempt from state taxes as well as federal taxes for residents of that state. These are often referred to as double tax-free. Some funds go one step further and offer triple tax-free funds, using debt securities that are exempt from local, state, and federal taxes.

The performance of these funds takes the tax exemption into account. They generally offer a lower overall yield than their taxable counterparts. In other words, by eliminating the calculation for taxes, the true yield is easily found— at least the one that doesn't take the fees into account.

About those fees.

Let's take a look at the top five money market funds in the taxable category, their yields (as of January 28, 2008), and their expense ratios.

	7-day Yield, %	Minimum Investment	Minimum IRA	Expense Ratio, %
Vanguard Prime MF 800–662–7447 Ticker: VMMXX	4.55	$3,000	$1,000	0.32
Vanguard Federal MF 800–662–7447 Ticker: VMFXX	4.35	$3,000	$1,000	0.32
DWS Scudder MMF 800–621–1048 Ticker: KMMXX	4.21	$1,000	$500	0.44
Transamerica Premier Cash Reserve Fund 800–892–7587 Ticker: TPCXX	4.17	$1,000	$250	0.74
Fidelity US Govt Reserves 800–343–3548 Ticker: FGRXX	4.12	$2,500	$2,500	0.34

Of these five top-yielding funds in the taxable category, Transamerica Premier Cash Reserve Fund has the highest expense ratio. Let's figure out our true yield with this additional piece of information.

We know we have a 28 percent tax bracket. So:

$100 - 28 = 72$ or 0.72

$0.72 \times 4.17\% = 3.00\%$ actual yield (more than the core rate of inflation rate, but less than the inflation rate for all goods).

$1,000 (the fund's minimum investment) $\times 3.00\%$ (or 0.03) = $30

Now deduct the cost of running the fund.

$30 $\times 0.74\%$ (or 0.0074) = $0.22 with $29.78.

That may not seem like much, but every penny counts in this type of investment.

Let's take a look at the top five tax-exempt money market funds.

	7-Day Yield, %	Minimum Investment	Expense Ratio, %
Alpine Municipal MMF 888–785–5578 Ticker: AMUXX	3.10	$2,500	0.32
Vanguard Tax-Exempt MMF 800–662–7447 Ticker: VMSXX	3.03	$3,000	0.17
DWS Scudder Tax-Exempt Money Fund 800–621–1048 Ticker: DTBXX	2.86	$1,000	0.37
American Century Tax-Free MMF 800–345–2021 Ticker: BNTXX	2.74	$2,500	0.51
T Rowe Price Tax-Exempt Money 800–638–5660 Ticker: PTEXX	2.63	$2,500	0.50

Let's do the same calculations, only without the need to consider your tax bracket. Once again, we will pick the fund with the highest expense ratio, the American Century Tax-Free MMF (also using numbers as of January 28, 2008):

$1,000 $\times 2.74\%$ (0.0274) = $27.40

Now we deduct the cost of running the fund.

$27.40 × 0.51% (0.0051) = $0.14 or $27.26 remaining

The difference between taxable and tax-exempt funds has a greater impact as your tax bracket increases. Even at 28 percent, there is a noticeable difference in what you take home.

Taxable (at 28%) = $29.78

Nontaxable = $27.26

Difference = $ 2.52

We will continue to build on some of the topics discussed here—taxes, fees, and yield—as we take a look at fixed-income investing using bond funds. These come with a whole array of different options for investors and for those planning on using these instruments as a means of protecting capital and generating income in their later years (sometimes called retirement).

CHAPTER 3

The Collective Investment Scheme

A s fate would have it, Yousef Madjidzadeh, the author of a three-volume history of Mesopotamia and a leading Iranian authority on the third millennium BC, found something that he had been looking for since his readmission to Iran following a cultural thaw in 1997. Madjidzadeh was a focused man who was convinced that the ancient city of Jiroft was more than a way station in Iran's rich archeological past. He believed that the city was instead a renowned Bronze Age capital. The problem was, he couldn't prove it.

As fate would have it, a flash flood in 2000 removed much of the topsoil at the site, revealing not only thousands of previously unknown graves, but also the possibility that Madjidzadeh was right in his assessment of the city. And then he found something else.

In the Real World... Language existed long before early man put his paintbrush to a cave wall. But when writing first began to take shape around 9,000 years ago, it was used largely to keep track of commerce, determine the worth of a man's land, or determine how much beer a citizen might receive.

The piece, found in 2005 as the site closed shop for the winter, was remarkable. It contained an ancient script, quite possibly the earliest evidence of a 4,000-year-old writing system. It wasn't the oldest written evidence of man's attempt at literacy, but it was enough to allow Madjidzadeh to make the claim of literacy for Jiroft. He believes that the city is actually Aratta, a somewhat mythological place of great wealth and civilization. Although many believe that Aratta was in Azerbaijan, or perhaps Baluchistan, or even the Persian Gulf, the find could prove significant.

Madjidzadeh has not been able to decipher the meaning of the inscriptions—three tablets in all were found, with 59 symbols—but I would be willing to bet that they involved money. They might even be an attempt to explain the terms of a debt.

The Scheme of Things

In the United States, mutual funds are almost never referred to as a collective investment scheme, but in truth, that is what they are. Numerous stock exchanges here and around the world recognize managed funds, mutual funds, or just plain old funds that allow a group of like-minded individuals to acquire a broad range of investments, far more than a single investor could hope to amass, and pay for them and any associated fees from a pool of cash.

The best thing a man can do for his culture when he is rich is to endeavor to carry out those schemes which he entertained when he was poor.

Henry David Thoreau

Mutual funds can be formed in numerous ways, but all such funds are governed by charters or statutes that give the investor in the scheme a sense of what the fund is trying to do. In essence, the charter sets certain limits on not only *what* the fund can invest in, but *how*. There may also be certain tax rules involved as well.

Generally, funds have five components. The *fund manager* or investment manager, who may or may not be an actual living person and may in some cases be a team of individuals, is at the helm of the fund, making the decisions. The manager's job is basically straightforward: follow the charter, invest wisely, and make money for the shareholders. We will discuss the role the manager plays throughout the book, but this is the person, persons, or computer that helps you achieve growth, capital appreciation, or safety. It is the manager that we credit or blame for the growth of our investment dollars or the lack thereof.

The *fund administrator* acts as the fund's accountant. The administrator manages the trading, makes fund reconciliations, and determines the fund's valuation and unit pricing. A recent job posting at Yahoo! HotJobs asked for the following credentials from applicants looking for a job as a fund administrator:

> - Specifically looking for someone to perform various Treasury functions, including allocation and preparation of fund expenses
>
> - Monitoring of expense accruals and expense ratio calculations. Need to be familiar with fund accounting (pricing, NAV calculation, etc.), and be familiar with issues relating to registered investment companies.

Watching over the activities of the fund is the *trustee* or *board of trustees*. Originally, the Investment Company Act of 1940 suggested that, in order to safeguard investors in the fund, a board of trustees should be appointed as a shareholder advocate. The trustees would oversee the fund, making sure that applicable laws and rules were followed; negotiate management contracts; and consider and approve advisory fees and other expenses that the fund would charge shareholders for their participation. This meant that the board would serve as a compliance office.

What to Say!

According to a paper written by Alan R. Palmiter of the Wake Forest University School of Law, mutual fund boards have failed miserably at the task they were assigned to do. Palmiter refers to them as a "curious institution" that has "not lived up to the hopes of the 1940 Act." They lack the leadership and supervision needed to make certain that management fees do not become too burdensome for the shareholders and to oversee the design and marketing of the fund. In his analysis of why these independent boards have failed, Mr. Palmiter writes: "The fund board is composed of part-timers who rely on the fund's management for information, direction and compensation. Even if they wanted to," he adds, "the fund's directors cannot realistically threaten to take the fund's business elsewhere. Negotiation on behalf of the fund's investors is understandably an empty ritual." Worse, he believes that fund boards are generally given the approval of the SEC. You can read the full paper on the subject at http://papers.ssrn.com/sol3/papers.cfm?abstract_id=1084876#PaperDownload.

The *shareholders* own or have a claim to the fund's assets, including the gains and losses of those assets and the associated income. Mutual fund investors come in a wide variety of shapes and sizes, but they have certain typical characteristics. A survey done by the Investment Company Institute, a trade group that advocates for and serves the mutual fund industry, found the typical investor in funds to be middle-aged, college-educated, employed, married or living with a partner with whom he or she shares investment decision making, of moderate financial means (household incomes between $68,700 and $125,000), and also an owner of individual stocks, although holding 47 percent of the household's financial assets in mutual funds. The typical investor generally has about $48,000 invested in four funds, with 56 percent of that investment is in equity (stock) funds; probably first purchased a fund in 1990; and has most, if not all, of his or her mutual fund assets locked up in some sort of retirement plan (defined-contribution plan). This 2004 survey also determined that these investors typically have a long-term horizon, redeem (sell) shares in the funds they own infrequently, understand risk, and are willing to take at least an average amount of it whatever fund they choose. They understand enough about risk to comprehend that market fluctuations tend to be short term and that funds are a good vehicle for achieving their financial goals.

Give a man a fish and he will eat for a day. Teach a man to fish and he will eat for a lifetime. Teach a man to create an artificial shortage of fish and he will eat steak.

Jay Leno

The last component of a mutual fund is the *marketing* or *distribution* arm of the company, which promotes and/or sells the fund. This is something we will get into in much greater detail later in the book, but at this point, I want you to consider how the fund company D.A. Davidson describes how its marketing expenses are handled in its disclosure to its investors:

Asset-Based Distribution/Service Fees (12b–1 Fees). Generally, these fees are taken out of a mutual fund's assets to cover a fund's marketing and distribution expenses. 12b–1 Fees reduce the overall returns of the particular mutual fund and are disclosed in a fund's prospectus. These fees are then shared between D.A. Davidson and the fund's distributor as set forth in the prospectus.

Nobel-winning scientist Eric Kandel once wrote: "Memory is the scaffold that holds our mental life together. One of its most remarkable characteristics is that it has no restraints on time or place." When Argentinean author Jorge Luis Borges wrote his landmark short story "Funes the Memorious" in 1942, the act of remembering was challenged in reverse. His main character cannot forget anything. He remembers every detail of his experiences, and through this device, Borges explores the unlimited capacity of the human brain. Even more interesting, Borges portrays himself in the story as a fictional character who meets the poor, illiterate farm boy whose life changed after a fall from a horse.

As we begin to look at bonds and, more specifically, the funds that invest in them, there will be a good deal of information that you must absorb. This so-called bondspeak relies on your memory more than on your investment acumen. While mutual funds that focus on equity investing are much more straightforward, despite what seem like innumerable nuances, bonds and bond funds are a wholly different world.

Before we get too far, let's discuss some of the bond terminology you will need if you are to make good financial decisions concerning this type of investment. We will do this before we discuss why, if ever, you would need a bond fund.

CHAPTER 4
Another Language

In general terms, a bond is fundamentally like a loan. More specifically, it is considered a negotiable instrument. Whereas a loan is a transaction between two parties, a negotiable instrument such as a bond is transferable. Both are contracts with set terms and periods of time over which the money needs to be repaid with interest, but the differences from that point on are quite substantial.

Bonds make periodic payments to the owner with the promise that the principal will be paid in full on a specified date, called the maturity date. When the government issues a bond, that bond is secured by the good faith and credit of the U.S. Treasury. Ironically, since there are no tangible assets backing the bond other than that promise to repay, the bond is considered unsecured.

If your city wishes to improve a road or build a bridge and expects the revenue (or the asset value) from that project to pay the interest and principal, this is considered a bond that is secured.

The contract that binds the issuer of the bond (the borrower) and the holder (the lender or investor) is referred to as an indenture. This document spells out all sorts of terms, such as when and how the bond will be repaid, what happens should the issuer be unable to pay the bond back (default), and what the holder can do if the issuer does default on its payments. Other terms included in the agreement, which are stated in the prospectus, are calls (which are basically prepayment options given the issuer) and sinking fund requirements (which is basically an obligation on the part of the issuer to repay a certain amount of the bond each year). Both calls and sinking funds are covered in a little more detail a little further along.

Virtually every bond has a maturity date, a point in the future when the holder can expect to be repaid the principal in full. Don't confuse this with the phrase *term to maturity*. That is simply the amount of time left before the maturity date.

To make mistakes is human; to stumble is commonplace; to be able to laugh at yourself is maturity.

William Arthur Ward

When an issue of bonds is sold to the holders, the entire issue generally has one set maturity date. If an issue has multiple maturity dates (and you will find this most often when municipalities issue bonds), the bonds are called serial bonds. That doesn't mean that there are no municipal bonds with a single maturity date. Such bonds exist. But many cities, counties, and states give the investor numerous maturity dates to choose from—and if you are already wondering why anyone would want to buy these investments outside of a fund, where a manager makes all of these decisions, you are not alone.

Do all bonds have maturity dates?

Yes and no. Perpetual bonds are a type of debt instrument that acts more like an equity, and the coupon payment is similar to the dividend payment an equity investor would receive with stock ownership. Without a fixed date in the future, these bonds do not mature. But they do have a finite worth as the value of the coupon is eroded over time. Interest will be paid, but its worth becomes the price of the bond. Yes, it pays interest forever. No, the interest after a period of time is not worth much.

Understanding the underlying terminology gives you an added sense of empowerment, especially when you are attempting to work your way through the prospectuses for these investments. So brave on just a little more as we look at more terms that are primarily related to bond investing.

A recent paper published by three Swedish medical educators, Anna Fyrenius, Charlotte Silén, and Staffan Wirell from the Faculty of Health Sciences, Linköping University, Linköping, Sweden, studied students' grasp of concepts, particularly in terms of how what they know relates to what they can diagnose. They were surprised to find that a large number of the students did not grasp some basic tenets of physiology. They were, according to their paper, published by the American Physiology Society, concerned about the students' understanding of body function timing, how the organs interact, and the timing of that interaction, and about their ability to make a decision on what to do. The paper suggests that the key to changing this inability to "problemize phenomena beyond long causal reasoning chains" will involve deeper understanding of how the cognitive processes can be changed. The entire paper can be read at http://advan.physiology.org/cgi/content/full/31/4/364.

Underlying Principles

Time is always a consideration when buying bonds, and this is why buying these investments through a bond fund is by far the best way to go. Short-term, intermediate-term, and long-term are sort of floating concepts, with no real written rules defining exactly what they mean. However, *short-term* is generally accepted as meaning a year or less, *intermediate-term* as one year to ten years, and *long-term* as having more than ten years to maturity.

No less important is the term *yield*. This (and we will discuss this again later) is nothing more than a way for the investor to determine the risk in the price. In short, the higher the yield, the greater the risk that the underlying bond might be subject to interest-rate fluctuations, the possibility that the credit markets might change during the time frame to maturity, and last, but not least, how quickly you can get your money back if you decide to sell the bond.

There is always the chance of default, often known as the *default risk*. This kind of risk plays a huge role in how the bond's yield is determined. Bonds issued by the federal government are considered default-free. Corporations sell bonds with higher risk, which are rated and assigned a risk grade. Municipalities also issue bonds that come with risk, albeit small. Bondholders who own high-default-risk debt are paid better than those who own safer, low-default bonds.

As we talk about Treasuries, you will stumble on the term *yield to maturity*. This is a method of determining yield that calculates the value of the interest payments, which are paid as coupons on a regular basis, and the change in price from purchase to maturity. This is probably the most accurate way to look at the actual worth of your investment. There are others. *Coupon yield* tallies the interest paid until the bond matures, and *current yield* looks at the current price of the bond and determines the income you will earn, expressed as a percentage.

A concept that isn't really so hard but is often considered confusing by the uninitiated bond investor (another reason to use bond funds) is this: as the price of a bond goes up, the yield the bond offers to its investors goes down. Investors buying bonds en masse will push the price of those bonds higher. Investors selling bonds will lower the price and increase the yield offered to the new purchasers. When bond investors sell, they believe that the risk is not worth the reward offered (in the form of yield). As the price goes up, the yield moves in the other direction. Investors who seek stability in fixed-income investments—in other words, no fluctuation in price or yield—look to short-term Treasuries.

The average investor can buy Treasuries either directly or through bond funds. A little further along, I'll point out the various reasons why bond funds are better for almost all bond investing—unless, of course, you are moving huge amounts of wealth around. So we'll take the opportunity now to give you some information about buying these kinds of fixed-income investments outside of a bond fund. Treasuries make great gifts!

There are certain things that a bond investor who is interested in U.S. Treasury offerings needs to keep in mind.

A U.S. Treasury–issued security, whether it is a bond, a note, a bill, TIPS, an I bond, an EE bond, an HH bond, or some other Treasury security, is considered a very liquid investment.

What's the difference between all those types of Treasuries?

Mostly, time.

Bonds, which are traditionally issued with 30-year maturities, offer a way to diversify an investment portfolio, help finance education expenses, and give retirees a steady income.

Minimum purchase: $1,000.

Investment increment: Multiples of $1,000.

Issue method: Electronic.

Rates and terms: Treasury bond rates are determined at auction, and the price depends on both the bond's yield to maturity and its interest rate. According to Treasury Direct, should the yield to maturity be greater than the interest rate, the price of the bond will be less than par value. If the price is greater than par, the interest rate will be greater than the yield to maturity. And should both the interest rate and the yield to maturity be the same, the price will be equal to par value (simply put, par is the original face value of the instrument; the par value of a $1,000 bond is $1,000).

This is perhaps best illustrated in the following table.

Condition	Type of Security	Yield at Auction	Interest Coupon Rate	Price
Discount (price below par) Issue date: 8/15/2005	30-year bond	4.35%	4.25%	98.333317 per $100

Here's why: The price at which that bond was auctioned, $98.33317, suggested that in order to get investors interested in buying the bond, the Treasury was forced to lower the price, which increased the yield. The below-par ($1,000) price was required to provide the required 4.35 percent yield.

Premium (price above par)	30-year bond	3.99%	4.25%	104.511963 per $100

Issue date: 9/15/2005

Here's why: Because the bond was auctioned at a price above par ($1,000), a higher price was required to provide the 3.99 percent yield.

The auction results done as I write this show how stable this type of bond can be.

Issue date: 2/15/2008		4.375%	4.449%	98.780998 per $100

Treasury notes (T-notes) are securities with maturities ranging from two years to ten years. T-notes are priced similarly to Treasury bonds. An investor might pay less than par value for the notes, which means that the yield to maturity would be greater than the interest rate (coupon yield); he or she might pay a price equal to par value, which means that the yield to maturity would be equal to the interest rate; or the investor might pay a price greater than par value, resulting in a yield to maturity that is less than the interest rate.

The original issue rate of a Treasury note is determined at auction. At a recent auction, a prospective buyer would have been offered a note with the following terms: A 2-year note sold on January 31, 2008, that would mature on January 31, 2010, had an interest rate of 2.125 percent and a rate at maturity of 2.237 percent, and cost the buyer $99.782126 per hundred dollars face value. (Just two years ago, this particular type of Treasury was yielding almost twice that amount, a sign of the willingness of the buyers of this type of Treasury to accept risk.)

Minimum purchase: $1,000.

Investment increment: Multiples of $1,000.

Issue method: Electronic.

Rates and terms: Treasury notes are issued for terms of 2, 3, 5, and 10 years in multiples of $1,000.

Treasury bills (T-bills) are short-term government securities with maturities ranging from a few days to 26 weeks. Bills are sold at a discount from their face value, which basically means that when you purchase a Treasury bill, you pay less than the face value. When the bill reaches maturity, the full face value is then received.

But keep this in mind: unlike notes, bonds, or TIPS (discussed later), Treasury bills pay the interest due on maturity. This is done because of the short-term nature of the investment.

There are some tax advantages. The interest received is exempt from state and local taxes, but the holder of the bill is taxed on a federal level.

The original issue rate of a Treasury bill is determined at auction. At a recent auction, a prospective buyer would have been offered a Treasury bill with the following terms: a 28-day bill sold on February 7, 2008, that would mature on March 6, 2008, had a discount rate of 2.210 percent and a rate at maturity of 2.251 percent, and cost the buyer $99.828111 per hundred dollar face value.

Minimum purchase: $1,000

Investment increment: Multiples of $1,000

Issue method: Electronic

Rates and terms: Treasury bills are issued for terms of 4, 13, and 26 weeks. Another type of Treasury bill, the cash management bill, is issued with variable terms, usually only a matter of days. The 4-week, 13-week, and 26-week bills are auctioned on a regular schedule, usually weekly. Cash management bills aren't auctioned on a regular schedule, and T-bills are always sold at a discount.

Rates of current auctions and purchasing information can be found at http://www.treasurydirect.gov/.

Treasury Inflation Protected Securities, or TIPS, as they are widely called, are issued for terms of 5, 10, and 20 years and essentially provide the fixed-income security of a Treasury issue, but with built-in inflation protection. These securities are indexed to the consumer price index (CPI), found at http://stats.bls.gov/cpi/.

The way these instruments work is simple. When inflation is rising, so is does the TIPS' principal. When inflation is declining (disinflation), the principal declines. When the TIPS reaches maturity, the owner of the security receives either the adjusted principal or the original investment, whichever is greater.

The interest is paid twice a year and, as with the principal, the amount of interest paid is adjusted upward when there is inflation and downward when there is deflation.

Minimum purchase: $1,000

Investment increment: Multiples of $1,000

Issue method: Electronic

I bonds are a low-risk, safe savings product that will pay the holder interest for up to 30 years based on current market rates.

Because they are sold at one-half the face value, they are a popular gift for young children. For instance, a $50 bond is sold for $25. As of this update, they are paying 1.20 percent through April 2008.

The I-bond holder must retain ownership for at least one year, and the interest-earning period is 30 years. If you cash them in within the first five years, you forfeit the three most recent months of interest payments.

They also have the same tax advantages: they are exempt from state and local taxes, but are subject to federal, state, and local estate, inheritance, gift, and other excise taxes—unless, of course, they are used for educational purposes.

Minimum purchase: $50

Investment increment: Multiples of $50, $75, $100, $200, $500, $1,000, $5,000, $10,000 (These bonds can also be purchased electronically from Treasury Direct for prices starting at $25.)

Issue method: Electronic

EE bonds replaced E bonds in 1980. Like the I-bond, these are accrual bonds, sold for half their face value, and upon maturity pay the bondholder the full value of the bond.

Minimum purchase: $50

Investment increment: $50, $75, $100, $200, $500, $1,000, $5,000, $10,000

Issue method: Paper, electronic

Rates and terms: EE bonds are sold at half their mature face value. The bond must be held at least 12 months before the investment can be sold. Selling the bond sooner incurs a penalty. An investor can buy up to $5,000 of EE paper bonds and $5,000 of series EE electronic bonds in a calendar year.

HH bonds can only be purchased by E, EE, or H-bond sellers. They are purchased in amounts beginning at $500 and mature in 20 years. They may be cashed in after six months.

The difference between the bid and the asking price on the fixed-income security you are looking for is usually very narrow. This makes it easier for investors to find the right security at the right price. The Treasury prices its offerings in 1/32 increments (or $3.125 per $10,000), which keeps price ranges (found most conveniently in the *Wall Street Journal*) very narrow. This makes their purchase very easy. Folks who want to buy Treasuries can do so directly through the Bureau of Public Debt.

The safety of these offerings, which are backed by the full faith and credit of the federal government, is no empty statement. This is the most trusted investment in the world. (There was a time, about a century ago, when a private banker, J. P. Morgan, had to bail the country out of a financial crisis.) Making good on this promise is why managing the economy is so important.

The Panic of 1907, the fourth such panic in the short span of 34 years, began with a stock market plunge and quickly turned into a run on the banks. At that particular time in our nation's economic history, banks held depositors' reserves and lent those deposits to borrowers. When a panic begins, depositors want their money back, largely because they have lost confidence in the banks. If a bank does not have the money available to cover these withdrawals, the bank can collapse, sending the economy plunging still further.

J. P. Morgan stepped in to prevent this from happening by organizing bankers into a trust of sorts; by doing so, he gave the banks the ability to borrow from one another. They bought stocks in companies whose shares had plummeted but that were otherwise considered to be healthy businesses. They secured credit lines overseas, which was easier for them to do as a group than individually. Not only did this action secure even more wealth for Morgan, but because of his influence, he was able to keep the panic small, and as a result, the economy emerged not much worse for wear.

It is always important to consider the tax implications of any investment. We will discuss this throughout the book. With Treasuries, the interest gained from these investments is not taxed at the state or local level. It is, however, taxed at the federal level in many instances. You will receive an exclusion from taxes on income from Treasury-issued debt if you use the proceeds from a Treasury security for education.

What are benchmarks?

This is as good a time as any to discuss benchmarks. Throughout the investment world, and in many other industries, there is a need for measurement. How well something is doing is of value, at least as a statistic, only if you can make some sort of comparison with something similar. Equity mutual funds seek a similar grouping of stocks to compare themselves with, and bonds often, but not exclusively, use a similar investment in Treasuries with similar maturity dates.

The best way to look at benchmarks, a term first used in surveying land, is the way legendary computer hacker and open source advocate Eric Raymond does. Computers are difficult to judge because there are no real discernible benchmarks. As a result, Eric Raymond defined a benchmark as "an inaccurate measure of computer performance" citing the "old hacker's saying" that "In the computer industry, there are three kinds of lies: lies, damn lies, and benchmarks." Mutual funds, when citing benchmarks for performance, are often guilty of the same crime. As I said, there will be a good deal of discussion about benchmarks as we move forward. Just keep Mr. Raymond's rather pessimistic outlook in mind.

Treasuries are used as a benchmark for similar types of securities. Comparing not only the maturity but also the yield to those of other offerings can be incredibly helpful when determining the amount of risk you are seeking.

There is a good chance that investors in Treasuries will be pleasantly surprised by the overall performance of their purchase. The tax advantage helps. The fact that there is no call risk on the offering (a distinct possibility with some fixed-income securities if the interest rate falls significantly and the issuer is permitted to "call" the bond) and no default risk (a problem if the borrower is no longer able to pay the bondholders) also adds to the stability of the debt. And should there be a financial crisis, a Treasury-issued security is usually where other investors, both domestically and globally, turn. This is often referred to as a "flight to quality," and it can also add to the offering's overall yield.

Art is not the application of a canon of beauty but what the instinct and the brain can conceive beyond any canon. When we love a woman we don't start measuring her limbs.

Pablo Picasso

With debt issued by government-sponsored enterprises (GSEs), a little care needs to be taken. To get the "full faith and credit" coverage of the government, the enterprise needs to be a government one. For instance, the Federal National Mortgage Association (Fannie Mae) and the Federal Home Loan Mortgage Corporation (Freddie Mac), although they are often considered to be government agencies, are actually publicly held companies. Also included in this list of publicly held GSEs are the Federal Home Loan Banks (FLHB) and the Tennessee Valley Authority (TVA). Not included is the Government National Mortgage Association (GNMA, or Ginnie Mae). This is in fact a true government agency, and any debt issued by GNMA carries the guarantee that you will be paid what is due to you.

Value Equal to, Greater Than, or Less Than

Although the concept is not impossible to grasp, the idea of par, premium, and discount does have its hurdles for the unfamiliar investor.

Let's look at a simple chart of how these three terms apply to the accounting for a bond.

Bond Sells	Proceeds from Issuance	Market Rate at Issuance	Coupon Payment
At par	= Par value	= Coupon rate	= Interest expense
At a discount	< Par value	> Coupon rate	< Interest expense
At a premium	> Par value	< Coupon rate	> Interest expense

Par is the same as face value. It is the original price of the bond that makes par equal to 100 percent. A $1,000 bond that is selling at par is selling at $1,000. Because bonds are bought and sold, not just held until maturity, the value of the bond changes with each trade. If the bond is in demand, the price can go higher. This is called a premium. If the bond is selling for less than face value or par, it is trading at a discount.

Ironically, a bond that is selling at a premium is actually better for the investor than one that is selling at par or at a discount. This is contrary to what we think we know or even how we react to the price of goods in the retail world. Studies have shown that we perceive a higher cost as actually being related to a better product—something we will discuss later when we tackle the topic of fees in equity funds. Yet a bond investor's reaction is contrary to that thinking, perhaps indicating the thinking inside a bond investor's brain.

Bonds that are priced at a premium—more expensive than par—give the investor the par value of the bond when the bond matures. The idea of paying more than face value deters investors from seeking bonds that are priced at a premium. This would be categorized as a good thing. Less investor interest means increased stability. Add this to what is known as the "amortization of premium," and the purchaser of a premium bond actually receives a higher annual payment.

What is amortization of premium?

As an investor, you paid a premium, or more than face value, for the bond you just purchased. To compensate you for this, part of the premium is subtracted from the interest you received on that debt. This is done in order to offset the premium you paid. As a reward, not only do you as the bondholder receive the periodic payment of interest, but part of the premium (over par) that you paid is subtracted. That special compensation makes premium bonds more attractive than those sold at par or at a discount.

Investors who buy bonds at a premium can also count on less interest-rate volatility. (Interest rates add to the risk of owning certain types of bonds.) There are tax positives for owning premium bonds that individual bondholders often overlook. Your bond fund manager, once again, has a better opportunity to control taxable events. The ability to write down this amortized premium gives these kinds of bonds an after-tax appeal.

There are other tax positives for owning premium bonds. Generally, the only taxes you owe are on the interest paid, which is taxed as income when sold before 12 months and as capital gains when sold after more than 12 months. This differs from what a discount bondholder would pay. In a discount situation, you owe taxes on the difference in the price of the discount and the par value. Depending on how many years you owned the bond, taxes would be based on a simple formula: divide the number of years until the bond matures by the difference in the purchase price to par, which is called the original issue discount. Each year you own the bond, you need to report this amount as income.

Credit Risks and Discounts

Interest rates on bonds are based on risk. The greater the risk, the higher the interest rate a bond is likely to offer investors. The lower the risk, such as in Treasuries, the lower the interest rate. Because of this sensitivity, bonds are often sold at a discount or a premium if the interest-rate environment is changing.

What we think of as our sensitivity is only the higher evolution of terror in a poor dumb beast. We suffer for nothing. Our own death wish is our only real tragedy.

Mario Puzo

Why, then, are bonds sold at a discount more attractive to investors than bonds sold at a premium? Hard to say. People are funny. It might be a case of the equity adage "buy low, sell high" being carried over as a kind of thinking for investors. The belief that buying something for less than par means that the investor has found a bargain is, at best, only an illusion. At tax time, the difference between par and the discount is considered to be a taxable gain to the investor. And should interest rates rise, the discount bondholder would pay the steepest price for the error of buying a discount bond based on price alone.

The manager of each type of bond fund must be able to execute a strategy with the investor in mind. As we look at some of the terms we just learned, we can see how they influence the type of fund you choose. Even with the most conservative investment, the government bond fund, its success is determined by the investor interest the manager attracts.

CHAPTER 5

Inside a Bond Fund—Government

◆▰▰▰▰▰▰▰▰▰▰▰▰▰▰▰▰▰▰▰▰▰▰▰◆

Like all the funds we will look at in this book, the government bond funds we highlight are chosen based on certain criteria. They must be highly regarded by the rating agencies that do in-depth research on the fund, such as Morningstar. They must be relatively inexpensive, which means that, if you were to group together all the funds in a particular sector and average their expense ratios, the funds we profile will fall below that average; if they are significantly below, all the better. The role of the portfolio manager is an important consideration as well. The normal template for judging a portfolio manager, and one that is used by most investors in funds, is based on tenure.

What is tenure?

A look at how universities award tenure to their faculty can give us some insight into how well a mutual fund manager who has been at a fund for a number of years might do. In fact, investors judge a fund manager using many of the same criteria that universities use. For instance, at Stevens Institute of Technology, tenure is awarded to teachers who exhibit high marks on research, teaching, and service. Research, according to the institute, involves the ability to add "quality, quantity, impact, and continuity," all the while finding a way to increase funding. Technically, we want no less from our fund managers. While we do not expect our fund managers to be teachers, we do expect them to have a certain methodology, to be innovative, and to stick to a certain style. The institute refers to service as peer recognition and the ability to represent and promote the school, all of which attract funding. The better a fund manager is considered to be in relation to her or his peer group can attract new investors, increasing the opportunities for the manager to grow the fund.

We are also looking for an easy entry point. Not all of us have tens of thousands of dollars to plunk down on a fund, nor is this book going to focus on the retirement component of a fund. Almost all funds offer a discount to investors who are planning to use the fund for retirement. These discounts can be relatively steep. We will talk about some strategies to use for funds both inside and outside these types of deferred tax accounts a little later on, but for now, we will concentrate on each type of fund as if you had to buy it as a stand-alone product.

In many instances, we will try to focus on the fund manager who has the longest record of accomplishment relative to his or her peers. The length of that record is not always easy to determine, however. For a short-term bond fund that invests in bonds with an average maturity of one to three years, judging the fund manager by a longer period of time, such as five years or even ten years, might not be the fairest approach. In equities, the longer a fund manager has been at the helm, the theory suggests, the greater the amount of time that manager has had to implement the fund's particular strategies.

You will often find that Vanguard funds meet this criterion more often than not. Consider the following three funds, one each in the short-term, intermediate-term, and long-term categories, all of which invest primarily in government fixed-income securities.

Over a three-year period, Ronald M. Reardon, the lead manager of Vanguard Short-Term Federal (VSGBX), has done quite well among his peers. His fund focuses on securities with a dollar-weighted average maturity of one to four years. The fund, which has an expense ratio of 0.20 percent (compared to the group average of 0.91 percent), invests at least 80 percent of its assets in short-term bonds issued by the U.S. government and its agencies and instrumentalities. These investments, as I noted earlier, are not necessarily backed by the full faith and credit of the U.S. government. This fund will cost you $3,000 as an initial investment, $0 if it is purchased in a retirement account.

(Just a little side note about these minimums. In Vanguard's case, until you reach that minimum balance, you will be charged some additional accounting fees for being underinvested in the fund, taking away some of the potential gain you might otherwise expect. Here is where you can download the prospectus as well as additional free prospectuses from the Vanguard fund family: http://yahoo.fundinfo.wilink.com/asp/F130_search_results_ENG.asp? nasdaq=vsgbx.)

Here are the top "short-term" government bond funds over a three-year period (with expense ratios):

Fund	Annual Return (at 2007 year-end)	Expense Ratio
Eaton Vance Government Obligations A EVGOX	4.78%	1.20%
Analytic Short-Term Govt Inc Instl ANSTX	4.71%	0.60%
Vanguard Short-Term Treasury Adm VFIRX	4.62%	0.10%*
Sit U.S. Government Securities SNGVX	4.57%	0.80%
Vanguard Short-Term Federal Adm VSGDX	4.51%	0.10%†
Vanguard Short-Term Treasury VFISX	4.47%	0.26%
Federated U.S. Govt: 2–5 Yr Instl FIGTX	4.46%	0.58%
Vanguard Short-Term Federal VSGBX	4.41%	0.20%
First American Interm Govt Bd Y FYGYX	4.40%	0.60%‡
State Farm Interim SFITX	4.25%	0.19%

* The difference between the expenses this fund charges shareholders and the industry average over a 10-year period is significant. If you held the fund for 10 years, the cost to you would be $128, compared to the industry average of $1,304.

† Mr. Reardon also manages this fund for Vanguard.

‡ This fund will charge you a million dollars for the privilege.

Thomas L. Pappas has been the lead manager of the Vanguard GNMA (VFIIX) fund since December 31, 1994. During that time, he has bested his peer group most of the time. The fund invests in securities that come with the full faith and credit guarantee, with at least 80 percent of its assets in Government National Mortgage Association certificates. The goal of the fund is to provide investors a moderate level of current income. The remainder of the cash on hand can be invested in other U.S. government obligations. This five-star fund has an attractive expense ratio of 0.21 percent (compared to its peer group average of 1.08 percent) and carries the minimum $3,000 initial investment requirement that Vanguard funds usually charge to nonretirement investors.

In the Real World...

Here are the top intermediate-term government bond funds over a three-year period (with expense ratios):

Fund	Annual Return (at 2007 year-end)	Expense Ratio
Vanguard Interm-Term U.S. Treas Adm VFIUX	5.50%	0.10%
PIMCO GNMA Instl PDMIX	5.40%	0.50%*
PIMCO Mortgage-Backed Securities Instl PTRIX	5.35%	0.50%*
Vanguard Interm-Term U.S. Treasury VFITX	5.33%	0.26%
Vanguard GNMA Adm VFIJX	5.19%	0.11%†
JPMorgan Government Bond Select HLGAX	5.18%	0.50%
Nationwide Government Bond Instl GGBIX	5.10%	0.72%
Federated Total Return Govt Inst FTRGX	5.10%	0.27%
Vanguard GNMA VFIIX	5.09%	0.21%
PIMCO Mortgage-Backed Securities Adm PMTAX	5.09%	0.75%

*This fund has a minimum initial investment of $5,000,000.00.

† Also managed by Mr. Pappas.

American Century Target Mat 2020 Inv (BTTTX), our long-tem government fund, has a manager who has not only an extensive financial background but also one that is grounded in law, Robert V. Gahagan.

He has been the lead manager since 2001 and an employee of American Century for almost 25 years. Mr. Gahagan is not only a vice president and portfolio manager for American Century Investments, but also a member of the Association for Investment Management and Research.

The fund he runs is focused on total return for the investor, and with an expense ratio of 0.57 percent (his peers in the category average 0.90 percent), he seems to be almost halfway there.

The fund invests in zero coupon U.S. Treasury securities and U.S. Treasury bills, notes, and bonds that will mature in 2020.

What does zero coupon mean?

A zero coupon U.S. Treasury security (or other fixed-income security, for that matter) does not pay interest. Instead, the security is sold at a discount and gradually increases to par value. This is sometimes referred to as imputed or phantom interest. Because no interest is actually paid out, the investor—in this case, the bond manager—does not face a reinvestment risk on the security. Reinvestment risk is something that all other bond investors, especially individual bond investors, face; in most instances, it is a greater risk with corporate bonds. Reinvestment risk is a very real concern among bond investors. The time between the purchase of the bond and its maturity date poses two risk-based questions: Will the yield over that time period be worth the investment, and will the maturity of the bond coincide with another, similar opportunity? Once the bond matures, the investor is looking for favorable terms for the next purchase. As we have seen recently, a lot can happen over the course of a relatively short time period in the world of investing.

We'll discuss the effects of this kind of risk and ways to control it in Chapter 7 when the subject of corporate bonds is in the spotlight.

The underlying investments in this fund will return a dollar amount that approximates the return on a direct investment in zero coupon securities for that year. Because the fund invests in long-term government funds with zero coupons, it can make relatively accurate predictions based on the time of investment. There are certain advantages to this investment style, which makes the fund a rock-solid investment for the long term. Mr. Gahagan is focusing on what are called disparities in prices and yields to get where he intends to be by 2020, when the fund will mature and be liquidated.

Here are the top long-term government bond funds over a three-year period (with expense ratios):

Fund	Annual Return (at 2007 year-end)	Expense Ratio
American Century Target Mat 2025 Inv BTTRX	9.51%	0.57%*
American Century Target Mat 2025 Adv ACTVX	9.25%	0.82%*
Wasatch-Hoisington U.S. Treasury WHOSX	8.03%	0.71%
American Century Target Mat 2020 Inv BTTTX	7.98%	0.57%
American Century Target Mat 2020 Adv ACTEX	7.72%	0.82%*
Vanguard Long-Term U.S. Treasury Adm VUSUX	6.90%	0.10%
Dreyfus U.S. Treasury Long-Term DRGBX	6.83%	0.65%
Vanguard Long-Term U.S. Treasury VUSTX	6.74%	0.26%
Rydex Govt Long Bond 1.2x Strategy Inv RYGBX	6.69%	0.96%
American Century Target Mat 2015 Inv BTFTX	6.43%	0.57%*

* Also managed by Mr. Gahagan.

Most people are aware of the social nature of fish. We think of them as swimming in schools, vast numbers of fish swimming with determination and purpose and with some unrehearsed synchronicity. On the nature channels, we have even seen them herd prey. However, the African Cichlids, a freshwater species, take this social activity one step further. They actually create a social home. Duties are dispersed among a group of about 10, all of whom support a breeding pair. By defending territory and maintaining nests, this support group keeps the area safe and secure. The breeding pair even leaves the menial task of tending the eggs to these lesser fish. In our next chapter, we will look at investing where you live. This sort of socially focused investing has some distinct advantages. And it often can reap some important tax advantages for investors who live close to the right municipality.

CHAPTER 6
Inside a Bond Fund—Municipal

◆◆◆◆◆◆◆◆◆◆◆◆◆◆◆◆◆◆◆◆◆◆◆◆◆◆◆◆◆◆◆◆◆◆◆

What the Experts Say

Your hometown is where they can't figure out how you did as well as you did.

Gertrude Stein

Sometimes the answer is right under our feet, literally. Science has always wondered when the crust of the earth first became solid enough to be considered more than molten slurry, and now they seem to have come a little closer to the answer.

In 1999, Minik Rosing and Robert Frei, both professors at the University of Copenhagen, Denmark, found the oldest evidence of fossilized bacteria in Greenland on what is known as the Isua Supercrustal Belt. The two scientists described their findings as the earliest form of photosynthesis and dated the find at 3.7 billion years ago. Up until this time, the earliest known fossilized evidence of this interaction of sunlight and living organisms was about a billion years later.

The reason the findings were doubted at first had to do with the earth's being perceived, at least up until that time, as being mostly ocean, with no solid landmasses. According to Hubert Staudigel of Scripps Institution of Oceanography at the University of California–San Diego, this rare outcropping of ophiolites is usually associated with mountains and plate tectonics. These kinds of rocks are identified by the green hue from the chlorite minerals within. Then it hit Harold Furnes of the University of Bergen in Norway. They were standing on an ancient ocean floor.

Investing in your home turf, be it city, county, or state, has long been touted as the best way for the rich to protect their money. The tax treatment of these investments has long been the draw. The interest income that many municipal bonds offer is exempt from federal income tax, and if you live in the state where the bond was issued, you may be free of state and local taxes as well.

On the surface, this seems like a win-win situation for the investor, but, as with so many financial no-brainers, there are caveats. Because we are talking about mutual funds, using a fund manager to sift through many of the details can be your best option.

Using a fund manager to determine the tax equivalent yield on municipal bonds compared to that of bonds with a similar coupon yield, maturity, and credit quality is priceless. Because municipal bonds are generally purchased at a discount, and we discussed earlier why this is perceived as being a better deal but actually is not, other tax consequences also need to be considered. Let the fund manager deal with the risk of the de minimis rule.

The name of the de minimis rule, or *de minimis non curat lex*, comes from Latin, as you may have guessed. It simply refers to the treatment of something that is too small to otherwise consider. In the U.S. tax code, the de minimis rule determines the borderline between what is considered capital gains on a discount bond and what is, at least for tax purposes, considered zero. For those who would like to do the math, here's how your fund manager makes the determination on whether the appreciation on a municipal bond held in the portfolio will or won't be taxed.

Take the face value of a bond, then subtract 0.25 percent of the value multiplied by the number of complete years between the bond's acquisition date and its maturity date. If this is more than the purchase price, the appreciation will not be taxed.

In the next chapter, we will cover some of the risks that all bond investors face, including credit risk, price risk, and the infamous yield curve. Bond investors understand that what is known as a secondary market—a place where, if you choose to do so, you can sell your bond—is virtually nonexistent when it comes to municipal bonds. The existence of a secondary market gives the more seasoned, hard-core bond investor the opportunity to pursue higher yields. Because of the lack of such a market, municipal bonds are much more illiquid and therefore more of a buy-and-hold investment.

The Better Deal

If you buy a fund that focuses on municipal bonds from, say, California, you can expect three things. First, if you live in California, the income produced from the fund will put you at a tax advantage. You won't necessarily be completely tax free, and I will tell you why when we profile a fund that successfully invests in municipal bonds from that state, but you will be pretty darned close.

The second feature is the fund's relative passivity. We will discuss the role of active and passive investing throughout the book, a discussion that will take us through the world of indexing, the tax advantages of both styles, and the costs of doing business using both methods, but when it comes to municipal bonds in a fund, passive investing is usually the best way to go.

This doesn't necessarily imply that a municipal bond fund is an index. What it does suggest is that many of the bonds from the same state that are included in a fund often have the same high credit rating and the same maturity. The cost of chasing down additional securities to enhance the fund's return is too high.

 Subtlety may deceive you; integrity never will.

Oliver Goldsmith

The third reason that municipal bond funds excel at purchasing these financial instruments is their ability to comprehend subtle differences in interest-rate fluctuations. Because these rates often defy prediction, making the use of the past performance of these funds as a measure of future performance virtually impossible, the only consideration for the investor looking for a tax-advantaged municipal bond fund is expenses.

The expenses of a municipal bond fund are the most important consideration in your purchase. Once you have determined what investment horizon you need and how much risk you are willing to take, looking for a fund that handles its investment expenses the way an equity index fund does can make all the difference in the end result: your return on your investment.

Insulated by Design

Because bonds are basically divided into taxable and nontaxable classes, with the latter being available only to citizens of a certain state or locality, the international investor is noticeably absent. This isolation from speculative overseas buyers looking to park cash from trade in U.S. dollars has created an insulated world that is free of the political or financial turmoil that usually forces investors worldwide to seek safety.

What is *flight to quality*?

I mentioned some of the problems that have faced numerous countries over the past few decades in the first chapter. Investors seeking higher than average returns move into a marketplace and position themselves to benefit from whatever economic activity a country might offer. But sometimes those opportunities either fail to materialize or do not pan out as these big investors had hoped. If the crisis is widespread and spills out onto the global economic scene, investors with billions of dollars will try to find something, anything, that will provide a safe haven until the unrest passes. This is called a *flight to quality*. These investors are looking for short-term safety. Unfortunately, sudden influxes of cash from anywhere create a certain turmoil in and of themselves.

Even investors from the United States are largely excluded from participating in localized municipal bond funds. Most investors realize that huge chunks of money are moving about the marketplace all the time. Pension funds and profit-sharing entities, for example, referred to as institutional investors, are always trolling for the best returns with the least amount of risk possible.

These types of entities are investing for the long term, having used actuarial tables to determine how much they will need to have on hand when the people they are investing for eventually need it. They seek growth, but conservatively. But because they are often investing for people in a number of states, municipal bonds are generally off-limits for them—at least from a tax-advantaged point of view.

 Pension fund managers are always on the lookout for changes in the economic scenery. Whenever you have a group of investors looking for the best return, the volatility of investments goes up. Municipal bonds are virtually free from this sort of speculation and from many of the strategies that bond investors (and some funds) employ. But that doesn't mean that these bonds are the ideal investment, and having a bond fund manager making the decisions helps you avoid making critical mistakes. For instance, while municipal bonds are tax-free today, they may not be tax-free tomorrow if a state's tax laws change. Municipal bonds tend to be long-term, and if the credit markets are in turmoil—and bond investors are always worried about one thing or another, even when there seems to be nothing of real concern—tying up your cash for too long can mean missed opportunities.

Why Muni Funds?

While on the surface, municipal bonds seem like the kind of thing that an average investor can buy outside of a mutual fund, there are additional considerations that a fund manager focuses on to provide the best return for the investor's money.

I mentioned the tax risk. Should a municipality change the way it treats its bonds, you could be subject to taxes that you were not expecting. Should the credit rating of the bonds change, you might be holding something with less stability than you may have previously thought. That could create an event that might trigger the alternative minimum tax (AMT).

What is the AMT and why does it affect me?

Think of the tax system as two parallel universes where two different sets of rules apply. In one universe you pay taxes and are allowed deductions in many instances for things like interest payments on your mortgage and the number of children or dependents you have. Even though the system seems burdensome and annoying, it doesn't seem poised to change anytime soon. You work. You pay taxes. As my late father once quipped, "It is one sure way to know you are still alive."

But in the alternative minimum tax universe, the rules are different. This place was once the haven of the few, the rich, the ones who avoided taxes through interesting schemes and shelters. Congress reacted and changed the code, setting a threshold for those who earned too much money and tried to deduct their way out of paying, what was considered by the much less rich, their just due.

Without going in too much detail, here's the way it works: If your gross income is above $75,000 and you are deducting personal exemptions and taxes you may have paid (such as property taxes and home-equity loan interest), if you exercised incentive stock options during the previous tax year, and the list goes on, you should do two sets of tax returns—one the way you always have done and one on a Form 6251. If you earn more than $100,000, you are probably in the wrong tax universe and owe the AMT.

The only consolation in this whole mess, that would never have happened had Congress built in some sort of inflation protection, is that millions of your fellow taxpayers are also caught in this universe. While your pay increased; so did your chances to get caught in the parallel universe, once the home of only the super-wealthy.

This is a very serious consideration. All municipal bond funds must disclose their potential exposure to such an event. Because some funds invest in municipal bonds that are subject to the AMT, and do so to attract investors with what is perceived to be a higher gross yield, reading the prospectus is very important. If you feel that you may have exposure to the AMT, simply eyeballing the municipal bond fund's return is not enough.

The reach of the AMT is likely to widen unless there are significant changes in the tax law. Currently, the preferred method of dealing with the problem is to offer patches, short-term fixes for a problem that is affecting more middle-class taxpayers each year. Although the AMT could be fixed by indexing it to inflation, lawmakers also recognize that the revenues brought in by this law are significant.

Using a municipal bond fund also lessens your exposure to credit risk. Municipal bonds come in two forms. General obligation bonds, which are used to fund municipal projects, are rated based on the creditworthiness of the issuer and (this is important) the ability of the municipality to tap the taxpayer if needed, while revenue bonds, also used for projects such as roads, depend on the success of the project and its ability to generate enough revenue to cover expenses *and* interest.

In Chapter 7, on corporate bond funds, we will discuss defaults in a little more detail—along with several other topics, such as calls, puts, risk, insurance, and yield curves—but for now the term relates to the ability of the bond to stay in effect until the maturity date. Municipal bonds have very little risk of collapsing, but there are exceptions. A good fund manager with a decent record should be able to spot these problems on the horizon.

A Careful Stroll

The funds listed here come from both the short-term category, usually holding investments with a maturity of $1^1/_2$ years or less, and the long-term category, investing in municipal bonds with maturities that can range from as little as 1 year to as much as 30 years. The top performers in these two groups are national funds (not the state and local varieties that give investors in a particular state additional tax-free opportunities), and the results listed here are based on a three-year average ending in 2007.

Fund	Annual Return (at 2007 year-end)	Expense Ratio
Evergreen Strategic Municipal Bd I VMPYX	3.66%	0.75%
Wells Fargo Advantage Ultra S/T Mun Inc I SMAIX	3.53%	0.37%
Wells Fargo Advantage S/T Muni Bd Inv STSMX	3.48%	0.66%
Alpine Ultra Short Tax Optimized Inc ATOIX	3.43%	0.60%
Evergreen Strategic Municipal Bd A VMPAX	3.38%	1.00%

You will notice that none of the three-year performers listed here call themselves tax-free. Most, if not all, come with disclaimers that read something like this: "The fund looks to invest in high after-tax current income consistent with the focus of those investments on preservation of capital. The assets in the fund are primarily municipal obligations that pay interest that is free from federal income taxes; there is a possibility that you might be subject to the AMT." Some of these funds actually own taxable debt obligations. Many of them will tell you the percentage of the bonds in the portfolio that are actually tax-free. Some of the funds in the previous table hold between 50 and 80 percent tax-free bonds. But in their defense, this is a very short-term category, and these funds look for municipal bonds on a national level. The expense average for this group is 0.85 percent.

Fund	Annual Return (at 2007 year-end)	Expense Ratio
Evergreen Strategic Municipal Bd I EIHMX	5.74%	0.38%
Eaton Vance National Municipals A EANAX	5.49%	0.63%
Wells Fargo Advantage Municipal Bond Inv SXFIX	4.85%	0.80%
Legg Mason Partners Managed Municipals I SMMYX	4.84%	0.52%
Pioneer AMT-Free Municipal A PBMFX	4.83%	0.86%

The funds in the above list use several strategies to give their investors not only preservation of capital but also exemption from federal taxes. Some, like the Pioneer AMT-Free Municipal A Fund, managed by Stephen C. Bauer since 1996, improve their overall returns by limiting the number of transactions, known as turnover; by seeking a wide range; by liberal use of the phrase *long term*—Mr. Bauer considers anything over one year long term—and by looking for bonds with lower ratings. Lower ratings, as we will find out when we discuss corporate bonds, usually translate into higher yield. The amount of municipal bonds from any one state that Mr. Bauer's fund can buy is limited, giving the fund "relative stability."

The expense ratio in this group averages around 1.10 percent.

Keep this in mind: the status of financial markets will seep into this group's return. Depending on what type of municipal bonds these funds hold and what those bonds actually were used by the localities to fund, the top performers as I write this may be totally different in just six months. Use these tables as illustrations of what the categories offer, not, by any means, as suggestions for purchase.

Because Treasuries may not offer a high enough expected return and because the investors may not live in the right municipality to take advantage of what investing locally has to offer, average investors will, more likely than not, seek what a corporate bond fund has to offer. In the next chapter, we will look at how corporations fund their businesses.

CHAPTER 7

Inside a Bond Fund—Corporate

◆◆◆◆◆◆◆◆◆◆◆◆◆◆◆◆◆◆◆◆◆◆◆◆◆◆◆◆◆◆◆◆◆◆◆◆◆

 I've refined my mechanics, refined my pitches. I've gotten more confidence, and I've gotten more determination. I've got a better idea what I'm doing out there.

Randy Johnson

The average person has probably never even heard of, let alone employed, a bootleg turn. A man named Robert Glen Johnson, Jr., more commonly known as Junior, invented the maneuver. The bootleg turn was used during police chases; when used properly, it turned the car 180 degrees, so that it was going in the opposite direction from the pursuers. Mr. Johnson ran moonshine up until 1955, when he decided to go legal and join the NASCAR circuit.

His experience as a moonshiner served him well on the racetrack. He is also credited with the unwitting creation of "drafting." This particular skill made use of physics—he had a much less capable car during his first race, and he discovered that he could keep up with a much faster car simply by riding directly behind it, almost locking bumpers.

The story became a legend. Not only did drafting give Mr. Johnson the aerodynamic edge, but because he was traveling so close to the car in front of him, a low-pressure area developed behind that car. That caused the glass in the lead car's rear window to pop out, distracting the driver enough to allow Johnson to win the race. That was 1953. Mr. Johnson has long since retired, but his use of the mechanics of the automobile he was driving and the nature of the driving experience gave him a long career, with 50 wins and 148 top 10 finishes.

There are ways to use corporate bond funds to your advantage, but doing so, as you will find when we get to the equity side of things, demands that you know something about the mechanics as well. You can call it a look under the hood if you like.

Bonds and the funds that invest in them must take many things into consideration. We have already covered some of these things: the difference between par, discount, and premium; what short, intermediate, and long term mean; taxes, yields, and economic influences. But to truly understand how corporate bonds work, there are some additional terms that you must make your own.

Potential Unrealized—Perhaps

An old football coach of mine told us after we lost a third game in a row that potential means "ain't done nothin' yet!" He was implying that we were not doing our job and therefore were not living up to his expectations and our potential. In bond investing, this is called a *call*. This is a feature that, if attached to a bond, can create a great deal of difficulty.

A call feature on a bond not only increases your risk—a topic that we will get to soon enough and will discuss over and over again afterward—but also thwarts what might otherwise have been a profitable situation. It is, in its simplest terms, permission to pay off what is owed without penalty. You may have this feature on your mortgage or your car loan. What it basically allows you to do is pay off the debt owed sooner than the terms dictate. But unlike the case with a loan, where the interest is usually covered first and the principal is paid off after that, with a bond, the prepayment or call can ruin some very good planning.

A great many municipal bonds carry just such a provision, as do some corporate bonds. Yield, as I mentioned earlier, is a reward for taking risk. When a bond is called, the reward is essentially reduced or nullified.

There is basically only one reason why a bond issuer would call its bonds. When the economic environment gets good enough—and, in a twist that may come as a surprise, when this happens, the economy will probably be doing a little worse—the bond issuer can refinance the debt that the bond is covering at a lower interest rate. The issuer calls the bond, pays off the principal, and issues a new set of bonds with a different maturity date and a lower interest rate. This is similar to what happens when you refinance your home at a lower rate: in effect, you pay off the original mortgage and start the loan process all over again at a lower, much more agreeable rate—at least for you. When this happens to a bond that you own, or one that you own inside a mutual fund, where there is a manager to cope with the problem, you lose the interest rate that you were counting on, and you have to accept another bond with a different due date. When this happens, the issuer of the bond must pay an agreed-upon sum over the par value of the bond. This is referred to as a *call premium* and acts as a sort of penalty for early redemption.

This can be problematic for any investor, but inside a mutual fund, it can be extremely difficult to deal with. Consider mortgage-backed securities. Most Americans had no idea what these somewhat shadowy investments were until late summer 2007. When the housing market started to shake at its foundation, it was this particular corner of the market that shook the most. Granted, folks lost their homes and stimulus packages were announced and everyone tried to save what they could, but the bond investor took a hit as well.

Mortgage-backed securities are big bundles of mortgages that are sold as an investment to bond funds and individuals. Like all loans, they have a period called the term. This can be used by the bond fund or investor as a way of determining how long it can expect the promised amount of interest.

If I can prepay my mortgage, and I do so, don't these mortgage-backed securities end up with something that they don't want: my money?

Yes. In a normal credit environment, when interest rates fall, the estimated principal payment period, something that is calculated for these securities as a precaution, gets shorter. The opposite is true if interest rates rise. The reason: people tend to refinance if there are lower rates available and hold on to their mortgages if rates rise. Bundling mortgages and selling these securities allowed banks and lenders to raise additional capital to lend to more home buyers. However, when the mortgage meltdown began, and home prices fell or at least stopped rising, something happened that caught folks completely off guard. When interest rates on numerous adjustable-rate mortgages packed inside these securities rose, the result was unexpected: people defaulted on their obligation to pay the principal. Foreclosures increased, and suddenly no one could make any good guesses as to how much trouble was still left inside these MBSs.

What might be considered the opposite of the call feature is the *put*. Bond issuers sometimes offer a put to investors who might be sensitive to interest-rate changes. If your bond fund manager owns bonds that have puts on them, the manager accepted a lower interest rate (paid a premium to par) for the option of bailing out of the bond early.

The Price of Risk

Basically, yield is compensation for taking a risk. The higher the yield a bond carries, the greater the risk that the bond issuer might default. Because yield can mean many things, it is probably easiest to list the different types.

Coupon yield. A coupon is your right to an interest payment on a fixed date. The coupon yield, whether it be a fixed or floating amount, is what the bondholder can expect each year until maturity.

Current yield. This is the yield based on the current price of the bond. If the price of the bond has fallen, the current yield is higher. If the bond is currently selling at a premium, the yield is lower.

Yield to maturity. This is a better kind of calculation; it takes into account not only what you can expect to earn (the interest payments), but also the price of the bond in relation to its value at maturity. If the bond has a call date, then the calculation uses that date instead of the maturity date and is aptly referred to as *yield to call.* A "yield-to-worst" bond has numerous call dates.

Tax equivalent yield. As we discuss throughout the book, taxes play a role in how much money you actually earn from any investment. If a bond is taxable, as corporate bonds are, understanding how much you *might* earn is a good way of determining the worth of a particular bond or fund given your particular situation. Because of the taxes involved, corporate bonds offer higher yields to attract investors and offset some of the taxes those investors might pay. They use the additional yield to compete with Treasuries, a much safer and federally tax-free investment.

SEC yield. This is a surprisingly deceptive indication of possible yield that is used primarily by mutual funds. When a fund calculates the SEC yield, it uses a number of tools, whether deliberately or not, to make the yield seem more attractive to investors than it really is—which is why we are spending some time discussing the underlying mechanics of the bond world. There are risks in fixed-income investing. It's unfortunate that some bond funds use investors' lack of knowledge to create a better-looking yield than they actually achieve. To do this, they purchase high-yield or riskier bonds and because the SEC yield is calculated on a 30-day basis, it gives the investor, who assumes that the SEC yield is a clear indication of the fund's expenses, the price of the bond as it moves to par, and the return on the bond based on the past 30 days, a false sense of worth. Because bond funds trade daily and investors rarely hold the bonds in their portfolios until they reach full maturity, the SEC yield gives the appearance of a more level playing field, when in fact, it is probably much different over a longer period.

The *yield curve,* as shown in the following diagram, gives different bond maturities along the horizontal axis and the yield or interest rate along the vertical axis. In normal times, the curve slopes upward toward longer maturities. On the other hand, in rougher times, the curve may actually invert or slope downward. These curves are an indication of economic health. Because yield is the price of risk and because time is also a consideration, the slope should indicate how much investors are willing to offer for the underlying bond. Yield curves can also be used to compare what Treasuries offer (the safest) and what corporations offer (riskier).

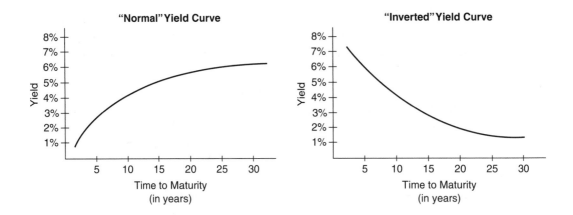

An Almost Perfect Peek Inside

Most investors need help. Not just the kind of guidance that a book like this can offer, but help from agencies that peer deeply into the inner workings of financial instruments and offer us an opinion. In bonds, such an opinion can come from numerous sources. The most commonly cited are the letter grades that Moody's and Standard & Poor's publish.

The following are summaries of the definitions of the ratings on long-term bonds.

Moody's	S&P	
Aaa	AAA	Best quality, with smallest degree of investment risk.
Aa	AA	High quality by all standards; together with the Aaa group, these are generally known as high-grade bonds.
A	A	Bonds with many favorable investment attributes; considered to be upper-medium-grade obligations.
Baa	BBB	Medium-grade obligations (neither highly protected nor poorly secured). Bonds rated Baa and above are considered investment grade.
Ba	BB	Bonds with speculative elements; the future is not as well assured. Bonds rated Ba and below are generally considered speculative.
B, Caa	B, CCC, CC	Generally lack the characteristics of a desirable investment.
Ca	C	Bonds of poor standing.
C	D	Lowest-rated class of bonds, with extremely poor prospects of ever attaining any real investment standing.

The letter grades assigned to fixed-income securities are not the same as the marks you received in grade school. While they are designed to give the investor some sort of idea of whether or not a bond will default (a nice way of saying that the money you invested will not be paid back), the same letters do not mean the same thing for all bonds.

There is a strong probability that a corporate bond receiving an AAA rating will not be nearly as good a municipal bond with the same rating and the same maturity.

Let's compare the differences. When Moody's published a paper looking back on the possibility of default, it wrote: "Moody's considers a default to have occurred if there was a missed or delayed debt service payment, if the bond obligor ceded its authority to make debt payments to a third party that resulted in the suspension of payments to bondholders, or if there was an exchange in which the bondholders accepted a package of securities that Moody's deemed to be of diminished financial obligation."

When you look at the following tables, abbreviated to consider only bonds with five- and ten-year maturities, municipal bonds would be the hands-down favorite if default records were used as the only guide. This is not to say that municipalities can't have financial difficulties. The paper actually lists numerous municipal problems that occurred during the study period.

Weighted-Average Letter Rating Cumulative Municipal Default Rates, 1970–2000		
	Year 5	**Year 10**
Aaa	0.0000%	0.0000%
Aa	0.0115%	0.0327%
A	0.0053%	0.0084%
Baa	0.0281%	0.0590%
Ba	0.4201%	1.3390%
B	3.9760%	3.9760%
Caa-C	10.5455%	10.5455%
All	0.0233%	0.0420%

Weighted-Average Letter Rating Cumulative Corporate Default Rates, 1970–2000		
	Year 5	Year 10
Aaa	0.1237%	0.6750%
Aa	0.2819%	0.8029%
A	0.4681%	1.4721%
Baa	1.8953%	4.8649%
Ba	11.4035%	21.2927%
B	30.5992%	47.3825%
Caa–C	57.7748%	76.7930%
All corporates	6.3025%	9.8363%

Risk Averted

To sum up, diversification gives the investor the opportunity to take a risk and be rewarded at the same time. Bond funds, like equity mutual funds, spread the risk by investing in a variety of holdings, giving the investor the opportunity to be exposed to many different types of securities, whether their payback is fixed, as in bonds, or not, as in stocks.

This principle comes into play when we discuss corporate bonds and the funds that hold them. Unlike Treasuries and many municipal bonds, corporate bond funds and the bonds they invest in are all taxable. The yields they offer take this into consideration, as well as the risk created by credit markets, inflation, the economy, and the ability of the corporation to survive in its own marketplace.

In bond funds, credit risk is interest-rate risk. You can achieve a near zero exposure to this problem by purchasing funds that invest only in Treasury offerings or only in the highest-quality bonds. But it is very difficult to diversify away this kind of risk. Historically, when there are interest-rate pressures, they affect both government and corporate bonds alike.

This inability to control a certain type of risk, such as interest-rate risk, is often called systemic risk. When you diversify your holdings, you add some control over the risk you are taking. This is called unsystematic risk.

Your bond fund manager must also contend with reinvestment risk. Laddering the underlying investments, a technique that is very difficult for individual investors of modest means to use, can often offset this risk. The idea of *laddering* is simple. By purchasing bonds that mature at different times, the bond fund manager can keep the fund's money invested without having to reinvest a large number of bonds that have matured at the same time. In a longer-term fund, owning bonds of different maturities enables the manager to avoid systemic risk (varying credit environments that happen over time). It also allows the manager to own bonds that may be less exposed to *inflation* (the risk that the purchasing power of the investors' return is less than what they assume it will be) and *events* (occurrences outside—usually—the corporate bond issuer's control; this could include anything from a natural disaster to an unnatural one, such as a terrorist attack).

Bond fund managers are generally expected to control tax risk as well. In corporate bonds, this risk is a given. In municipal bond funds, this risk is still very real. If the tax treatment that municipal bonds enjoy were suddenly no longer available, investors might decide that the risk was not worth the reward. Holding a municipal bond with a long maturity would be disastrous.

The last kind of risk is the most difficult kind of systemic risk to manage, more so for the holder of a bond fund than for the holder of an individual bond. The volatility of the fund is directly related to how the fund manager reacts to certain situations.

What the Experts Say

Build for your team a feeling of oneness, of dependence on one another and of strength to be derived by unity.

Vince Lombardi

In municipal bonds, the biggest risk is often passed on to taxpayers of the municipality. The credit problems I have mentioned throughout the book will not last forever, but, as I mentioned, their occurrence gives us an opportunity to examine what could happen to a wide variety of bonds that are dependent on the availability of a certain amount of credit.

A recent auction for municipal bonds was withdrawn because no one wanted to buy the bonds. Because of this, taxpayers in those municipalities will be forced to pay higher taxes to cover the expenses that the bonds would have funded. When a muni defaults, it is also the taxpayers who are forced to make good on the obligation or have the municipality's credit rating slashed.

Treasuries, on the other hand, do not default. Instead, the value of these bonds is slashed when inflation rises. The longer the term of the bond, the greater the risk that inflation will outpace the return that it offers.

Inside a bond fund, the manager is worried not only about your money and your satisfaction, but about his job as well. In a crisis, buying Treasuries is not exactly a bad move jobwise, but for the shareholders, the expected returns are lowered, and if inflation has reared its ugly head, you might even lose money as a result. This is called *agency risk*.

Agency risk is very real, and it is worth considering when you buy a bond fund. Before we discuss some of the best funds available, I want to take a brief moment to discuss insurance.

When a bond is issued and the credit rating is secured, the company that issues the credit rating purchases insurance, and the cost of both the rating and the insurance is passed on to the issuer, who then passes it on to the bond purchaser. In the rest of the financial world, insurance is used to cover the potential risk of loss.

 You are thinking about buying a bond fund because you want to control the risk on some of your portfolio and you want to be able to see some capital appreciation and yield for your efforts. You want to buy a fund because you hope that the manager will work out the details of the portfolio, assessing risk, taxes, inflation, maturities, and so on. So what would you make of the headlines in many of the online news publications on February 15, 2008?

"Can the Real Bond Insurance Regulator Please Stand Up?"—*Wall Street Journal Online*, Feb. 15, 2008, 3:53 p.m.

"Treasurys Rise on Credit Jitters, Manufacturing, Confidence Data"—*Wall Street Journal Online*, Feb. 15, 2008, 3:52 p.m.

"Buffett's Bond Plan Offers Little to Insurers"—*Smart Money*, Feb. 15, 2008, 3:45 p.m.

"Bond Insurer FGIC Wants to Split in Two"—*ABC News*, Feb. 15, 2008, 3:43 p.m.

"Muni Bond Regulator Seeks Transparency"—*Forbes.com*, Feb. 15, 2008

Would you answer that question with a question or two: "Shouldn't bonds be safer than this? What is Warren Buffett doing running around with bonds? Was I wrong in thinking that munis were a relatively straightforward investment?

Relax. To use a popular phrase, "It is what it is." *Flak* magazine offered this explanation of that particular idiom: "'It is what it is,' means what it means. Depending on context, it can be a statement of resignation or of defiance, but in neither case does it connote the optimistic good humor of 'It's all good.' If anything, it expresses the absence of emotion, the abdication of feeling."

That is how the bond insurers such as MBIA, AMBAC, FSA, FGIC, XLCA, Assured Guaranty, and CIFG feel as their ability to assess risk is questioned and, because they are insurers, their ability to make good on the claims that are bound to surface is also questioned.

Bond funds that invest in Fannie Mae and Freddie Mac mortgages do not need to worry, at least on the surface. The government guarantees any default issues that these two GSEs might encounter. And as we have learned, taxpayers underwrite municipalities, and if you'll notice, the federal government is the largest municipality that issues bonds and guarantees them with its "full faith and credit." So in the vicious cycle of investing in fixed income, taxpayers will foot the bill, and if we are busy paying taxes, we are not spending, and that means that we probably are not investing, so corporate bonds are not being bought and growth begins to slow. Can you see where this is going?

Warren Buffett is there because he sees an opportunity to make a couple of gazillion additional dollars for his company by insuring the insurers. And because everyone knows that Buffett isn't known for making unwise investment decisions, the fixed-income world is supposed to breathe a sigh of relief. The Oracle of Omaha has come to the rescue! It is what it is.

How Business Is Run

The market for corporate bonds is much larger than the market for municipal bonds. They are used for a variety of purposes, from building or expanding the current business to refinancing previous debt obligations that may have been incurred when the credit environment was not so good. Just as you would if you were buying or building a house or refinancing your mortgage, businesses run on borrowed money so that they can stay nimble in a competitive global world.

The problem is, even with that straightforward explanation, corporate bonds are not well understood by the investing public. As of June 6, 2006, there was about $5.3 trillion in outstanding bonds, and, surprisingly, there are few ways to measure how well investors do. Corporate bonds are often compared to Treasuries, which requires a little more than simple math to do correctly. Algorithmic calibrations and credit risk pricing models that need to factor in characteristics such as liquidity, taxes, and aggregate market risk variables make the at-a-glance comparisons that the average investor is likely to make and the bond fund manager is likely to use seem almost a futile exercise. The so-called spread between corporates, as corporate bonds are often called, and Treasuries does not capture the true nature of what the bond is worth.

Some have suggested that a better measure might be credit default swaps (CDSs) and what is known as latent liquidity.

 What is a CDS?

A CDS is generally described as: "a barometer of the market's collective judgment of the credit risk of the bonds issued by an obligor. The CDS price is thus a proxy for the premium attached to credit risk, although it may itself be affected by market frictions." At the beginning of 2008, investors purchased CDSs as way to hedge against what, in the early part of that year, proved to be numerous unknown risks. Bill Gross of the PIMCO funds warned that at some point in 2008, CDSs might be valued as being worth more than the bonds themselves.

When Amrut J. Nashikkar, Marti G. Subrahmanyam, and Sriketan Mahanti of the New York University Department of Finance tackled this subject in a paper published in the fall of 2007, they saw the inability to get a good comparison as simply an error made for lack of a better tool.

Their paper, titled "Latent Liquidity and Corporate Bond Yield Spreads," focused on a different method. They suggested that "our measure of liquidity does not use transactional information; instead, it uses information about the ownership of securities to measure the accessibility of a security by a securities dealer." This definition of liquidity requires that several elements be present. For instance, the holdings within a bond fund should not only be rated highly but also have some distinct characteristics. The authors believe that the bonds that are least likely to default are those that are backed by tangible assets (real property that can be liquidated if there is some sort of financial crisis), have leverage, which they relate to the ability to maintain not only share price but all other debts as well, and are strong on something that they call the current ratio, or the ability to meet short-term (one-year) debt obligations without causing problems for longer-term outstanding debt.

The Upside of Corporates

Corporate bonds have some distinct characteristics, not the least of which is a much higher yield than those offered by Treasuries or municipal bonds. That yield, as we now know, is actually higher to offset the taxable nature of the bond and to attract investors.

In spite of having higher default rates than Treasuries or munis, corporate bonds are still considered a mostly safe investment for people who are looking for a steady stream of income and the eventual repayment of principal when the bond matures.

And while we understand how many different types of risks are faced by any type of bond, the funds that invest in corporate bonds are able to choose from a wide variety of sectors (public utilities, transportation companies, industrial corporations, financial services companies, and conglomerates) and structures (maturities and yields), and because not all credit offerings come with the same ratings, different credit-quality characteristics.

There is also the added plus of marketability. Because of the sheer size of the market for corporate bonds, liquidity, or the ability to sell a bond that has yet to mature to another investor, is much greater.

We will eventually get to the techniques for building a portfolio, and yes, one that might suit even the most conservative investor interested in owning only bond funds; however, for the average bond investor who is looking to own something safe, it would be wise to avoid the words "high yield." Generally, the best yields come with the highest risk, and consequently, the lowest letter grade applied by the agencies that do that sort of thing.

It is difficult for the average investor, and often for the bond fund manager, to predict or in some instances even react to the problems that could affect the company that issued a particular bond. For this reason alone, individual bond investors are more likely to make mistakes and misunderstand how the various risks involved can affect what they perceive to be their return. Even bond managers, who are supposed to be the experts in the field, have some difficulty.

Suppose a hurricane makes landfall, with epic force winds, rain, and flooding. Companies that are in its path can be severely damaged. Even if they have adequate insurance, they may be faced with staggering losses. However, unless your bond fund is sharply focused, as some exchange-traded funds (ETFs) can be, a bond problem like this inside a bond fund may have a negligible effect on the overall holdings that the manager has assembled.

Just as hard on the bond fund manager is a severe economic disruption such as a recession or a depression. Even with diversification (something that the individual bondholder rarely has), a bond fund could run into difficulties. For that reason, the best performers should be those whose bonds have an intermediate exposure—too long and the underlying investments might not beat inflation; too short and the bond might not offer a yield that is sufficient to offset the tax issue.

We have mentioned taxes alongside every discussion of your return on investment (ROI). They work as a counterbalance to our enthusiasm and should be considered with every investment decision.

Corporate bonds have different tax considerations from equities. Unlike the interest from Treasuries and municipal bond funds, the interest that you receive from corporate bonds is subject to federal and state income tax. Individual investors treat this as ordinary income.

A mutual fund may refer to these payments of interest as dividends, but unlike equity dividends, which are profit returned to investors, they are fully taxable as ordinary income (be sure to check with your tax advisor).

You can create capital gains and get that 15 percent capital gains rate that you hear about so often, the one that is set to expire in 2010, if a bond that you own or that your mutual fund owns is sold at a profit before the bond matures. If you sell a bond before you have owned it for a year, however, the gain will be taxed as ordinary income. This is important for bond fund investors. You should always scan the prospectus for turnover ratios. If they are too high, the tax efficiency of the fund might be low, and the taxes could eat up all those expected returns.

On the flip side, you could lose money. This creates a capital loss, which, while painful, can be used to offset any gains you may have made, dollar for dollar, to keep your taxes low. Once again, check with your tax preparer. This is the only time a loss will work to your advantage.

When we discussed zero coupon bonds and bonds sold at a discount, I mentioned some special tax situations that may require a personal consultation with your tax attorney or advisor. Discount bonds are taxed a little at a time, with taxes being paid on a portion of the discount each year. Think of it as a prepayment of taxes, with the result that when your bond matures, you do not pay capital gains or other taxes on the difference between the face value (what you received when the bond matured) and the price you paid for the bond (at a discount). You have been incrementally taxed on that difference while holding the bond to maturity.

Who, What, When, and How (Much)

Corporate bond interest is usually paid on a semiannual basis, with the payment being called a coupon. This is why "who" you are buying the bond from is just as important as "what" you are buying. And it is another reason why we spent some quality time discussing the inner workings of this type of investment. Zero coupon bonds, as we have learned, pay no periodic interest.

Although it is often considered a requirement, registering trademarks is not necessary. In the United States, first-use rules apply, and the symbol ™ suggests that any number of things (shapes, sounds, smells, moving images, taste, and any other sensory experiences considered proprietary to the business) are in fact owned by the business and are not generally available for anyone to use. The symbol ® offers proof of registration; however, this is a legal requirement only in countries that do not recognize first-use laws, but instead enforce "first to file" rules. Companies that do register their brand or logo do so with the U.S. Patent and Trademark Office (USPTO).

Your fund manager will be faced with numerous types of corporate bonds to purchase, each with a different structure and purpose. Generally, corporate bonds are *registered* bonds. In this case, the issuer gives the bondholder a certificate of ownership, and the bondholder (or fund) needs to do nothing more than wait for the interest payments to begin. There are no physical coupons that must be sent in if the bondholder is to get paid. When the bond matures, the principal is repaid.

Bearer bonds are no longer issued, but some of them still exist. Dan Brown, author of *The DaVinci Code,* puts these obscure bonds in the briefcase of Bishop Aringarosa, who is looking to finance some nefarious scheme anonymously. (It should also be noted, while we are on the topic of Mr. Brown's book, that the name of the French detective, Bezu Fache, is one of the greatest fiction names of all time.) These bonds are anonymous; they can be used just like cash wherever bearer bonds are still accepted, and because of that, they are highly negotiable.

By far the most common type of bond is the *book-entry* bond. With this type of arrangement, the bondholders receive nothing physical, neither a bond nor coupons. The certificate is considered global and is held at a securities depository. If the bond is held individually, it may be held in the investor's brokerage account, which receives all of the interest and principal payments.

As we outline various types of bond funds here, you will find that many of them require that outsized amounts be purchased if an investor is to be involved in the fund. While they have good reasons for this, the individual investor who is interested in rounding out his portfolio risk with a bond fund may find that the best of the best are too pricey for him. Individually, bonds can be purchased over the counter (OTC) for as little as $5,000. Most, however, sell for $10,000.

We don't often think of bonds in a physical form anymore. At one time they did come to the investor upon purchase as actual pieces of paper containing the obligation of the issuer written where one could actually see it and hold it. The history of these types of bonds, now almost completely issued by electronic means, is now a colorful oddity. The largest bond ever printed was sized at two feet by three feet including the coupons, which could be torn off for redemption. The face value of this bond was $1,000 and was issued by the New York Cable railway in 1884. The smallest in size was a baby bond issued by the state of Louisiana in $5 increments, written on paper not much bigger than a business card. In terms of denomination, the largest bond ever issued came from the New York Central & Hudson River Railroad. It was a 100-year bond backed by gold for $42,110,000. Paying the bondholder 4.5 percent, this series A bond will mature in 2013.

I would still discourage the average investor from using the individual bond route. Taxes are always a consideration. Laddering requires the ability to buy bonds with various maturities to offset different economic conditions, not the least of which is inflation. The bond funds that we will look at in the next couple of pages have low entry fees, low turnover, and intermediate maturities (but remember, the terms *short-*, *intermediate-*, and *long-term* are rather vague), and should provide us with a decent yield while providing some asset protection.

The marketability of a corporate bond is considered superior in many respects. There is a great deal of demand (under normal circumstances), and there are a large number of available bonds to purchase at any one given time. As I mentioned earlier, this is also called liquidity.

Individuals will pay a broker's fee; mutual fund bond investors will pay fees as well. Throughout the book, the cost of owning the fund will always be provided side by side with the return that the fund has posted. Occasionally we will note how much the fund may have cost as compared to the industry average (the average for the sector that the fund focuses on).

From Ultra-Short to Much Longer

In the world of ultra-short-term bond funds, Pacific Investment Management Company (PIMCO) rules. However, because these funds generally charge upwards of $5 million to join, and I'm guessing that most of us do not have that kind of money to put into play, despite windfalls, we will not examine them here.

Ultra-short-term funds generally focus on current income consistent with capital preservation. Many of them break down their strategies without exposing their hand. Thomas M. Price, manager of the Wells Fargo Advantage Ultra S/T Inc I, invests at least 80 percent of his available assets (investors' cash) in income-producing debt securities. His portfolio at any one time could contain U.S. dollar–denominated debt securities of foreign issuers (up to 25 percent); to boost returns, he also discloses a much riskier position in below-investment-grade debt securities with at least a BB rating by Standard & Poor's.

I have included, alongside the expense ratio, the turnover percentage. The average turnover for the ultra-short-term group of bond funds listed here as the best over the last three years is 0.76 percent.

Fund	Annual Return (at 2007 year-end)	Expense Ratio/ Turnover
STI Classic Ultra-Short Bond I SISSX	4.36%	0.26%/96%
Wells Fargo Advantage Ultra S/T Inc I SADIX	4.36%	0.38%/28%
Pacific Capital U.S Govt Short F/I Y PSGYX	4.35%	0.39%/81%
Trust For Credit Unions Ultr-Sht Dur Gov TCUUX	4.32%	0.35%/107%
STI Classic Limited Duration I SAMLX	4.32%	0.14%/185%

Short-term bond funds often resemble the Wild West of bond trading. Some of the best funds can turn a portfolio over at a clip that is five times the sector average (which is already a high 94 percent) and go well over the category's average expenses (also 94 percent). Robert F. Auwaerter, vice president and portfolio manager with the Vanguard Group, has overseen all of the Fixed Income Group's portfolio management activities since 2003. As the lead manager of the Vanguard Short-Term Investment-Grade (VFSTX) since 1983, his fund, which has low sensitivity to interest-rate risk while investing in good-quality bonds with high credit ratings, has put an emphasis on current income.

In this fund, 80 percent of the assets are in short- and intermediate-term corporate bonds and other corporate fixed-income obligations, which can vary greatly throughout this corner of the bond world. This could signal some positioning on his part in anticipation of some economic event.

Mr. Auwaerter considers short-term to be an average weighted maturity of between one and three years. As I write this, the fund currently has 15 percent of its assets as cash. A portion of the fund may, at any one time, consist of bank obligations, commercial paper, repurchase agreements, and/or dollar-denominated foreign securities.

Fund	Annual Return (at 2007 year-end)	Expense Ratio/ Turnover
Diversified Short Horizon Instl DISHX	4.79%	0.10%/76%
Vanguard Short-Term Investment-Grade Adm VFSUX	4.60%	0.21%/43%
DWS Short Duration Plus S DBPIX	4.46%	73%/57%
Diversified Short Horizon Inv DVCSX	4.42%	10%/76%
American Performance Intrm Bd N/L Inv APFB	4.39%	73%/31%

Daniel J. Fuss, executive vice president, director, and managing partner of Loomis, Sayles & Company, heads up the Managers Bond fund (MGFIX) and has done so since 1983. This intermediate-term bond fund may be experiencing more than just a little bit of trouble if its focus remains the same. This is where you are most likely to come into contact with those mortgage-backed securities that I mentioned earlier.

This fund is decidedly focused on earning a high level of current income. At this particular moment in time, Mr. Fuss is still keeping 80 percent of the fund's assets in investment-grade corporate bonds and mortgage-related and other asset-backed securities.

In a year-ending note, Loomis, Sayles & Company offered a "no recession call" for several reasons. (Only you, the reader, will know whether they were right because recessions are generally identified either after they have already taken hold or months after they end.) The company believes that banks, despite their unfolding credit issues, will "lead us out of this credit crunch," even with the possibility of higher oil prices and a continued decline in housing prices. It even notes that whatever this economy faces before 2009, we can expect higher rates of corporate bond defaults than we have been used to (they have recently dropped to an all-time low of 0.81 percent) and slower profit growth.

The fund also has hedged its bets with securities issued or guaranteed by the U.S. government or its agencies or instrumentalities. The three-year best for the sector have a relatively high turnover (196 percent) and what I would consider a higher than necessary expense ratio (1.00 percent).

Fund	Annual Return (at 2007 year end)	Expense Ratio/ Turnover
ISI North American Government Bond A NOAMX	6.51%	1.06%/49%
Managers Bond MGFIX	6.17%	0.99%/46%
Loomis Sayles Investment Grade Bond C LGBCX	6.05%	1.57%/35%*
Loomis Sayles Investment Grade Bond B LGBBX	5.99%	1.70%/35%†
Frontegra Columbus Core Plus FRTRX	5.92%	0.20%/958%
ISI North American Government Bond C NORCX	5.83%	1.72%/49%‡

* This fund is also managed by Mr. Fuss.

† This fund is also managed by Mr. Fuss but carries a 5 percent deferred sales charge (also known as a closed-end fund, which we will get to later).

‡ The cost of this expense ratio should be considered. Based on an investment of $10,000, this fund would cost investors almost $2,030 in fees and expenses. The sector average expense ratio at 1.00 percent over the same period would cost the investor $1,440.

Vanguard's Bond Index Group flexes its indexing muscles best in the long-term bond category. Kenneth Volpert, lead manager for Vanguard Long-Term Bond Index (VBLTX), keeps it inexpensive (with a 0.18 percent expense ratio compared to the sector average of 0.83 percent, which leaves you with an additional $1,000 or more in your pocket when you keep $10,000 with him for 10 years), keeps it consistent (turnover for the sector is over 144 percent; this fund is at 55 percent), and focuses almost exclusively on U.S. Treasuries (or otherwise dollar-denominated securities, most of which carry a AAA rating).

Fund	Annual Return (at 2007 year-end)	Expense Ratio/ Turnover
Vanguard Long-Term Bond Index VBLTX	5.81%	0.18%/55%
Delaware Extended Duration Bond A DEEAX	4.87%	0.25%/15%
Maxim Federated Bond Portfolio N/A	4.47%	0.70%/63%

Where Risk Rules

Most bond advisors worth their salt will carefully examine how you have structured your portfolio before recommending hybrid, high-yield, emerging-market, or world bond funds. Those same bond advisors, even your broker, who still subscribes to the 60/40 equity-to-bond split for a good portfolio, should know that risk is better managed on the equity side. In *Retirement Planning for the Utterly Confused*, I suggested that eliminating the bond part of the equation altogether would be better for someone who is focused on growing as much money as possible in a tax-deferred account. Bond funds do have a place in a portfolio, but they should be held outside of a retirement plan.

We look to bond funds for capital preservation, income, and a small amount of risk. Once investors begin eyeballing the high-yield side of the equation, it may be difficult to convince them that the increased risk—which should be on the equity side of the balance sheet—is quite different once you begin looking at risky bond funds.

High yield is, as we now know, a reward for taking unusually large risk on less than good-quality bonds. If liquidity is the ability to be able to get out of the investment on a moment's notice, high-yield bonds offer unwary investors the opposite. High-yield bonds always have a lower rating, and because of that, most of them come with a call feature. For whatever reason, the bond issuer's credit rating could improve, and that would allow it to refinance its debt sooner than anticipated. On the opposite end from good news for a company, the possibility of default exists.

When authors Richard J. Herrnstein and Charles Murray wrote *The Bell Curve* in 1994, they hoped that the book would clarify how intelligence and class structure in American life could be charted. The book was met with a great deal of criticism, largely because it offered a way to predict financial income, job performance, unwed pregnancy, and crime based on intelligence rather than on a parent's socioeconomic status or education level. Initially, the book was well received and sold over 500,000 hardcover copies. It eventually became deeply divisive and was criticized as being a distortion of the truth. But the popularity of the "bell curve" stuck. I have seen it used to represent how grades are awarded, how emotions are tracked, and even how a product might be received.

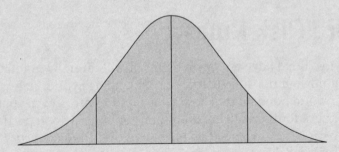

If high-yield bonds were put on the bell curve, they would experience what is known as kurtosis. A bell curve enables you to pick a middle ground (the most common values); as it slopes away in either direction, it graphs the extremes (special circumstances). Kurtosis in bond investing shows the special cases that occur more or less often than they normally would have. High yields show a high kurtosis; lower kurtosis equates to lower than expected yields. The more the investors are misled by high kurtosis, or the belief that these outsized returns are normal, the more dangerous the bond becomes.

Adding to the risk is the inability to accurately compare such a bond, or a fund that invests in these types of securities, with similar types of investments.

So who actually invests in high-yield bonds, knowing that should a recession take hold of the economy, the prices of those bonds may decline? Who actually is willing to take the high default risk involved with this type of bond, fully understanding that all the issuer needs to do is not make good on a payment of interest or, worse, the repayment of principal?

All sorts of events can make high-yield bonds an extremely hazardous place for a fixed-income investor's money. High-yield investors will need to understand that if a credit rating company such as Moody's lowers its rating on the bond, the price will take a nosedive. Rising interest rates can have the same effect on a bond's price, as can a recession on the other side of the economic coin.

If the average bondholder is indeed a worrier—sensitive to any sort of bad news, pricing in both good news and bad, looking long-range and short for any troubling event on the horizon, from oil prices to inflation to international acts of terror—then a high-yield investor would indeed be throwing caution to the wind. News from within an issuing company's industry can do as much damage as if the issuing company had released the bad news on its own financial status. Natural or unnatural, movements in high-yield bonds are a knee-jerk reaction to numerous events and newsworthy items.

And what kind of investor buys something that he or she may not be able to sell? High-yield bonds can be highly illiquid, even more so than investment-grade bonds.

But on the off-chance none of these things might happen, high-yield bond-holders and those who invest in funds that hold them will find several almost risk-worthy reasons why they might use these types of investments.

The Upside of High Yield

High-yield bond investors also see great reward. Given the right state of economic affairs, a high rate of current income is the reward for taking the risk when the issuer offers high interest rates. Given the right set of circumstances, the company that issued the bond could have its credit rating changed for the better, and that would mean capital appreciation.

And then there is the one thing I have yet to mention: should a company be liquidated for one reason or another, bondholders stand in line ahead of owners of common and preferred stock. That alone would make the risk more palatable and even more conservative than betting on the company in the stock market.

What is risk worth if it is not taken? Is it reward not realized? Potential not fulfilled? Denial? Or is it safety as a result of a well-informed decision? How do we make an informed decision based on a handful of variables that could change in a hurry?

Everyone who has ever tried to help folks embrace their inner risk taker understands how difficult the subject is. In *Investing for the Utterly Confused*, I looked at the NBC game show *Deal or No Deal*. It has been called the best-contrived economics test ever. Where else can one find out how people might react in the face of huge amounts of money, often without the clinical atmosphere found in economics studies? It is an unequivocal hit, even though no one has won the million-dollar prize, despite the fact that the show has increased the number of $1 million opportunities on the board to, at last check, 13 of 26 chances. The game requires no skill, no knowledge (not even at the fifth-grade level), and no physical abilities (although one contestant had her husband suspended from a platform). The 26 high-definition gorgeous models help the show along. Howie Mandell provides the suspense. A shadowy figure called the banker entices, angers, tempts, and cajoles with either ascending or descending offers to take the money or take the risk that the suitcase the contestant has chosen at the beginning of the show contains one of the million-dollar prizes.

I suppose, for the investor who is willing to take the risk, the answers to those questions would be: All risk is worth taking. Risk not taken is reward not realized, thrills not experienced, and the belief that this is the right decision. Denial is not the same thing as being in denial. Good investors assemble as much knowledge as they can and go with it regardless of the outcome. Unforeseen events are just that: things that are not easily predicted and aren't always on the loss side. Just as often, perhaps more so, the coin flip comes up heads.

Using a bond fund manager helps.

The Best High-Yield Opportunities

John Moody, the financial publisher who began Moody's Investors Service, which briefly was absorbed by Dun & Bradstreet and then later became independent again, did not like the term *junk*. His preferred term for non-investment-grade, below-investment-grade, less-than-investment-grade, or speculative-grade bonds was *high-yield*.

Moody saw the use of these bonds, which first came into existence in the early 1920s, as an opportunity for some investors to profit from less-than-stellar companies' need to seek financing and overcome the weaknesses that the market attached to their balance sheets. Bonds are, for want of a better description, the grease that keeps business moving. The ability of a company to raise money through bond offerings was essential when it came to mergers and acquisitions, leveraged buyouts, or even hostile takeovers.

The term *junk* did not disappear from the marketplace simply because Moody chose to give these bonds a more appealing name. Junk has a purpose.

When John Moody began his investment rating firm in 1909, investors needed to know whether the obscure but highly lucrative securities issued by railroads and corporations were worth the risk, and if so, how much risk they were actually taking. This was a departure from Moody's previous journalistic venture of simply discussing property, management, and company valuations. By 1924, helped by the fact that many of the companies he reviewed for his widely read manuals had defaulted on their bonds, Moody's covered 100 percent of the bond market, including not only corporate offerings but municipal bonds as well.

If you fast-forward past the Great Depression, where Moody gained even more recognition for the number of companies that he rated highly that did not fail, past the days of Michael Milken, the bond trader who took "junk" bonds to new levels in the 1980s, to the state of the bond markets in 2008 and beyond, you will find that the company still offers a letter grade to help investors determine risk.

But what does that letter signify? In a paper published by Grais & Ellsworth LLP, New York, the reliability of those letter grades was called into question when a defamation suit was brought against Moody's. In 1999, a school district attempted to sell bonds that had not previously been rated by the service. Several hours into the auction, Moody's offered an outlook via its electronic publication and stated that the district's "obligation debt is negative, reflecting the district's ongoing financial pressures." That was enough to kill the offering, and the school district sued, in part because of the rating. The bonds needed to be repriced and offered again at a much higher yield. The court did not side with the school district, suggesting that the rating, no matter when it was issued, was too vague to be considered "provably false."

Gregory Husisian was the first to call the grade offered by Moody's "the world's shortest editorial," and because it is considered to be a journalistic opinion, it is protected by the First Amendment. Add to this the fact that companies like Moody's, Fitch, and Standard & Poor's have been given the blessing of the SEC through its designation of them as NRSROs (National Recognized Statistical Rating Organizations), and because of that, actually charge bond issuers a fee to give their offerings ratings, and you have an idea of why so much of what is unfolding in the credit markets is confusing.

Junk bonds allow otherwise unsecured and poorly financed companies to raise capital without further diluting their stock. (Each time a company issues additional shares, the value of each share falls for two reasons: first, when the income statement is issued, the number of shares outstanding is divided into the profit to get the earnings per share, and having a larger number of shares lowers that number, and second, stock is a much longer-term commitment, lacking the maturity date offered by bonds.) Junk also gives foreign securities an opportunity to enter a marketplace that otherwise might have been closed to them. Mortgage-backed securities (MBS) offerings would not have been possible had investors not embraced the risk. When Arthur Stone Dewing suggested that default losses and price instability were not enough to make this type of investment less attractive, especially to those who were willing to take the increased risk, and that these bonds were only slightly worse than bonds that were covered (secured), he legitimized their use in a portfolio.

The question is, do they belong in your portfolio? There are several considerations that you must entertain before you answer. Each of the funds listed here makes no bones about what its goal is or how it hopes to achieve that goal. Many investors, including Gary Pokrzywinski, lead manager of the Principal Inv High Yield II Inst (PHYTX), look to high-yield, high-risk, below-investment-grade fixed-income securities to provide higher than average returns through current income. The fund may invest in foreign funds, it may borrow funds to do so, and it may hold convertible securities and preferred stocks. Many of the fund's holdings are rated lower than BBB by S&P or Fitch or lower than Baa by Moody's.

What to Ask?

What are convertible securities and preferred stocks, and why do so many high-yield bond funds invest in them?

A *convertible security* gives the investor and/or the company the right to convert the security from a bond to common stock. The downside is that once the company converts the bond to common stock, the steady stream of income and the expected principal payment at maturity no longer exist. A *preferred stock* is like a common stock with two basic differences: it has many of the features that a debt security like a bond might have (a fixed rate of return and pricing that is based more on how interest rates move than on the price that the equity markets put on common stock), and the holders of preferred stock have a place in line ahead of the holders of common stock (but behind bondholders) should the company ever declare bankruptcy.

(You can read more about convertible securities at http://www.sec.gov/answers/convertibles.htm.

You can read more abut preferred stocks at http://www.mojolaw.com/info/is09.)

Mr. Pokrzywinski's fund is given five stars by Morningstar (a mutual fund rating service that offers an "opinion" much the way Moody's does), its highest rating. Many of the funds in this particular corner of the investment world charge fees in excess of 1.24 percent and often have turnover rates for their portfolios of 117 percent. Mr. Pokrzywinski's fund offers a much lower fee structure and less than half of the turnover of his peer group.

Fund	Annual Return (at 2007 year-end)	Expense Ratio/ Turnover
Principal Inv High Yield II Inst PHYTX	9.53%	53%/47%
John Hancock High-Yield A JHHBX	9.38%	93%/47%
Fidelity Advisor High Income Advantage I FAHCX	8.99%	81%/35%

What's Next ▷ The huge bell towers you often see pictured in so many photos of rustic Italian villages are called campaniles. Italians, who are fiercely devoted to the place where they live, with an undying love for their home, their city, or their region, have a spirit of campanilismo. And while we may find that having all of our investments on the ground we are most familiar with will suit our needs, there are opportunities to be had in other countries. In the next chapter we will look at international bond funds and their much riskier brother, the emerging-market funds.

CHAPTER 8

Inside a Bond Fund—International

◆◆◆◆◆◆◆◆◆◆◆◆◆◆◆◆◆◆◆◆◆◆◆◆◆◆

U ntil now, we have mainly focused on what this country has to offer. Looking at foreign-based bond funds requires two things, both of which involve a certain amount of additional risk and, with that, the potential for a certain amount of increased reward. If the underlying bonds in the fund are dollar-denominated, any fluctuations in interest rates that have an effect on U.S.-based bonds (prices go up if rates are falling and vice versa) will have a similar effect on foreign-based dollar-denominated bonds. If the bonds are linked to the currency of the foreign country (or company) issuing the bond, the changes in rates and prices in the United States may actually have the opposite effect on those securities.

If you are buying bond funds to avoid credit risk, it would be far wiser to stick with U.S. Treasury offerings or bond funds that invest in AAA-rated securities. With foreign bonds, in addition to the possibility that you might face some interest-rate risk, the currency risk also needs to be considered.

Currency risk does not come with any sort of premium. It is unpredictable and hard to price into the security. Unlike the duration risk (the possibility that a bond is called), the credit risk (the possibility that the bond issuer's ratings change), and the equity risk (the possibility that the company defaults), currency risk is not easy to assess, and because of that, it defies categorization for investors who are looking for some safety, expected returns, and with any luck, capital preservation.

If you feel that the risk is worth taking, it would be prudent to look at funds that invest in a limited number of countries, preferably well-established economies (rather than emerging markets, which we will get to next) and that do not expose you to maturities much beyond 10 years.

These types of funds are often called world funds, and some of them—those that were immune to the recent credit problems here in the United States—have done quite well. The turnover is generally higher in this group than in any of the previous sectors we have so far explored, with average turnover exceeding 200 percent. Expenses are generally high as well (1.27 percent).

The Oppenheimer International Bond fund and the Alliance Bernstein fund group dominate the three-year best of category. Both funds, offering both closed-end and front-load funds (I discuss the merits of each kind further in the section on equity mutual funds), have managed to control their turnover and expenses.

 You know them by name. The writers and artists Ernest Hemingway, F. Scott Fitzgerald, T. S. Eliot, Ezra Pound, Gertrude Stein, Josephine Baker, Langston Hughes, Richard Wright, James Baldwin, Miles Davis, Charlie Parker, Allen Ginsberg, William S. Burroughs, Harold Norse, Tom Ford, Patrick Kelly, and Marc Jacobs were all expatriates, living abroad in centers of culture and art such as Munich or Paris, enjoying the ability to travel and live abroad even as millions of Europeans were making their way to American shores. They seldom became citizens of the countries they lived in, but they flourished in those surroundings. The opening lines of Lillian Lida Bell's novel *The Expatriates* explain it best: "It was Paris. It was May."

World funds or international bond funds generally are not as risky as some people might suppose. The bond rating companies generally offer a letter grade for overseas offerings if the country is large enough or the assets of a corporation are transparent.

Arthur P. Steinmet has been the lead manager since 2004 not only of the Oppenheimer Y Fund but of the classes of bond shares known as A, B, C, and N, all offering a variety of entry points, differing load features, and dissimilar expenses. Essentially, the prospectus for these different fund classes is the same, as are the objectives spelled out this 52-page prospectus.

Mr. Steinmet is interested in fixed-income securities that, as a whole, provide better returns than those offered in the United States. Basically the fund is looking for total return, but he also seeks compensation for the added risk of investing overseas. Some of the fund's top holdings include securities issued by the Republic of Italy (4.38 percent) and U.S. Treasury notes (3.65 percent), as well as securities issued by Japan (2.73 percent), New South

Wales Treasury (2.47 percent), and the Federal Republic of Germany (2.15 percent). None of his top holdings would be considered especially risky. The fund invests at least 80 percent of its assets in bonds. (The full prospectus is available for downloading at http://www.oppenheimerfunds.com.)

Fund	Annual Return (at 2007 year-end)	Expense Ratio/ Turnover
Oppenheimer International Bond Y OIBYX	10.13%	54%/68%
Alliance Bernstein Global Gov Inc Tr In A ANAGX	9.33%	1.05%/170%

Investing Bravely

I briefly explained how some countries faced credit crises when investors, seeking risk and the hope of reward, piled into nations such as Argentina, Mexico, and Brazil. These were the emerging markets of the last century. Today, markets of this type can be found wherever there is a lack of economic stability, but the countries are moving toward open accountability, seeking economic reform, and hoping that by doing so, they will add transparency. Mostly, these are economies that are growing but still lack the confidence to compete on the world stage.

The greater that confidence becomes, the more the economy attracts investors who are willing to take risks. Those risks can and often do greatly outweigh the reward.

In the Real World...

Antoine W. van Agtmael of the International Finance Corporation of the World Bank did not like the term *third world*. It seemed to him that it was too derogatory a label to be applied to developing nations. Credited with coining the phrase *emerging markets* to describe developing economic nations, Mr. van Agtmael understands the importance of investments to help increase the per capita incomes of the country's low- to middle-income citizens and aid in instituting economic development and reform. With such investments, these countries can "emerge" onto the world stage and be able to compete. His latest book, *The Emerging Markets Century: How a New Breed of World-Class Companies Is Overtaking the World*, offers a glimpse of how these economies grow and, in so doing, increase the quality of life in these economically underdeveloped nations.

Not all emerging-market economies are without turmoil. In countries where there is a threat of civil unrest, unstable elections or oppressive regimes, or the threat of revolution, and in those whose banking systems do not have the infrastructure needed to provide an atmosphere that is conducive to growth, investors find the capital markets with the greatest need for monetary infusions. They also find an increase in the overall chances that they will lose everything if the economy turns bad.

Brett Diment heads up the DWS Emerging Markets Fixed Income S (SCEMX) fund for Aberdeen Asset Management. His approach to his fund offers a bit of insight into the need to be nimble in what could be considered to be an ever-shifting landscape. Although his primary holdings are in seemingly stable outposts like Brazil, Argentina, and the Philippines, he is much higher than the sector average (87 percent) when it comes to turnover. But that can be expected from a fund that looks for current income first, with long-term capital appreciation second.

Because of the nature of emerging markets, investing in debt is especially risky. Many experts believe that the strategy of owning an emerging-market bond fund such as this, despite its outsized returns, belongs in the riskiest part of your portfolio—the equity side. Many of these funds have the same risk potential as stock funds that invest in the businesses in those countries. With that in mind, and considering the usual conservative nature of the bond fund investor, a fund like Mr. Diment's is not for the faint of heart.

The fund places assets in high-yielding (lower-rated) debt issued by governments and corporations in emerging-market countries. Granted, many of those debt instruments use the dollar as a currency, but nonetheless the risk can fluctuate wildly.

If you do go into this area, avoid funds that charge loads (which we will discuss soon), and watch those turnover ratios. I emphasize these because of the trading costs; overseas, in emerging markets, these costs can be a tremendous drag on returns.

Fund	Annual Return (at 2007 year-end)	Expense Ratio/ Turnover
WS Emerging Markets Fixed Income S SCEMX	11.47%	1.15%/173%*
Goldman Sachs Emerging Market Debt A GSDAX	11.27%	1.23%/48%†

* The sector averages 1.40 percent in expenses.

† This fund has a front-end load charge of 4.50 percent.

It's a known fact that those patients scheduled for chest or abdominal surgery who have the largest networks of social support in place often have lower levels of pain and anxiety, not only before the operation, but afterward. This can also be said for the investor who seeks mutual funds as the investment of choice. In the next chapter, we will take a look at the equity side of investing in mutual funds. Like bond funds, equity mutual funds have an underlying mechanism, with all parts making up a whole in the attempt to achieve an investor-worthy return. But each component is important, and how well those elements appeal to the potential investor is important to the success of the fund.

CHAPTER 9
The Bandwagon Effect

I n 1998, Albert Mehrabian published a paper in the *Journal of Applied Social Psychology* that looked at how information that suggested that one candidate was leading the other prior to voting could influence the outcome of an election. The article, "Effects of Poll Reports on Voter Preferences," offered insight into the way voters seemed to gravitate toward the candidate who seemed the most popular, while ignoring another candidate who might have addressed all of the same issues.

Mutual funds provide the same type of psychological comfort zone for investors. We like winners. We all want to believe that when we, as a group of investors, are behind a fund manager with all the right qualities—the winning numbers, the just-right amount of tenure with the fund, and billions upon billions of dollars under his care—we too will win. Picking a winning fund manager assures us that we have made the right choice and that our money will grow, exponentially, forever, just because we have "jumped on the bandwagon," so to speak. We want to believe that this is the best way to pick a fund. But we are only half right.

What the Experts Say

If you're not making mistakes, you're not taking risks, and that means you're not going anywhere. The key is to make mistakes faster than the competition, so you have more chances to learn and win.

John W. Holt, Jr.

As we have discussed, mutual funds are complex structures with a good deal of underlying mechanics that need to be discussed. We have looked at the five basic components of a fund: the managers, the administrator, the board of trustees, marketing and distribution, and, finally, the shareholders (see Chapter 3). We began to discuss risk in the form of credit risk, inflation risk, and tax risk, and how investors are rewarded for their ability to accept risk. In bond funds, we learned that risk is rewarded with yield (see Chapter 4).

Fund managers were back in the spotlight in the next chapter as we discussed the importance of a manager's tenure. Getting some insight into the way the fund manager operates is a good way to pick a fund—in almost every circumstance. Does this mean that a new fund manager will not give her investors a good return? Absolutely not, but, as we will discuss throughout this section on mutual funds that invest in equities, there is a good deal of housecleaning, rearranging of the fund's investments, and the application of fresh philosophies that accompanies the changing of the guard. That same time frame of three years minimum that we applied to the bond funds we spotlighted (for example purposes only) will be used in this section of the book as well (see Chapter 5).

More important than who is running the mutual fund is the effect that expenses have on your return. These are a very real deduction that affects how much money you actually make. And your fund manager has control over these expenses. In addition, there is another expense looming if the fund manager does not properly manage how the assets are bought or sold, when and why they are sold, and the tax implications of those moves for the shareholder: taxes. While no fund will ever be without them unless our tax code is improved, your fund manager walks a fine line between working for you and working for the IRS (see Chapter 6).

The stock market is tied to the bond market. Understanding yield is just as important in determining the quality of an equity fund that you are investing in as it is when you are considering a bond fund specializing in corporate offerings.

Many people believe that the value of the stock market should be independent of whatever happens to interest rates. We have found that interest rates determine the cost of borrowing money. Because much of the money that businesses need is raised in the bond market, knowing the rate that the company needs to pay investors in its bonds often communicates the overall health of the company to equity investors (see Chapter 7).

And finally, we took a look at things that what we have no control over. For bonds, that is the high-yield and high-risk world of emerging-market investing. Both imply that rewards are available to the strong of heart and the fierce of will, but that these rewards may not materialize because of factors beyond the investors' control. If that sounds like a Twilight Zone introduction, it should. And as Larry Swedroe, bond manager from Buckingham Asset Management, often tells it: "If you want risk, buy equities." His advice also suggests that investors in bonds should stick to AAA and AA fixed-income offerings (see Chapter 8).

As we begin our look at equity funds, we will move in the opposite direction from that we took with bonds. Whereas when we looked at bond investments, we went from the safest to the least safe, we begin our look at investing in equity mutual funds with the most volatile and proceed to the least volatile.

The Attraction of a Well-Spoken Pitch

My son Andre owns a small search engine marketing (SEM) firm in Bend, Oregon. This is a well-saturated business, with new "experts" in the field offering tips on how to give every Web site top positioning in the search engines. In the end, it is the sites with the deepest bankrolls that win, and the SEM firms that can court those clients rise to the top of their field. No matter whom you are trying to sell your strategy to, having the perfect sales pitch is the key. He learns his at the local community college.

Every semester, he dons his "Professor of Search" cap and leads a class full of small business owners, a total of 26 students, on a quest to learn how to become a presence online despite a low budget. What he gains from the class—he donates the money he receives and seems to share the joy when his students succeed—is a look into the businessperson's mind, the person who is in control of many more marketing dollars than his students are. With this information, he has honed his sales pitch to those company leaders, who ask the same questions and face the same challenges as his students and, at the end of the day, just want to be able to sleep knowing that they have made the right decision.

Mutual funds aim their pitch at a much wider range of people. Their pitch must appeal to financial advisors (people who, often masquerading as brokers, can offer you, the individual investor, a basket of mutual funds from which to choose your portfolio), you, and institutional investors (pension funds, insurance companies, banks, hedge funds, and sometimes mutual funds that are designed to manage large group portfolios).

What is an institutional investor?

Institutional investors are market movers. They have large portfolios that they invest with certain return goals in mind. For a pension fund, the goal might be to ensure that the investments in the portfolio will adequately cover the needs of current retirees from a company or a union and those of workers yet to retire. An insurance company may be investing to maintain and grow its current reserves; because, like pensions, its requirements are tied to actuarial tables; or because it is hedging its bets against future claims. The Employee Retirement Income Security Act (ERISA) usually keeps a close eye on these groups of accredited investors.

The rules describing who is an institutional investor can include a person with an income of $200,000 and/or a net worth of $1 million. They can also include charities, endowments, brokerages, and investment banks. Hedge funds generally qualify as well.

What group mutual funds are pitching to is just as important as what they say. For financial advisors or institutional investors looking at how well a fund performs, the focus might be on any of a number of things. For instance, the focus might be on *technology* (what kind of tools the fund manager and her team use to gain a competitive edge), *competitive analysis* (picking the correct benchmark to compare the fund to, focusing on how well it did under certain economic and marketplace challenges, and, with any luck, choosing just the right length of time to highlight its success), or perhaps even *what sort of edge the fund might have over its competitors* (once a fund determines whom it is trying to beat, it can focus on strategy, capitalizing on the nuances of the sector). The fund manager might emphasize *the fund's value* (this is a nice way of boasting about his execution, disclosing future growth projections, offering market forecasts and prognostications, and telling these savvy investors how much better he can do it and do it for cheaper than the other fund), or *his market reputation* (making it into the top 10 of any category for one week, one month, one quarter, one year, three years, or any other period means more investor dollars coming in, and that, coupled with the fund's returns, can create a certain investment mystique that cannot be ignored), or even *his innovative edge* (if he is not indexing, as so many actively managers of mutual funds tend to do to stay in the race, what new thing he saw that others missed). The last part of the pitch might include a comment on whether, when the going got tough (and it always does), all of these qualities were strong enough to keep investors hanging around for the market to recover—in other words, how good is the fund's *after-sales service level.*

Something in that pitch will no doubt grab your attention if you are an individual investor. Often, the technology and innovation are left out of the pitch to the individual investor, with the emphasis being how well a fund did, what it was focused on, and what kind of an edge it may have over the competition.

Too often, mutual funds pick the wrong indexes to compare themselves to, and although they have improved in this area, they underplay how they do what they do.

 The problem that most of us have is not whether we accept what is being offered as reliable information, but sifting through the information provided to determine what is relevant to us. For that, we need to use the same techniques most often suggested by experts as ways to resist buying something. Increasing your level of skepticism can make you a better consumer and, in the case of mutual funds, a better investor.

Buying a Fund

Most consumer advocates would suggest that you avoid the sales pitch in the first place. But with mutual funds, that is almost impossible. If the fund family isn't selling itself as a whole, individual funds are using every medium they can to lure you into investing. This is fine, but the pitch, as we explain throughout the book, is often skewed. Unfortunately, the mutual fund industry knows that you will not browse through hundreds of funds in order to pick just the right one. You have already decided to buy; now for the follow-through.

Your alternatives will be numerous, and in some cases there will be only slight differences in performance, in execution, and in other factors such as unnecessary expenses. Sifting through these choices requires at least an educated guess about the level of risk you are comfortable with. Once you determine that, you are ready to narrow the field further by selecting a category (growth, value, small cap, large cap—more on these in the next chapters); then, pitting them against one another based on the criteria mentioned earlier, you pick a few that you think would work for you.

Unfortunately, there are only a few venues where mutual funds are available. The first is by direct contact through a Web site where you can download prospectuses for the top fund families (there will be a list of these in the back of the book), or you can call a toll-free number and ask.

You may, for one reason or another, already have a brokerage account. When you purchase a mutual fund through a broker, you should use additional vigilance. For one thing, brokers are not investment advisors, although they often pose as such. Arbitrators have ruled that the rule that applies to "advisors" does not apply to brokers.

People who represent themselves to clients as investment advisors, as explained by the Securities and Exchange Commission (SEC), must have those clients' best interest in mind. Brokers, while they may represent themselves as advisors, do not have any kind of regulation governing this practice.

Brokers are, for all intents and purposes, sellers and buyers of securities. Governed by the National Association of Securities Dealers (NASD), brokers are subject to a slightly different standard from the one applied to investment advisors by the SEC.

Brokers are subject to a suitability standard when making suggestions to their clients, a more vague version of the fiduciary responsibility required of advisors.

In 1999, brokers won an important change in regulations that allowed them to change their pay structure from one that is based solely on transactions to one that is based on fees. With this change, the income from clients with large portfolios was no longer dependent on the number of trades done in a given year. But once fees were allowed, brokers took on some of the aspects of an investment advisor. They began to offer numerous products, such as mutual funds. Mutual fund families offered the brokers incentives, and that is where the difference becomes the most glaring.

Brokers do not have to disclose these fees or the fact that their firm may actually be spotlighting certain investments. If they deem a pitch "suitable" for a client, it can pass the test. If investment advisors recommend a product, they must disclose the fee structure and their potential for compensation.

One other important distinction lies in your ability to take legal action if you feel that any of these rules and regulations were violated. Brokerage contracts often require you to turn any complaint over to an arbitrator, while investment advisors can be sued.

One final comparison is often the most problematic for folks: what is the difference between an investment advisor and a financial planner? Briefly, an investment advisor can structure a portfolio of products that are suited for your goals. They are generally used by people who need to invest large sums of money, perhaps from an unexpected windfall such as an inheritance, or to protect the gain they may have made on the sale of a property.

A financial planner can be someone in a small office in your hometown who, acting as an advisor, will tailor a whole array of products to your needs. Most of the people who use financial planners could do the work themselves. In many cases, you already have numerous products available to you. Financial planners sell from a basket of goods and, for a fee, take much of the legwork out of the process. Do you really need yet another fee to make your money work?

You can read the rules governing investment advisors at http://www.sec.gov/about/laws/iaa40.pdf. For the regulations that brokers must follow, the NASD offers numerous links at http://www.finra.org/RulesRegulation/index.htm.

Mutual funds should be a mainstay of your retirement accounts. Within these accounts, your choices may be limited to a selection of perhaps 10 funds across a broad swath of the market; they may include tens of hundreds of funds from numerous fund families; or they may include all the offerings from a fund family such as Vanguard or Fidelity. Often these plans try too hard to provide what they assume all investors want: choice and diversification.

Almost every plan offers some sort of S&P 500 index fund, one that follows the activity of the 500 most prominent companies on the stock exchange. Beyond this, they break down the market into smaller pieces, each with its own kind of risk and mostly indexed to a particular sector of the markets. Some plans offer access to actively managed mutual funds, where a fund manager takes a stab at investing in a certain way, perhaps adding more risk or perhaps taking away some of the risk that index fund investors might have. There has been considerable growth of lifestyle funds (investments that shift from a more aggressive growth style to a more conservative wealth preservation style as time passes) in recent years, and there are always balanced funds that offer a split between bonds and stocks for those closest to retirement. Some plans offer bond funds, and all have a money market fund of some sort.

 Wealth can only be accumulated by the earnings of industry and the savings of frugality.

John Tyler

These funds come with no transaction fees—that are clearly visible. But the smaller plans can cost the employee in terms of choice. While the funds offered inside the plan seem to be priced competitively, many fund families offer less expensive alternatives to the general investing public. (In *Retirement Planning for the Utterly Confused*, I take a long, hard look at how these plans are structured and offer some ideas on how to use them to your best advantage.)

 In the next chapter, we will continue our conversation on how to buy a fund with a look at some of the tools that mutual fund families use to convince you to invest with them. The material they provide in the prospectus, many of which can be downloaded to your computer's desktop, can help you make the right choice—if, that is, you know how to read it and, more importantly, take the time to do so. That will lead to the next step: understanding the differences between load and no-load funds and knowing when one is more beneficial than the other. In addition, we will take a look at making some critical comparisons to determine just how well a fund is doing.

CHAPTER 10
The Fine Print

◆◆◆◆◆◆◆◆◆◆◆◆◆◆◆◆◆◆◆◆◆◆◆◆◆◆◆◆◆◆◆◆◆◆◆◆◆◆◆

About 18 years ago, a Canadian computer scientist began to harness the power of his machines to solve the game of checkers, often using more than 200 additional computers. The program recently finished its quest to play out over 39 trillion games that Jonathan Schaeffer had been running nonstop.

That sort of computing power once required almost 80 percent of all of the available Internet space to run, but in the end it answered the question: is winning at the game of checkers a function of human intuition or the player's ability? It turns out that the answer is actually neither of those, but rather a tactic that Schaeffer calls "brute force." Rather than play with the full number of checkers, his technique challenged the computers to win the game with only 10 pieces on the board.

What he found out, though, was something of a disappointment. If the game of checkers is played perfectly, much like a game of tic-tac-toe, it will always end in a draw.

Will the same kind of thing result no matter how much information you gather about a mutual fund? Is all you can hope for, despite all your efforts, a return that is just average?

No.

When you gather enough information together in one place, as a prospectus does, the jumble of facts and figures and investment managers' opinions fosters the underlying hope that, going forward into the future, you can achieve the returns mentioned throughout the document as having existed in the past.

Can we take what has happened and learn from it? Or is history, as they sometimes say, doomed not to repeat itself but simply to rhyme?

The Prospectus

 History is fables agreed upon.

Voltaire

Probably the best way to see how a prospectus works is to dissect one. And because in the next chapter we will begin looking at funds, starting with the riskiest and moving toward the not-so-daring, we should look at the prospectus of one of the more volatile kinds of fund.

The front cover of the Fidelity International Discovery Fund (FIGRX) prospectus comes with the following standard disclaimer. "Like securities of all mutual funds, these securities have not been approved or disapproved by the Securities and Exchange Commission, and the Securities and Exchange Commission has not determined if this prospectus is accurate or complete." This page also carries a date. Had any those statements been subject to review, they would have been printed in red. Mutual funds, unlike individual stocks, publish a final prospectus complete with all the necessary filings.

The *fund summary* outlines what this fund consists of. In the case of the Discover fund, multiple classes of shares are issued. These share classes offer different opportunities to different investors. Allowing investors to pay the fees up front (front load), pay them after they sell the shares (closed-end), or not pay any fees to join or exit (no-load) makes numerous entry points into the fund available.

Load versus no-load: is there a difference to the average investor?

According to a paper written by James Kuhle and Ralph Pope in 2000, it is often assumed that a fund for which a load is paid either at the beginning of the investor's time in the fund or at the end, when the investor sells the shares, must be more profitable in terms of return on investment than the no-load offerings sold right alongside it.

But those assumptions are wrong. A side-by-side comparison will always show the no-load fund doing better than the closed-end or the front-load fund, but for those comparisons to work, the investment needs some time to show those benefits. Look at the example given here. In it, an investor has three choices (classes) for same fund: one is a no-load that not only charges no fees to join but also does not charge 12b–1 fees (a cost for marketing the fund to other investors, which is a good idea—not charging the fee, but attempting to grow the fund provides numerous additional opportunities for the fund to expand its investment base), one is a front-load fund charging 5 percent, and one is a closed-end (redemption-type) fund that levies a 2.75 percent fee against assets accumulated over the time the investor was involved. Most load funds continue to charge 12b–1 fees even when the fund is closed to new investors, but we will discuss this fee a little further along. For now, let's assume that our fund does not have 12b–1 fees associated with it. Keep in mind that a fund that claims to be 100 percent no-load has no 12b–1 fees.

You begin with $2,500, the minimum entry point for the fund we are discussing. The average front load charged by funds in this category is 5.34 percent, so for the sake of this example, we will use that number. The average back-end load for this type of fund, a foreign large-cap blend of companies, is 2.75 percent. And to be even more realistic, we will give our fund a very modest 5 percent return for the year. (As I write this, the fund is down over 9 percent, but in the year ending 2007, the fund was up 34.85 percent.)

	Start	Year 1	Year 2	Year 3
No-load	$2,500	$2,625	$2,756	$2,893
5.34% front-end load	$2,365	$2,483	$2,607	$2,737
2.75% back-end load	$2,500	$2,625	$2,756	$2,813*

*Value of the fund if you sold it, with the 2.75 percent calculated into the return.

In that paper, "A Comprehensive Long-Term Performance Analysis of Load versus No-Load Mutual Funds," published by the *Journal of Financial and Strategic Decisions*, Mssrs. Kuhle and Pope wonder why, if investors understand how these fees affect the fund's overall return, they continue to use them. One argument is higher overall returns because the fee pays for increased investor services.

But that is simply not true. About 50 years ago, at a time when 12b–1 fees were significantly higher, numerous studies by other researchers (Friend, 1962; Treynor, 1965; Sharpe, 1966; Jensen, 1968) concluded that there is no direct correlation between how a fund performed and how the fees were assessed. The only difference would be if the no-load fund had higher annual expenses, and that seemed to do little more than mute the results. In the end, they both returned the same.

Perhaps turnover ratios, an expense that the fund incurs when the stocks it holds change frequently, have an effect. We began to monitor those rates in the bond funds we looked at earlier. One study began with the possibility that funds that charged more in fees and annual expenses and turned their portfolios over more frequently did better. What the study proved was a case for efficient trading and information gathering, making those additional fees, once again, of little or no difference in how the fund performed.

The question later researchers asked was whether mutual fund managers did better in a load fund or a no-load fund. The results showed no significant difference in the return for the time period studied. The following year, yet another study suggested that there might be something hidden in how these funds were analyzed. However, dissecting performance evaluation techniques did little to find that one type of fund fee led to different performance from the nonexistent one in no-loads.

Researchers continued to shake, roll, and rattle the funds, looking for something that would allow them to conclude that load funds had some additional value to the investor. They looked at size, goals, management fees, expense ratios, primary objectives, turnover rates, and relationships between past and future performance and found no evidence that paying more meant getting better results. Each time they attempted to examine the industry, they widened their scope, not only in terms of the total number of funds analyzed, but in the length of time as well. So why, if investors are not compensated for the higher cost of load funds, do they use them?

Okay, buying wine is not the same as purchasing a mutual fund. One is infinitely easier and gives you a feeling of relaxation. The other is just an investment. But as researchers try to uncover what makes our brains do what appear to be irrational things, we are forced to deal with what seems to be some sort of cranial hardwiring.

Suppose you were given five samples of wine to taste, each labeled with a different price for a bottle: $5, $10, $35, $45, and $90. Antonio Rangel, associate professor of economics at the California Institute of Technology, chose 20 volunteers who, by their own account, knew enough about wines to know what they liked but did not consider themselves experts by any means. The results of the test on the five samples of wine were unexpected.

Mr. Rangel fooled the volunteers by actually using only three bottles of wine. The $5 wine did in fact cost only $5, but the same wine was also used for the bottle labeled $45. The $90 wine really cost $90, but it was also used for the bottle labeled $10. Only the $35 bottle was priced entirely correctly.

The volunteers in the test were allowed to taste all five bottles (but, in actuality, just three wines), and were asked to rank them on taste. The bottles labeled $45 and $90 (which were the $5 and $10 bottles) were ranked the best. The medial orbital prefrontal cortex showed unusually strong activity during monitoring when the subjects believed they were sipping the most expensive wine and the least amount of pleasure when they were tasting the least expensive bottle.

George Loewenstein, professor of economics and psychology at Carnegie Mellon University, has been doing similar research on this type of activity, suggesting that "price is one of the many attributes that people pay attention to, and it affects how we perceive things as a consumer."

But Mssrs. Kuhle and Pope began by stripping away the fundamental difference between the two types of funds: the load. Once that was done, the funds could be compared like apples and apples. 12b–1 and other management fees, reinvested income and capital gains distributions, and net asset value month over month were calculated for the time period of 10 years (this allowed for short-term fluctuations in the market to be dropped from the equation).

The load funds, the authors found, did outperform the no-load funds but usually in the short term (less than five years); the no-load funds began to do better as a group once the 10-year mark was hit. There are several possible reasons for this: the group was large, with many diverse investments, some of which do better in one economic environment than in another; some are more conservative and laced with bonds, while others target overseas markets or smaller-capitalization companies.

The Fund Summary

The fund we are using as an example is described as one that seeks "long-term growth of capital." The strategy section of the fund's prospectus identifies how it plans to invest your money. Because this is an international fund, it should come as no surprise that the fund buys common stock in companies doing business in different countries and regions. The focus, in this particular case, is on non-U.S. securities.

As we learned in the earlier discussion on overseas and emerging-markets bond funds, the regulations and rules governing securities issued outside the United States are often quite different. The activities surrounding something as routine (to us) as an election can have long-term adverse effects on a country's stock exchange. For this reason, the fund seeks to warn you of this potential.

Stock market volatility is a measure of how deep a correction might go or how high a bull run might progress. Given our fund's overseas position, investors should know that this is a risky fund, where the rewards and the risks can be outsized compared to what happens in the United States. You may find, as the prospectus claims, that "your shares"—your stake in the fund—"may be worth more or less than what you paid for them, which means that you could lose money."

Performance—the Disclaimer

This is where that famous warning is found. In the case of the International Discover fund, another consideration is mentioned. Not only are you warned that the "fund's historical performance may not represent its current invest-ment policies," but you are told that such changes literally make any kind of comparison a waste of time. When a fund has major policy changes, it tells the investors who are currently in the fund. But new investors have little to go on aside from historical evidence that what the fund now claims is not relevant.

By page seven, the disclaimer is reiterated with a few more details, including who does the legwork for the fund manager, whose name is William J. Kennedy and who has not previously been mentioned (page 22 of 26 total). Relying on the Fidelity Management and Research Company (FMR) allows the manager to make investment decisions based on the FMR's analysis of a company's financial condition, how the company does within its industry, and what, if any, effect economic and political influences might have on how well the common stock of those companies might perform.

What is a futures contract?

When you hear the evening news report that a barrel of oil is worth $100, that quote is the price of a futures contract. It is a promise to buy a security or investment at some time in the future at a price that was contracted for today. If the contract is profitable, you will have bought an investment for one price and sold it at a higher price when the contract reaches its delivered date. Futures contracts actually demand that the delivery be made to whoever owns the contract. They come with obligations. *Option contracts*, on the other hand, do not impose an obligation to buy. (That is the really short explanation. It can get much more complicated.)

The fund's strategies allow it to invest in futures contracts and exchange-traded funds (which we will get to in Chapter 15). The common stock of these foreign entities is often subject to different securities laws. In the United States, the common shareholders are the last in line when a company goes bankrupt, receiving whatever may be left after first the bondholders and then the preferred stockholders are satisfied. Foreign laws may have different voting and dividend rights as well.

Other conditions also need to be considered with a fund of this type, including the way the common stock is priced, which currency is used and how it is valued, and how liquid the overall market is. For this reason, this fund will charge an investor 1.00 percent of assets if the investment is held for less than 30 days. Some online brokers also charge a fee if the fund is held for less than one month, or sometimes three.

The fund wants $2,500 from an investor who does not come into it via a retirement plan. If the fund balance falls below $2,000, you will be charged a $12 "small balance maintenance fee." Some funds will charge this even if you open an IRA with a lower required initial minimum balance.

The Reinvestment Option

Most folks assume that dividends and capital gains earned in the fund are automatically reinvested (a term used when the fund shareholder allows the fund manager to purchase more shares of the fund for the shareholder), mostly because in tax-deferred retirement accounts, the funds reinvest them without giving you an alternative. But in funds held outside of these plans, you can choose to receive distributions of income directly.

A dividend in a mutual fund is much like a dividend paid by an individual stock. It is paid to shareholders for a variety of reasons. Larger mature companies pay dividends to their shareholders when they have profits that are greater than the opportunities to reinvest in and thus grow the business. In mutual fund holding companies like Fidelity, the dividends paid by companies whose stock the fund owns are collected and distributed to the fund's shareholders. If you opt for reinvestment, the fund automatically buys additional shares for you.

Capital gains (or losses) are the result of selling a common stock at a profit (or a loss). Gains can be reinvested. At Fidelity, you can authorize the company to use these payments to purchase additional shares in other Fidelity funds.

A Statement on Taxes

Dividends and other distributions of cash are taxed differently from capital gains. The former are treated as ordinary income, while the latter are taxed, at least until 2010, at the current 15 percent rate—unless of course, the fund does not own the stock in the company for the full 12 months the IRS requires for the gain to be considered long-term.

The timing of buying this type of fund—or any fund, for that matter—should be taken into consideration. Funds like the International Discover fund will make a realized distribution of income and capital gains before it is actually distributed. If you buy into a mutual fund during this period, you may be buying the dividend, and you could be socked with the tax bill for that quarter, making your membership into a no-load fund seem front-loaded.

You will also need to keep track of your purchase price. If you decide to sell your holdings in the fund, you will be liable for the difference between what you paid for it and what you sold it for.

Some Do, Some Don't

The prospectus we dissected was unexpectedly clutter-free and relatively straightforward. Many prospectuses are littered with important footnotes (which should be read and understood—it is your investment's fine print!). In many cases, the prospectus is sort of like a first date. Not until after you commit (your money) will the fund manager let you know her thoughts on where she believes the fund is headed, what has derailed it recently, or what influenced it to have such a stellar year. These notes add to the fund owner's reading enjoyment but do little to validate what happened. It often seems like an additional pitch to current customers.

These postinvestment prospectuses are much more detailed in terms of what the company actually invests your money in. Sites such as finance.yahoo.com/funds can offer you a look, albeit in the past, at the holdings of the fund.

Information in these prospectuses may include how the management is compensated. Some fund managers are required to buy shares in the funds they manage. Most people skim over this section, hoping, if not fully expecting, that the fund manager will have a *vested* interest in the fund.

Some prospectuses will go to great lengths to explain the risk that they and you as an investor face. This acts almost like a disclaimer, a sort of I-tried-to-tell-you-so. But the investors need to be aware of the risk factors facing them and the headwind their fund faces. All of these are principal-altering events.

Active Investor Risk

This kind of risk is a distinct possibility if professional money managers or investors also use the fund you have chosen. These types of investors may trade mutual funds frequently, making quick in-and-out trades and shifting their positions before the fund manager has the opportunity to make the new investment work. On the flip side, if investors cash out too quickly, then the fund manager may have to sell shares to accommodate the seller. The result is increased fund turnover, and if you are looking at turnover as a determining factor in your investment decision, you may end up avoiding what would normally have been a good fund. If your prospectus comes as a quarterly statement, and you notice that your fund's turnover has spiked for no good reason, call. Ask why.

The 30-day fee that was assessed on investors who fail to stay in our International Discover fund can help stop this sort of frequent trading. Unfortunately, the penalty may not fit the crime. If traders decide that a 1 percent fine on assets is not nearly penalty enough, trading will take place regardless.

Aggressive Investment Risk

Most folks think of mutual funds as a plain vanilla investment. But some funds, like our example fund, use other instruments to shore up gains and profits. Not only do some funds use futures contracts and often options on those contracts, but they may also use other types of investments with less transparency to the average investor. (The investment world is always in search of transparency, or the ability to see what is going on, when it happened, and with what. Transparency is a good thing. Just remember, the lack of it spells added risk.) Most of the time, things like swap agreements make up such a small part of the overall trading strategy as to be almost negligible.

Concentration Risks

While this is much more problematic in funds that focus on a single industry, or at least complementary ones, and is often more prevalent in exchange-traded funds, it can occur in some funds that promise to diversify. When a certain sector gets "hot," such as the way the Internet fueled the equity bubble almost 10 years ago, the temptation to invest in that sector in order to stay competitive becomes great, and the possibility that the manager will do so needs to be spelled out in the prospectus. Some funds specifically designate where they will invest and how many companies they will hold. The risk increases when an industry receives some bad news about future earnings growth and all related companies feel the pain.

What the Experts Say

The average man does not want to be free. He simply wants to be safe.

H. L. Mencken

Correlation Risk

When is a benchmark not a benchmark? When the correlation risk is high. If you calculate all the fees, expenses, transaction costs, trading costs, and leverage costs, and also consider the fund's inability to own every stock in whatever benchmark it has chosen to be compared to, you now have the risk that the benchmark, usually an index, will outperform the fund. Does this mean that an index is the better investment? Not necessarily, but I will save that pro/con argument for the point in the book where we discuss index funds. Can actively managed mutual funds overcome this correlation risk? Absolutely.

Credit Risk

At any given time, a company's financial rating can be downgraded by the bond rating industry. This can have a direct effect on the company's share price and is largely beyond the fund's control (aside from doing research that might foresee the problem). Equity funds generally do not face any direct risk from debt instruments the way bond funds do, but how well those debt securities perform may have some crossover effects on the company's share price.

Once a company's credit has been downgraded, the share price usually comes under scrutiny. Was the share price too high, or, as the industry likes to say, was the stock overvalued? The stock market, which is often referred to as a living, breathing entity, is believed to be able to take all of the available information into account and make a decision about the worth of a company. There are numerous factors that go into a company's share price, but the lion's share is a vote in the form of money.

Early Close/Trading Halt Risk

This is rare, but it is a problem that can arise when markets suddenly become turbulent. It can happen in one of two ways. News that might affect a company's share price can force a trading halt to allow investors to digest the news without needing to react to rumors. This is called a *regulatory* halt. Alternatively, an entire exchange such as the NYSE (New York Stock Exchange) or the AMEX (American Stock Exchange) can halt trading when there is an extreme movement of prices on that exchange. When this happens, sellers may be forced to take a price below what they want, and buyers, in the reverse, may pay more for a stock than they had anticipated. This is referred to as a *nonregulatory* halt. It acts a sort of cooling-off period. The Nasdaq does not halt or delay trading, although it may open late or close early, depending on the reason.

Mutual funds are just as vulnerable to these stoppages as individual investors are. Trades that have been scheduled may not be completed, and this could make pricing of the fund, something that must be achieved by 4 p.m., difficult.

What is volatility?

Generally, the word is defined as the difference between the price for a stock or commodity in one time period as compared to the price for the same item at a later date. This is used to determine the risk of that stock or commodity and becomes a forward expectation of where the price might be in the future. The Chicago Board Options Exchange monitors the volatility in the stock market with an index based on options (the right, but not the obligation, to buy a stock or contract in the future) on the S&P 500 (VIX), the Nasdaq 100 (VXN), and the Dow Jones Industrial Average (VXD). Because the S&P 500 provides a much broader look at the overall market, this is often the index that active traders look at in hopes of divining some sort of sign as to what to buy (or sell) and more importantly, when.

Equity Risk

In brief, this risk is based on volatility. This is why your money may gain ground or lose it. This is also why mutual fund investors have the upper hand over individual traders. Because of the expertise of the fund manager, the ability of his research team to dig through the vast amounts of information circulating around the markets in any one day, and the fact that a mutual fund is able to spread the risk across numerous investments, the volatility is, at least in theory, reduced.

And, the more volatile the marketplace that the fund manager is focused on, the more volatile the fund will be. When we begin the actual profiling of funds in the next chapter, we will go from the most volatile—emerging markets—to the least—indexes based on large-cap stocks.

Foreign Currency/Investment Risk

This is the same type of risk that is present in bond funds that invest internationally. It is generally accepted that an investment traded in the currency of another nation is not as safe as an investment traded in dollars. And, although you may have been unaware of this, the dollar, along with other nations' currencies, is also traded on the open market.

If the dollar rises in value, an investment that is based on another currency could lose value. Numerous factors can enter into the reasons why this happens, from economic and political developments in the country where the investment is based to a lack of dependable information (transparency) on which to base good decisions.

This type of risk tumbles over into the quality of the information available. Often, generally accepted accounting principles (GAAP) are lacking in foreign markets; the markets themselves may lack what traders like to call efficiency; companies may have failed to disclose relevant information, such as hiding health and safety risks from investors; and generally, overall standards are lower than those that are taken for granted here in the United States.

With greater transparency will come greater accountability and better corporate behaviour. Rather than engage in futile resistance to it, firms should actively embrace transparency and rethink their values and generally get in better shape.

Don Tapscott, coauthor of *The Naked Corporation*

Geographic Risk

Funds that offer more specific types of investment disciplines can be much more volatile. This is because of the narrowness of the market and the possible lack of additional ways to wiggle free of problems that are developing in a particular sector. While there are many different ways to capitalize on a specific market, and funds that are very narrowly focused often have a great deal of leeway when trying to protect their shareholders' money, this risk is very real.

Some fund families may invest in precious metals, short selling of foreign countries, or even gambling with currencies. See the previous discussion of foreign currency/investment risk.

Growth Risk

Dividends to investors are paid out of profits. The companies that pay dividends are generally established businesses that have succeeded in creating value for their shareholders. While these companies may be growing, they are not considered growth companies.

Growth stocks are often considered to be those of smaller and midsized companies that have larger exposure to market conditions. There are large-cap companies that are considered growth stocks, but the field is often more narrow. If things go bad, the growth of these companies is affected. Investors are keenly aware of earnings and earnings potential, forecasts offered by the company, and the condition of the overall market.

In a mutual fund in which growing your money is key to the fund's success, the lack of dividends adds to the volatility of the fund. Without that steady stream of income, the fund is directly affected by the shifts in the marketplace, be they good or bad. Once again, because funds spread that risk over numerous companies, the impact is less than that faced by the individual investor.

Liquidity Risk

Depending on what your mutual fund is allowed to do, something that is specifically spelled out in the charter/prospectus, this can be high or almost nonexistent. Liquidity is an investor's ability to turn an investment into cash. In funds that are permitted to invest overseas, where a specific country's markets may not be as easy to navigate during turbulent times, or in illiquid investments such as derivatives [described as financial instruments that are valued based on the worth of something else, such as stocks, bonds, interest rates, exchange rates, or indexes (such as a stock market index, the consumer price index, weather conditions, commodities, or even other derivatives)].

Since the fund manager may be unable to react in a timely manner to changes in these investments, the risk is much greater when redemptions are higher than normal. This lack of liquidity also hampers potential gains, may prevent the fund manager from limiting losses, and, worse, may make the correlation to the benchmark more difficult.

Value Risk

When a fund invests in value stocks, it is looking for opportunities in companies that have been ignored by the markets and, because of that, are considered undervalued. The risk here is smaller than that with growth companies. These stocks might even pay dividends. Where then is the risk?

For a fund manager, the risk in this type of investment is your lack of patience as an investor. It may take a long time for the market to realize that the price it has given a particular stock is lower than the true value. The fund manager also runs the risk that, even after holding the company for a length of time, she was, in fact, wrong, in her assumption and the stock she believed was undervalued was actually priced correctly or, worse, overvalued. The latter is far worse than the former and could result in a further price per share decline.

Value stocks in a fund's portfolio often face a different type of external pressure. Should the company have a bad earnings report, forecast a worse-than-anticipated earnings future, be subject to political or economic pressures, or simply be punished by market forces, the likelihood of a recovery in the share price is much lower than that of a growth stock. The risks may seem, on the surface at least, to be muted, but they are very real. In times of turbulence, though, value funds may actually outperform growth funds as investors look for more stable places to put their money.

What's Next Often considered to be woven frescoes, tapestries offer the art lover something that paint on canvas cannot. Their intricacies and attention to detail are often overlooked because, as culture writer Matthew Gurewitsch suggests, "Every gesture and field is built up point by single color point. Technically sharp edges are impossible, and so is blur. Instead," he continues, "tapestries can possess a granular sparkle that plays across their entire surface—each stitch, as it were, a pixel." Mutual funds possess the same qualities. Unlike paintings, which are more like stocks (rich and vibrant and beholden), tapestries have the reputation of being dull and dusty, antiquated, and, in the right light, tranquil and obscure.

In the next chapter we will begin to explore the wide variety of stitching that goes into the fabric of numerous types of retirement plans, investigate the nuances of pageantry that lie hidden from the eye, and with any luck, reveal what is the true nature of the mutual fund.

CHAPTER 11
Inside an Equity Fund—International

◆◆◆◆◆◆◆◆◆◆◆◆◆◆◆◆◆◆◆◆◆◆◆◆◆◆◆◆◆◆◆◆◆◆◆◆

Writing about mutual funds, or about personal finance in general, often makes me feel like a biographer. There is often an enormous amount of material to sift through that needs to be parsed, dissected, and then, through the magic of words, turned into something understandable, timeless, even narrative. Just as often, those attempts fall short.

There is an old Zen saying: "Before enlightenment, chop wood; carry water. After enlightenment, chop wood; carry water." And like water, nothing in the world of money stands still. We can enjoy the bucolic scene at the edge of a babbling brook but fail to realize that it is changing with every passing second. There is a certain fluidity in the financial markets: obstructions such as the credit mess that greeted 2008, the dam that the weak dollar threatens to become, or even the push for regulatory changes, congressional help, or monetary policy interventions all leave us wishing for the free-flowing wildness that is the hallmark of more prosperous times.

As we begin to look at equity funds, we are forced to look at the past, glance at the future, and hope for the best. Some of the best biographers have suggested that, oddly enough, knowing too much about their subject can make things more difficult. Others have suggested that biographers should be humbled by the experience. Still others want you to believe that their biographical words can elevate their subject to a mythical status.

The World

 The most incomprehensible thing about the world is that it is at all comprehensible.

Albert Einstein

As promised, we will begin the discussion of equity, or stock, mutual funds with a look at the riskiest funds, then move on toward the least risky. The risk involved in mutual funds that invest in stocks is far greater than the risk involved in those that invest in bonds, or fixed-income securities, and the risk is even greater with those that invest offshore in countries that do not regulate their markets as well as we do here in the United States.

There are some basic things about looking abroad for investment options that you need to understand. For instance, a global mutual fund is not necessarily an international fund, and an international fund is not necessarily an emerging-markets fund.

Let's begin our journey offshore with a look at global funds. When a mutual fund manager like David J. Schoenwald of New Alternatives (NALFX) invests, he has a wide range of options available to him. However, as far-reaching as those options may seem—the ability to buy any companies that fit his fund's charter, both from the United States and from any foreign country—his focus is exceedingly narrow but nonetheless popular. He is looking for companies that have clean and sustainable business practices and that are focused on producing energy alternatives.

As a disclaimer, the choice of Mr. Schoenwald as a manager to profile is based on the fact that he meets the same type of criteria we set out in our discussion on bond funds. We are looking for some of the best three-year performers, and as fate, and a little bit of investment skill, would have it, his fund fit the category.

He runs what is known in the business as a socially responsible fund, and although we will explore this type of investing a little further on, these types of funds focused on the environment have gained in popularity over the last several years for the obvious reasons.

What is a socially responsible mutual fund?

Simply put, the focus of a socially responsible fund is much the same as that of any other mutual fund: growth of assets and capital gain. However, socially responsible investments (SRIs) focus on investing in companies that are doing good work on environmental, human rights, health, labor, and corporate governance issues. Some funds, like the newly created Blue Large Cap Fund run by Daniel de Faro Adamson, take this so-called green investing a step further. According to Mr. Adamson, ethics should also play a role. He believes that investing "in companies with progressive leaders—leaders who recognize the link between long-term shareholder value creation and core values like environmental sustainability, respect for human rights, diversity, fair treatment of employees, responsible corporate governance and active community participation" is equally important.

Investors now have placed one of every nine dollars invested in these types of funds. Cheryl Smith, an executive vice president and senior portfolio manager at Trillium Asset Management, confirms those numbers, saying, "Increasingly, money managers are incorporating social and environmental factors into their investing practices, acknowledging the demand for social investing products and services from institutional and individual investors, socially concerned high-net-worth clients, individuals seeking SRI options in their retirement and college-savings plans, and 'mission-driven' institutions including foundations, endowments, labor unions, and faith-based investors."

Mr. Schoenwald came to fund management after working careers as both a newspaper reporter and a lawyer at a firm providing aid to the poor. His fund qualifies not only as a global fund and a socially responsible fund, but also as a more narrowly focused sector fund (we will talk more about sector funds in Chapter 16). He focuses on energy companies that are working to develop fuels like ethanol and energy sources like wind, solar, and geothermal power. And because he finds the current government support for companies doing these things lacking here in the United States, he has gone abroad in search of countries that do provide that support.

In a global fund, the focus usually is on larger companies that dominate their particular market. Mr. Schoenwald's New Alternatives fund invests in companies like Q-Cells AG, a German-based company that is active in the field of photovoltaics; Vestas Wind Systems A/S, a Danish-based company that is active in the wind power industry; Spanish Gamesa Corporacion Tecnologica, S.A., which engages in the manufacture, supply, and installation of products in the renewable energy sector; and Renewable Energy Corporation ASA (REC), a Norway-based company operating in the solar energy industry.

But like their bond brethren, funds investing in the stock of companies operating in foreign lands are subject to the vagaries of those countries' political and economic situations, which may be vastly different from those we normally accept as stable and accountable. But unlike their counterparts in fixed income, global stock funds, or, as they are often referred to, "world funds," are difficult to pin down. They are attractive, but they often don't fit snugly into a portfolio that is attempting to allocate assets in a certain way.

Asset allocation became the buzzword for smart investing soon after that infamous bubble in technology and Internet stocks burst (it was really more of a correction, albeit one that happened quickly; it certainly didn't burst the way we imagine such bubbles to do). In its simplest terms, asset allocation means spreading the risk across numerous industries, with a wide variety of investment strategies and a number of diverse investments. It doesn't sound simple, does it? Mutual funds can do this for you, but they cannot do it if you don't know what they are doing.

Asset allocation forces you to spread your risk. You can do this in numerous ways. An all-stock index such as the Wilshire 5000 (which does not, whatever the name implies, invest in every company trading on any exchange) will create diversity but not necessarily asset allocation. An index fund on the Wilshire 5000, as we will discuss in Chapter 12 as part of our discussion of indexes, would create volatility in the shares of the smallest companies, which are generally thinly traded and usually don't have enough shares to go around if a behemoth like an index fund comes shopping. Another way is to focus on size, such as funds that buy large, medium, or small companies exclusively. Perhaps a focus on growth or value (not to worry, we will discuss these as well) might add the allocation that is needed in the perfectly built portfolio.

William Sharpe, in an article titled "Asset Allocation: Management Style and Performance Measurement," which appeared in the Winter 1992 issue of the *Journal of Portfolio Management*, identifies these asset classes as falling into 12 categories.

Bills

Cash equivalents with less than three months to maturity

Index: Salomon Brothers' 90-day Treasury bill index

Intermediate-Term Government Bonds

Government bonds with less than 10 years to maturity

Index: Lehman Brothers' Intermediate-Term Government Bond Index

Long-Term Government Bonds

Government bonds with more than 10 years to maturity

Index: Lehman Brothers' Long-Term Government Bond Index

Corporate Bonds

Corporate bonds with ratings of at least Baa by Moody's or BBB by Standard & Poor's

Index: Lehman Brothers' Corporate Bond Index

Mortgage-Related Securities

Mortgage-backed and mortgage-related securities

Index: Lehman Brothers' Mortgage-Backed Securities Index

Large-Capitalization Value Stocks

Stocks in Standard & Poor's 500 index with high book-to-price ratios

Index: Sharpe/BARRA Value Stock Index

Large-Capitalization Growth Stocks

Stocks in Standard & Poor's 500 index with low book-to-price ratios

Index: Sharpe/BARRA Growth Stock Index

Medium-Capitalization Stocks

Stocks in the top 80 percent of capitalization in the U.S. equity universe after the exclusion of stocks in the Standard & Poor's 500 index

Index: Sharpe/BARRA Medium Capitalization Stock Index

Small-Capitalization Stocks

Stocks in the bottom 20 percent of capitalization in the U.S. equity universe after the exclusion of stocks in the Standard & Poor's 500 index

Index: Sharpe/BARRA Small Capitalization Stock Index

Non-U.S. Bonds

    Bonds issued outside the United States and Canada

    Index: Salomon Brothers' Non-U.S. Government Bond Index

European Stocks

    European and non-Japanese Pacific Basin stocks

    Index: FTA Euro-Pacific Ex Japan Index

Japanese Stocks

    Japanese Stocks

    Index: FTA Japan Index

Sharpe believes that these 12 asset classes, each with its associated passive index, are all that is needed for comparison of how well you might be doing. But the lines blur when these indexes are broken down between value and growth and between small and large.

Global or world funds are hard to keep track of, especially because of the differences in where they invest. Some of them may hold portfolios that have up to 60 percent of their holdings in U.S.–based companies. However, if you have built a portfolio that allocates only a small percentage of your investments to a global fund, hoping that this fund gives you some exposure to companies in other countries, you may find that the fund you thought was providing you with some sort of diversity is actually invested in companies that may already be in your portfolio through other funds. This defeats the whole purpose of asset allocation.

Mr. Schoenwald's fund does not seem to fit into that category, but its charter does allow him to invest up to 25 percent of the fund's assets in one company. Suppose he decides that the company that best fits his "green" profile is GE? This would present problems if you held an index of the top 500 companies, or if you owned a fund that actively prowls the exchanges for the best large-cap companies. This sort of cross-contamination of investments can wreak havoc on a poorly planned portfolio if, for some reason, the markets turned sour.

The New Alternatives fund has had a rough time as I write this. (I do not shy away from using funds that have had a bad year because of problems that may well be beyond their control.) You will find that a good many of the funds that I profile in the coming pages have negative numbers on a year-to-date basis, but may have done well over a three-, five-, or ten-year stretch. As with our profiles of bond funds, we will use three years as a guide, and look for a fund manager who manages to trade infrequently, or at least less than his peers in the same sector do; does so without charging an arm and leg for expenses; and may charge a fee up front, at the end, or even none at all.

Global funds tend to charge 1.53 percent on average, and yes, that is starting to get up there in terms of expense ratio. The front-end load that Mr. Schoenwald charges his investors, 4.75 percent, is less than the sector average of 5.24 percent. Turnover, or the number of times a portfolio of stock changes in a given year, is around 58 percent for all global funds. As I write this, the fund is down 15.57 percent year to date:

Fund	Annual Return (over three years)	Expense Ratio/ Turnover
New Alternatives NALFX	26.12%	1.25%/40%

International—European Flair

 Change of fashions is the tax which industry imposes on the vanity of the rich.

Sebastien-Roch-Nicolas de Chamfort

In recent years, it became quite the vogue, I believe the expression goes, to invest in what Europe had to offer. Europe had what it took. The euro was moving significantly higher than the dollar, for reasons too numerous to get into here, and the growth on the Continent was on the rise. Unlike some other countries, this was not an emerging marketplace, but instead a mature continent that was undergoing some changes for the good—once again, for reasons too numerous to discuss.

American investors poured money into European stocks in 2007, looking for something that they presumed could not be found in the United States. And for the most part, Europe delivered. But it did so because, despite our general perception of Europe, it is actually two places that have been coexisting for decades, one of which was for a long time virtually hidden behind the iron curtain. Because of that, Europe is not just the mature marketplace exemplified by Britain, France, and Germany; it is also an emerging market, with Poland, the Czech Republic, and Bulgaria, to name but a few, offering investors added risk.

By way of example, we could look at one of the top three-year performers that focus on these growing economies, looking for their place on the world stage. The Metzler/Payden European Emerging Markets fund (MPYMX), managed by Markus Brueck since 2002, is an excellent example of this risky, yet not too risky part of the world. Many of the countries that this fund focuses on have much of their political turmoil behind them, and in order to join the European Union, they must keep it that way.

Countries like Hungary, Russia, and Turkey understand the economic importance of remaining focused on the big prize: capitalism. When the world perceives that doing business in a particular country does not entail any unnecessary risk, that country will literally "emerge."

But there are risks. Energy prices could continue to climb. The exchange rate could swing in the other direction or, worse, continue to work against the dollar.

What does the dollar have to do with risk in overseas investments?

The short explanation for the dollar's role is that it depends on who is the buyer and who is the seller. If these fledgling economies are to grow, they need to sell goods. If those goods are priced in dollars, and the dollar is weak, these exporters might not be so anxious to sell. If the dollar goes up in value against the price these foreign companies charge, the rate of exchange from dollars to euros falls, and the emerging-market producers end up selling for less than what they perceive their products are worth.

Edward Kerschner, chief investment strategist for Citi Global Wealth Management, believes that the success of these emerging markets depends on how well they handle growth, and this depends on how they stay focused on the task at hand. These markets, Mr. Kerschner suggests, require a good balance between growth and consumerism, both at the higher end of the spectrum and for domestic goods.

Because all emerging markets require power, their ability to embrace newer technology is the key to their success over a long period. That sort of forward thinking, if properly supported by a stable political environment, leads to increased service-sector productivity, the first stable sign that a country has emerged.

Mr. Brueck's fund keeps over 80 percent of its money invested in the emerging markets of Europe. Beware though: all dividends received are paid in euros, making the current exchange rate as of the first of April 2008 not so good. Every euro received in dividends is equivalent to 63 cents in dollars. The question is, should this be factored into the yield?

How does the dollar affect an emerging-markets fund such as Metzler/Payden European Emerging Markets?

I phoned the company directly at its Los Angeles headquarters and asked just that. This company, a 50–50 joint venture between the 400-year-old German Metzler Bank and U.S.-based Payden-Rygel, is truly focused on giving the investor exposure to European securities, so much so that purchases and dividends need to be factored into the equation. The fund pays in euros.

The representative of the fund that I spoke with, Vladimir Milev, was quick to point out that no matter what currency the fund uses, investors should be aware of the high risk involved when using such a fund. He said that the fund employs forward currency contracts, among other things, to protect against open currency exposure (a technical way to describe the methods that traders use to protect their investments in numerous markets).

Mr. Milev did point out that a neutral market, in which the current level of the dollar has not changed from its level when you purchased your investment, will give you the truest and most easily measurable yield on your investment. If the dollar falls from the point at which you made your investment, this bodes well for U.S. investors when the currency is converted back to U.S. dollars. But if the dollar's value overseas increases after you have purchased shares, your yield will be affected. As Mr. Milev said, "These funds have risk and should be used as part of a portfolio that is diversified."

It should be noted that the Metzler/Payden European Emerging Markets fund invests in markets that trade in currencies other than the euro, giving this fund an opportunity to employ numerous strategies to net the best return for the investor. If this helps, Morningstar has rated this fund with five stars for five years running.

The risks do not stop there. We have mentioned that political and market-place turmoil can have an effect on your investments, and that lack of liquidity in some companies and the inability to raise cash in some situations could choke off the possibility of continued growth and development, not only for specific companies, but for countries as a whole. Legal recourse is also worth considering, but not so much given the underlying diversity of a mutual fund.

Most emerging-markets funds do a great deal of trading, and Mr. Brueck's fund is no exception. His turnover is higher than that of his contemporaries, but his lack of load fees allows him to recover many of those costs. The average for the sector is a greater than acceptable 1.62 percent in total fees, which, over a three-year period, could mean that you would pay almost a third more than our profile fund charges. The fund has faced some headwinds in 2008 and at the time of this writing is down 10 percent in the first quarter

Fund	Annual Return (over three years)	Expense Ratio/ Turnover
Metzler/Payden European Emerging Markets MPYMX	38.77%	1.24%/128%

International—Europe, Sliced

On the other side of the Continent is the Europe that many of us think of when we think of traveling abroad. These are countries that have a more stable economic standing, whose politics are well known, and whose markets are regulated in many of the same ways as ours. Some of the legal barriers are lessened, but the nagging question about exchange rates still remains.

Trygve Toraasen's Fidelity Nordic Fund (FNORX) is a good example of this style of investment. About 80 percent of this fund's assets are in securities of Danish, Finnish, Norwegian, and Swedish issuers. It may invest the balance, however, in securities of other European companies.

It is important to note that these countries have a very limited number of companies whose stocks actually trade. The Swedish index listed as few as 310 stocks when it merged with the Nasdaq recently, shortly after many of the Nordic countries merged into one exchange. This growth in trading transparency is better for the stocks, and combining several exchanges into one, the Nasdaq OMX, with 3,900 companies, has certainly made it easier for investors to reach beyond their own borders.

Offering investors an opportunity to take advantage of the cyclical nature of the European region has proven very profitable for funds that have looked for large-cap investments in a stable part of the world.

Mr. Toraasen has led his fund since the late 1990s, and has done so with below-average expenses (the category averages 1.62 percent), no loads, and half of the average turnover of his cohorts. His fund has seen slower growth as economies around the world respond to the 2008 recession in the United States, but it has lost less ground than the S&P 500 index.

Fund	Annual Return (over three years)	Expense Ratio/ Turnover
Fidelity Nordic Fund FNORX	27.38%	1.03%/62%

International—Europe as a Whole

 Albert Camus, the European philosopher, can be seen either as eloquent and enlightened or as foolish for his observation that moderation and responsibility could solve the world's ills. Most of what he believed in centered on this simple division of ideologies, boiling down to "two types of thought: a destructive one, rooted only in History, absolute, messianic, reducing everything in its path to ideological abstractions; and a life-affirming one, in which History and Nature balance one another, an outlook which is modest and respectful of limits."

Increasingly, Europe as an investment has grown in attractiveness over the last four or five years, while nonfinancial companies on the American stock exchanges languished. But even as this happened, the world was shrinking. U.S. companies were growing outside the American borders, looking for more accommodating business environments, tax-friendly situations, and more importantly, if only for shareholders, less regulation to stop or impede future earnings. This period of euphoria lasted until, skirting many of those regulations, the U.S. markets began to teeter on the edge. If anything worth noting has come from the downturn in 2008, it was the lack of immunity that the rest of the world had to what occurred. No longer could the international markets ignore the way in which the world's financial and investment systems were intertwined. While the old adage about the spread of financial problems, "when the United States sneezes, the world gets a cold," might no longer hold the way it once did, it is still true that "when we get a cold, everyone in the playpen gets the sniffles." The unexpected effect of globalization has not eliminated economic and financial downturns, but simply made them less devastating.

Philippe Brugere-Trelat of Franklin Templeton Investments runs one of the best funds investing in the whole of the European continent. His Mutual European Z (MEURX) fund focuses on European companies, investing a minimum of the fund's assets in continental heavyweights such as Siemens, Daimler, and Nestlé. The investment charter gives him some leeway when strategizing. He may invest in some U.S. companies (up to 20 percent), but his current holdings do not show any such positions. The fund can buy debt securities like bonds, and if Mr. Brugere-Trelat is worried about exchange risk, he hedges against the possibility.

What to Ask?

What is a hedge?

Essentially, a hedge is a method of eliminating financial risk by taking two opposing positions. If one loses, the other wins.

Expenses for the fund are a third less than the category average and come without any load fees. Its turnover—or should I say lack of it—makes it a much better bargain than its peer group, which averages a complete change of portfolio over the course of a year. As a reminder, turnover is calculated by dividing the average assets held during a given period, usually a year, by the lesser of the value of purchases or the value of sales during the same period. High turnover ratios often result in higher overall fund expenses (trading costs and research), and if the fund is selling stocks that have done well, it pays higher capital gains taxes.

Fund	Annual Return (over three years)	Expense Ratio/ Turnover
Mutual European Z MEURX	15.74%	1.04%/38%

International—Japan

The world owes all its onward impulses to men ill at ease. The happy man inevitably confines himself within ancient limits.

Nathaniel Hawthorne

Japan, at least these days, is often mentioned as a comparison country, although not necessarily in a good way. The country's economy has remained motionless for over two decades, garnering the unflattering remark from Edward Cartwright of KGR Capital that it was a "slow boat going nowhere." This wasn't always the case.

Japan is the fourth largest economy after China, India, and the United States. The country's post–World War II economy grew at an unsustainably high rate. It needed trade to obtain raw materials. By exporting new technologies built on mature industries and an industrious workforce, it was able to maintain the typical Japanese cooperation between manufacturers, their suppliers, subsequent distributors, and the banks that invested heavily in them. The stock market soared as exports rose. Savings grew, and the Japanese currency, the yen, became more valuable (much the way the euro has become more valuable against the weak dollar, creating a buyer's market for those holding the euro and a seller's market for those pricing in U.S. currency).

But the country's high savings rate, along with some other indigenous economic policies, put the country's economy at odds with other emerging markets in Asia, which could produce for less. The Nikkei stock market in Japan plummeted, and the price of housing skyrocketed. No one was spending money, and the economy deflated. (More on the effects of deflation, inflation, and stagflation later in the chapter.)

Even today, almost 20 years later, investors question whether Japan is worth the time and money when other markets offer substantially better reward for the risk.

Japan faces many problems, and investors should be aware that the risk here is different. Without going into too much detail, the Japanese are caught between the proverbial rock and hard place. Their currency, the yen, is being used in global financing in a way that the country should not necessarily be pleased about. The yen carry trade, as it is called, allows those big-boy/girl investors to borrow money in yen, pay a very low interest rate on the loan, and then take that cash and buy other investments with it. For example, if you could borrow money at 1 percent and then turn around and reinvest that money at 5 percent, your profit would be 4 percent.

Because the yen carry trade plays such an important role in global financing, the Japanese government is reluctant to raise the interest rate. To stay competitive, companies in Japan are more importers than exporters. They use other cheaper countries as their assemblers and finish the product in Japan. This makes it very difficult from an investment perspective, and using a mutual fund to invest in the country, or even in the area known as the Pacific Rim, can be very difficult.

It is often considered a given that when markets are cheap, as the Japanese markets are and have been, they are considered a good value. But if the reason for investing in a country like Japan is based on the appearance of inexpensive investments as a result of ongoing deflation, the value is quickly eroded.

 Deflation, especially in the Japanese situation, results from the relationship between high commodity prices and the prices that producers can charge. If producers are unable to raise prices and the costs of raw materials increase, they must increase their exports to recover those costs. To keep prices low for Japanese consumers, wages were kept low. This forces the consumer to save rather than spend, keep rather than borrow. This is a rather simple explanation of what brought the economy of Japan to a standstill. In the meantime, as the Japanese continue to sort out these economic and monetary policy situations at home, the rest of the world's economy moved on.

Stagflation, a word that no economy wants to hear, stems from not just slow economic growth, but high unemployment as well. It can easily overtake a mature economy if prices for commodities that the country needs rise to levels that make it difficult to buy them. Once prices increase to cover these higher costs, inflation takes hold. We will see how inflation affects your investments further along.

For that reason, I have chosen to use a fund that isn't purely a Japanese fund. There are numerous other actively managed mutual funds that can position an investor for better returns. But much of what would be considered "better" does not fit our profile of portfolio turnover. Some funds turn their underlying portfolio of equities 12 to 15 times in a given year. The sector average is $1^1/_2$ times, or 148 percent. That many exchanges of stock begin to erode any yield you might receive.

Kenji Chihara, the former Japanese equity fund manager at Okasan Investment Management, directs the DWS Japan Equity S fund (FJESX). Attempting to offset the risk and possibly increase investor returns, the fund commits 80 percent of its assets to companies that would be considered Japanese. There is no limit to the size of the companies that Mr. Chihara can purchase. This enables him to look at less-exposed companies that might offer the fund additional growth.

While this type of investment strategy would normally warrant numerous position changes in the fund, he has kept his portfolio turnover relatively staid by comparison. Another huge selling point for this no-load fund is lower fees and expenses than the sector average.

Fund	Annual Return (over three years)	Expense Ratio/ Turnover
DWS Japan Equity S FJESX	11.82%	1.37%/120%

International—ex-Japan

Because of the drag that Japan can put on an investor's returns, funds that specifically exclude Japan now number almost a hundred. Some of the ex-Japan funds look at the countries in the Pacific Rim, running all the way up to China and Korea; others focus on the subcontinent of India. The risk here is of a different kind and depends on the primary investments in the fund.

In terms of returns, few countries can beat what is happening in China. From a purely economic point of view, its growth resembles that of Japan during its heyday. And so far, the difficulty in controlling such exuberant growth has not been too much for the ruling party. But the kind of capitalism that China embraces does not necessarily mesh with the government's philosophy. That sort of risk is not present in many other international marketplaces. While China may be called a bubble economy, there is no way to tell how big the bubble actually is. When you couple that with the unusual political pressures that the country has to deal with (political pressure normally percolates from within a country, forcing changes that usually have economic effects; China faces opposition to its policies from its trading partners), you have the potential for increased risk.

The question is: is the risk worth taking? Yes and no. If you are the slightest bit squeamish about the way governments in this part of the world (and, as a rule, in almost all of the emerging-market countries) handle their economies, the answer is no. This type of social investing has taken hold. (In the United States, social investing refers to companies that are responsible with regard to not only the environment but also their employees and customers.) Human rights issues, who is being left behind in a quickly growing economy, and what effect all this sudden prosperity has on the environment all must be factored into an investor's perception of value, yield, and return.

But if your concerns are more about making money, few parts of the world pay you as well for the risk you take than this type of investment. In many cases, this type of growth cannot last. But while it does, investors see opportunity, and those that pick investments in this part of the world see a risk that is worth taking. J. Frederick Copper does.

Mr. Copper has headed up the Columbia Greater China Z fund (LNGZX) since 2005. His fund understands that China is more a region than a country, with numerous neighbors that are economically tethered to the nation's success. His fund uses 80 percent of its available assets to buy companies in this neck of the woods.

Generally, funds of this type use numerous other tactics to offset what they consider a riskier than usual investment. Columbia Greater China Z is no different. The fund not only invests in common stock, but also may try to increase investor value by using preferred stock, warrants, convertible debt, ADRs, and GDRs. [*Preferred stock* is a sort of half-stock, half-bond instrument that pays dividends and therefore offers fixed income the way a bond would, but that, if the company fails, does not give the investor the same recourse in recovering funds that a pure bondholder would have; some preferred stocks may be convertible into common stock. A *warrant* is simply, and I mean really simply, a contract to buy stock at a specific price in the future; it is usually issued in connection with some sort of bond issue. *Convertible debt* is debt that carries a much lower interest payment than other debt issued by the company but that gives the holder the option of turning the investment into common stock; once that happens, the per-share value of the common stock is diluted by the additional shares. An *ADR* (American depository receipt) is an investment that involves taking a foreign company's stock and reissuing it on an American stock exchange, thus taking the currency risk and the risk imposed by foreign exchanges out of the investment picture, but leaving the investor with the illusion (all ADRs are sold for between $10 and $100, even if a single share of an ADR might represent numerous shares of the company as sold on its own exchange) that the underlying investment is healthier than it might be. *GDR*s are similar to ADRs using banks instead of stock exchanges.]

Expenses run high in this group of funds, with the sector average being 1.90 percent. With expenses that are lower by a third and offering its services with no up-front or closed-end loads, the Columbia Greater China Z fund has been able to put more money to work in this region than similar funds that may charge as much as 5.31 percent (front-load average) and 2.31 percent (deferred sales costs) for the same kind of nuanced strategy.

I know I spend a lot of time emphasizing turnover. Too much turnover, as I have said, costs you money in the form of additional trading costs, research costs, and taxes if what is being sold is sold for too small profit, and if the fund appears to be chasing an index too closely. Those funds don't charge the same low fees that index funds do despite the outright mimicry. Mr. Copper's fund falls about halfway, selling the underlying portfolio roughly half the number of times as the rest of the sector (76.27 percent).

Fund	Annual Return (over three years)	Expense Ratio/ Turnover
Columbia Greater China Z LNGZX	47.22%	1.34%/36%

International—Pacific Rim

To begin a discussion about the Pacific Rim, you first need to look at how big a geographic space this sector covers. The top economic centers on the Pacific Rim, excluding San Francisco, Seattle, San Diego, Portland, Honolulu, and Vancouver, are Hong Kong, Singapore, Seoul, Tokyo, Manila, Lima, Los Angeles, Shanghai, Taipei, Ho Chi Minh City, Sydney, Melbourne, Brisbane, Auckland, and Santiago. This is considered the most economically diverse region of the world, and because of its size, it encompasses both economically mature countries and newer emerging markets as well.

So is the risk less because there are so many stable countries in which a fund manager could make less risky bets? Once again, yes and no. Many of these "mature" economies depend on the emergence of their neighbors and tend to encourage growth through investments. But as is often the case, the answer could just as well be yes.

There are numerous countries and numerous currency, political, and economic pressures that are all at play, with no one nation emerging as the stalwart in the event of an economic downturn. As long as the global economy remains strong (and much of that strength still comes from the U.S. consumer), everything hums along quite nicely. And the earnings from this area over the last three to five years definitely signal that the upward trend has been strong. But how long can it last?

The answer to that question provides the key to all the investment knowledge you will ever need. The quick answer hinges on China. The long answer involves the ability of these countries to continue to outpace the United States in terms of real growth in gross domestic product (GDP). Over the last decade, this has proved to be easy to do, and the improvement in the economies of virtually all the Pacific Rim nations, even Japan, is largely believed to be likely to continue.

Some disagree, citing too much dependence of these countries on the U.S. consumer as the real problem. Any decline in the purchasing power of the American consumer, whether it will be called a recession in the history books or not, will have some sort of effect on these nations and the survival of their underlying economies.

What the Experts Say

At the start of 2008, the economic outlook for the Asia Pacific region is more uncertain than it has been since the 1997–98 Asian Financial Crisis. With the full consequences of the sub-prime loan problem in the United States still playing out, the potential for turbulence in the financial markets to spill over into the real economy remains a serious concern. Notwithstanding these and other risks, the economic outlook for the Asia Pacific region is cautiously optimistic.

Council on Foreign Affairs (http://cfr.org)

These economies will suffer from some of the same pressures that we are fighting so diligently here in the United States. Inflation is forcing prices up in many regions, including the economic giant, China. The influence that China has on the region cannot be discounted, but some are worried that the perceived failure of the Chinese government to adjust its own trade imbalance (it still exports far more than it imports) will lead to increased developmental risk in the area. This risk, which will be due to short- and long-term imbalances of both an economic and an environmental nature, will make investing here much more difficult. Because of that, the Pacific Economic Cooperation Council expects China's economy to surpass the U.S. economy within the next 10 to 12 years.

John R. Alkire, lead fund manager of the Morgan Stanley Pacific Growth D fund (TGRDX) since 1998, tempers that risk somewhat by focusing the lion's share of his assets on Asia, Australia, and New Zealand. While this does not free him from the influences of the region on stock prices, as many of the countries have significant investments in the surrounding geographical area, it does limit the risk the fund may be exposed to as a result of the way the markets in those countries operate.

Mr. Alkire's blended style, which focuses on larger-capitalization stocks, keeps the portfolio turnover on the lower side of his peers, and because of that, his expenses tend to be lower as well.

Fund	Annual Return (over three years)	Expense Ratio/ Turnover
Morgan Stanley Pacific Growth D TGRDX	25.97%	1.43%/50%

International—Latin America

Right in our own backyard, albeit on the other side of the tracks, lies one of the hottest and riskiest investments around. The region is dependent on foreign investment, and when it becomes a political hot spot (we discussed several instances of this in the first chapter), these economies can quickly go from belle of the ball to redheaded stepchild. This fire/ice relationship has had its ebbs and flows throughout the years. According to a publication by

PricewaterhouseCoopers, "Investing in Latin America: When, Where, and How," the attractiveness of the region is returning.

But it still remains a case study in foreign risk. The growth of these economies is still unpredictable and often hinges on weather or, worse, the whim of a large consumer. Politics plays a huge role in how well these economies perform. It's no wonder that companies are reluctant to invest in places where the safety of their people may be at risk. Political upheaval disrupts the human capital needed to grow any business.

Challenges with currencies and often devaluations can have an effect on how well a portfolio of investments does. As with the emerging European market fund strategies mentioned earlier by Mr. Milev, forward currency contracts can eliminate a good deal of risk for even the most ambitious investor.

In the Real World... Currency trading on the Forex can involve mind-boggling complexity. Forward currency contracts are one of the tools used in those trades. According to John Nobile, a senior account executive at CFOS/FX (http://cfosfx.com), an online Forex spot and options brokerage, here is the idea behind this vehicle: "Foreign currency forward contracts are used as a foreign currency hedge when an investor has an obligation to either make or take a foreign currency payment at some point in the future. If the date of the foreign currency payment and the last trading date of the foreign currency forward contract are matched up, the investor has in effect 'locked in' the exchange rate payment amount." This strategy basically allows the fund manager or any investor to target the rate of exchange for a specific currency at a certain date in the future, allowing her to make specific investment decisions.

One of the key elements in the success of an emerging market is its ability to access capital markets, or lenders who see the possibility of growth as being worth the risk of their monetary commitment to the region. If they see too much risk, no matter how good the possibilities for a particular country or industry may be, they simply will not finance it.

Some countries simply make doing business there too expensive. Puerto Rico was once a haven for companies looking to invest in the region. It had a favorable tax system, a good economy, and the default protection of being a territory of the United States. However, changes in the tax laws pushed much of the investment to the Dominican Republic.

How product moves one place to another is also part of the equation. Mexico has airfreight laws that prohibit some types of product movement, for example. This can be a result of what Renato Santos of the Coca-Cola Latin American group explains as the inability to follow the "rules of the game and the environment," which, he says, "change suddenly."

In many places, it is the local governments that make many of the determinations when it comes to how foreign investors are handled should legal questions arise. These highly unreliable courts must decide who owns what in the event of a dispute. Even national governments have sometimes shown their political inexperience. One border dispute can send two countries and sometimes their allies into a downward economic spiral.

But despite all this risk, the Wharton School of Business at the University of Pennsylvania speculates, "Some investors are beginning to sense opportunity in Latin America. Rising stock markets, strengthening currencies and, perhaps most important, the first glimmers of activity in the U.S. mergers and acquisitions business, are seen as early clues that Latin America will present more investment opportunities than obstacles over the next year or two."

The Fidelity Latin America fund (FLATX) agrees and has been doing quite well since some time before Brian Bottamini took over the helm of the fund in 2005. Instead of speculating, the fund takes a large-company, long-term growth of capital approach when looking for investments in the region. Although these larger companies are not entirely immune from the risk that their own countries may pose, their ability to raise capital and to acquire markets in which to sell their goods is far better than that of their smaller counterparts. Foreign investment is likely to be better positioned to fund future growth and perhaps even insulate the company through diversification of holdings and industries.

Mr. Bottamini's fund is largely invested in common stock, spreading the risk across numerous countries. His large-cap positioning has also enabled him to keep his turnover in check, offer his fund as a no-load, and charge fees that are about half of what the rest of the sector levies.

Fund	Annual Return (over three years)	Expense Ratio/ Turnover
Fidelity Latin America FLATX	51.23%	0.98%/52.00%

International—Emerging Markets

Fund managers who attempt to operate a purely emerging-markets fund must be nimble, be wary, and probably keep copious lists. Peter Mark Roget was one who did so; he developed the ability to categorize the world not as a long list of synonyms, but as a relationship of concepts, only a small part of which he considered successful. Roget was a philosopher, a doctor who focused his efforts on public health procedures and, because of his work on physiology, was instrumental in the creation of the moving picture. But his lists, compiled as a thesaurus, gave him the money and fame to dabble in his science.

How would a fund manager who is trying to put her investors' money to work do so if she did not keep a list of who is who, what is what, and where in the world is that company from anyway?

Managers who focus their attention on the emerging markets of the world can be forgiven for focusing their efforts on large-cap companies, as those companies are easier to keep track of. They can be forgiven for investing in banking in India and oil from Russia or Brazil, or even for loading up their portfolios, as so many have done, with companies in China that are growing at astronomical rates. They can be forgiven in some instances, for portfolio turnover.

However, despite all of the risks around the world, these funds cannot be forgiven for trying to be what they are not. Many of these funds look not just for companies in emerging markets, but for businesses doing business with emerging-market companies. While this isn't cheating, it is a slight bending of the rules. The fact that a company has a Brazilian headquarters, as Esso and Texaco do, does not make investing in that company the same thing as buying shares in BR Distribuidora, a Brazilian-based company in the same business. Nor is the recent trend in reverse any easier for these fund managers to comprehend.

What happens when Indian auto parts maker Bharat Forge Ltd. buys Imatra Kilsta AB of Sweden? Or when Cemex SA of Mexico takes a stake in the European cement-making business, paying $4.1 billion in 2004 for RMC Group PLC of the U.K.? In such a case, is the country or the business still classified as emerging? China, as we have discussed, is an emerging-markets darling; after China's Lenovo Group Ltd. bought the personal computer division of International Business Machines Corp., is it still emerging? When Orascom Telecom, owned by billionaire Naguib Sawiris, buys a controlling stake in the Italian mobile and fixed-line phone operator Wind Telecommunicazioni from the Italian utility Enel SpA, is the company as much of a risk as its country as a whole is? China's Cnooc Ltd. withdrew an offer to buy oil and gas producer Unocal Corp for $18.5 billion after Washington questioned the purchase for political reasons. How are these entities to be classified? As these companies strive to become stable and mature, do they deserve to be punished by being assigned the emerging-markets moniker simply because they are based in countries that have bad tax laws, poor trade rules, political unrest, and questionable legal systems?

Emery R. Brewer has the less-than-enviable job of sifting through this wide mix of global giants and newly minted players from still developing countries and making the investment moves for his Driehaus Emerging Markets Growth fund (DREGX). He has been doing this since 1997.

This fund takes the emerging markets by the horns, giving Mr. Brewer enough leeway to expand his investment horizon to companies that may be little known or thinly traded. This often leads to a much higher turnover than we have found acceptable in many of the previous funds we have looked at and many of the funds we have yet to explore.

Mr. Brewer's fund expenses are no lower or higher than those of his peers.

Fund	Annual Return (over three years)	Expense Ratio/ Turnover
Driehaus Emerging Markets Growth DREGX	51.23%	1.78%/181.00%

Size Matters

It would be not be wholly correct to end right there. As a number of funds further diversify into investments in companies of various sizes, the risk is often increased as each nuance is added. Foreign companies that would barely qualify for the Russell 2000 index of small companies doing business in the United States would not get a second glance from most investors unless those investors only looked at the returns that these funds have posted.

Many funds investing in this area have had stellar runs and have the fees and turnover to prove it. Many are of them front-loaded, scraping off as much as 5.50 percent before your first dollar is invested. Many face some less-than-stable situations while also facing some of the same problems that small companies in American markets face. They still remain volatile, are unproven in the long run, and may have limited access to new inexpensive financing at the time when they need it most.

Consider, for example, AIM International Small Company A (IEGAX), run by Jason T. Holzer. This fund has had an enviable run over the last three years, as it focuses on international companies, with some small caveats: it may, if it so chooses, buy companies in developing countries or spend 20 percent of its investors' dollars on U.S. companies.

Fund	Annual Return (over three years)	Expense Ratio/ Turnover
AIM International Small Company A IEGAX	31.70%	1.54%/69.00%

What's Next: As we move into the next chapter of this book, I want you to be aware of the things that I am aware of. I know that the fount of information that this book is turning out to be may make it harder for you to buy a mutual fund—at least, if you listen to Dhananjay Nayakankuppam. This assistant professor of marketing at the University of Iowa has found that consumers are happier with a purchase when they have limited knowledge of what it is.

What Professor Nayakankuppam found was that the more vague a product appeared upon first inspection, the more attractive it was to consumers. In other words, less is more. He actually describes people as "cognitive misers" who use only as much thinking and research as is needed before making a decision. This is why I have chosen a much more conversational route when discussing these funds. I could delve into their deepest depths, but that wouldn't give you any more impetus to invest or give you a much better clue as to where to put your money once we get into that portion of the book.

As we move into the next chapter, we will be examining the mutual funds that will make up the largest percentage of your portfolio, those that invest in U.S. equities.

CHAPTER 12
Inside an Equity Fund—Growth

Much has been written about both the small-stock and the value/growth phenomena. While the terms "value" and "growth" reflect common usage in the investment profession, they serve only as convenient names for stocks that tend to be similar in several respects.

William Sharpe

We have covered a lot of ground so far, and there is a good reason why I have chosen the progression that we have taken: from the most conservative of money funds to the bond funds. We then worked our way through the bond funds, starting with conservative funds that invest primarily in bonds issued by the federal government and moving on to the risky business of looking to far-off corners of the world where risk can be determined by the kind of news headlines the region receives.

Continuing the conversation about risk, we jumped from risky international and emerging-markets bond funds to risky international and emerging-markets stock funds. Here we explored some of the risks that those types of investments present, and showed that outsized returns often accompany those risks.

Once again, those risks are affected by a wide variety of influences that come from the regions of the world in which these fund managers invest your money. Political strife, currency exchange rates, and even legal systems all play a role in how well stocks do or not.

As we have meandered along, we have uncovered a wide variety of influences that may or may not have been a consideration before. There are investors who seek risk and will do just about anything to achieve even the most marginal of gains. They will borrow cheap money and buy risky investments, and when they do, they take your money for the same ride. Should they sour on an international region, for whatever reason, your investment can go sour as well.

Finding a good fund manager is extremely important when looking around the world. The manager needs to be nimble, well attuned to subtle changes in faraway markets, and most of all, focused on what seem to be the almost innumerable influences that could affect your return. In the end, the equation works like this: the better the return, the higher the likelihood that new investors will come into the fund and old investors will stay and invest more. The lifeblood of a fund is cash.

Each time an opportunity presents itself, a fund manager needs money to chase it down. When things are going well, the money pours in. When things are not doing so well, investors have a totally opposite reaction. They either don't continue to fund their investment or head for the doors.

On Being Counterintuitive

In the book *Investing for the Utterly Confused*, I refer to this type of reaction to the markets as the inability to control the mental maniac inside each of us. I wrote the following:

> Investing is three things at once. The first: it is an achievable gain. The second: it is an avoidable loss. The third is much more difficult and personal. It involves mastering the mental maniac in all of us.
>
> That mental maniac wants to make rash decisions; wants to follow the markets with great intent; wants to be where the in-crowd is; wants to take huge risks in the face of reason; wants to sell low and buy high instead of vice versa.

When we look for a fund in which to invest our money, we are often confronted with thousands of choices. Narrowing down those choices is not that hard, and in the coming pages, we will look at how this process should take place. But we are a nation of list makers. We like to rank who is best, and we believe that those at the top are there because of their superior performance, excellence in execution, and single-minded dedication to a goal.

Mutual funds are no different. They are ranked on the basis of performance, and the amount of money any fund receives depends on those rankings. Fund managers will do almost anything to achieve better returns, as they know that if they do succeed in picking the right underlying investments and the market forces align themselves just right, they will show a positive return. And investors, like fish to the bait, will rise up and bite.

One of the first treatises on fishing came from Isaak Walton, who in 1676 wrote in his final revision of his book *The Compleat Angler, Or, The Contemplative Man's Recreation* that "art was not to be taught by words, but practice: and so must Angling. For Angling may be said to be so like mathematicks (sic), that it can never be fully learnt; at least not so fully, but that there will still be more new experiments left for the trial of other men that succeed us." As Walton fished with hooks without barbs and respected his bait—apparently frogs were given the best opportunity to live as long as possible while dangled on a hook—he offered us a look at life and, more importantly, an approach to investing. His belief that there will be anglers who follow him who will have greater skill suggests that even though he had made it his work to write an account of how to fish and what to fish for, he knew it would not be the final chapter on the sport. Any writer claiming to have the be-all and end-all answer would show himself to be a fool.

Mutual fund managers live for those rankings. The question is: how much of a fund's performance is luck and how much is skill? This question was posed in a paper written in 2005 by Malcolm Baker [Harvard Business School and the National Bureau of Economic Research (NBER)], Lubomir Litov (NYU Stern School of Business), Jessica A. Wachter (University of Pennsylvania Wharton School and NBER), and Jeffrey Wurgler (NYU Stern School of Business and NBER). In this paper, the authors asked how well mutual fund managers could pick stocks in their portfolios. The best way to judge this so-called skill was to test it against the earnings announcements of those stocks after the fact.

Companies make earnings announcements and predictions of future earnings to analysts who follow the sectors in which the companies operate. If the forecast for the next year is good, the stock may rise on that news. If the earnings meet the expectations based on the analysis of these Wall Street insiders, the stock will also rise, as investors, not wanting to be left out of the good news announcement, pile in. The authors believed that, if there was indeed a skill in picking stocks for a mutual fund, the best measure of how well the fund manager did should be based on the trades he or she made prior to these market-moving announcements.

With $3.57 trillion invested by households (and nonprofits) as of March 2008 (you can see the complete assets and liabilities of the nation in a report published by the Federal Reserve, "Flow of Funds," http://www.federalreserve.gov/releases/z1/Current/data.htm), answering the question of which managers can pick the best stocks for their investors is a serious undertaking. The authors believe that they have hit upon the right way to judge those managers based on the idea "to associate skill with the tendency to hold stocks that are about to enjoy high returns around their next quarterly earnings announcement, and to avoid stocks that are about to suffer low earnings announcement returns." This leaves the fund manager with the unenviable problem of making fundamental forecasts.

The authors do admit that there are also some basic underlying conditions on a fund manager's ability to pick stocks for the fund. "According to our measures of skill," they write, "certain funds perform persistently better than others, and the best performers tend to have a growth objective, large size, high turnover, and use incentive fees to motivate managers."

Until this point, we have considered turnover as having a negative effect on your returns. Despite what the authors of this paper, which can be downloaded as a PDF file (http://pages.stern.nyu.edu/~jwurgler/papers/blww021605.pdf), argue, we will continue to make turnover a subject and a condition of which fund is preferable in this discussion.

Inside a Fund—Aggressive Growth

In the world of equity funds, this is your Ferrari. We all understand that the speed that can be attained when we drive a beautifully built fast car transcends anything we may have previously known. Even if you don't relish the idea of going a hundred miles an hour, surrounded on all sides by elegant craftsmanship, you can certainly appreciate the skill involved not only in building such a mechanical marvel but also in piloting such a machine.

The real appreciation comes from getting somewhere faster. This is what life inside the charter of aggressive growth is like. Growth, in and of itself, implies a forward motion, and in mutual funds, this motion is achieved by a fund manager's use of the stocks of companies that are younger and more energetic. These companies are carving away at their niche and looking for a place among the pantheon of big business. They are developing new things, innovating where necessary, and implementing ideas and products that they think the world needs. They must be nimble, ready to change at a moment's notice. These companies are usually small.

While the attraction of this kind of cutting-edge business comes from its potential, the risks need to be factored in.

Equity mutual funds basically can be divided into three types. Growth funds invest in companies of all sizes, but mainly focus on companies that are growing in market share, stature, and profit. A large-cap growth fund might be looking at companies like Research in Motion and First Solar.

Value funds look at older, more established companies that may be growing by acquisition rather than innovation. A fund that is looking for value seeks capital preservation with a limited amount of risk. The companies that these funds and their managers like to invest in frequently pay a dividend instead of plowing every dime back into the business. Such a company might be so large that it has many businesses under one logo. Think of Monsanto or DuPont.

The third type is a combination of the two, divided in any number of ways. While index funds and to some extent exchange-traded funds might be considered a fourth category, they are in many ways a separate type.

Then, we will break these variously risky funds down into the traditional small-capitalization (small-cap), mid-cap, and large-cap categories. Market capitalization, or cap, is the worth of the company as determined by its stock price multiplied by the number of shares that are available to trade. In smaller companies, the amount of stock available on the exchanges is usually far less than that of mid- or large-cap companies. And because many of these companies are risky investments even for individual investors, the price of their shares is often, at least on the surface, pretty inexpensive. For example, if a company had 10 million shares issued to investors (many of which are held by insiders in small companies) and the shares were worth $30, the company would have a capitalization of $300 million. It would be on the far edge of the small-cap universe, which, depending on who you listen to, can run up to $2 billion. But that is a relatively safe range. Companies with smaller capitalization are considered micro-caps (we'll have a little talk about them soon).

Mid-cap funds focus on companies that have a capitalization of $2 to $10 billion. These are businesses that are still on the move, looking to dominate whatever space they can. But they can also be slower moving, more calculated in how they grow. More Camry than Ferrari.

Then there are the large-cap companies, the ones that have slowed down, pay dividends because their profits are far greater than their ability to spend them, and have grown their business model about as much as they can. They are not down and out by any means, but they have settled into a routine that shareholders expect. More like a Buick.

Fund managers who are involved in the aggressive growth end of the mutual fund world seek to make their investors' money grow in a relatively short period of time. The very moniker implies impatience.

These managers look for small-cap companies and what they often promise they will do. Many are based on a idea, often quite a bit more viable than the I've-got-the-next-new-thing Internet companies that attracted so much attention in 2000, and the stock market is how these companies raise money. That presents a problem for the fund manager. When there isn't a lot of stock to buy, how does a fund manager get the best price without tipping her hand and letting the rest of the marketplace know that she considers this company to be a good buy?

If a company has a promising innovation and the stock, which is attractively priced because no one really knows the details of what this fledgling operation has to offer, is not too widely available, the mutual fund manager may have to file with the SEC. This would ruin his opportunity to get a good price. Because the fund manager needs to buy more than just a few thousand shares to make the purchase worthwhile, he will tend to focus on companies with lots of stock.

I have yet to meet a man as fond of high moral conduct as he is of outward appearances.

Confucius

Perhaps the best way to approach this is to look at some of the best performers in each of these groups based on size. We will retain the same format, looking at three-year performance, expenses, and turnover. However, we'll add another number to consider: the index that the fund claims to be doing better than. Funds need something for you, the investor, to compare their performance against. Often the index that a firm uses is the wrong one. Also, driven by the urge to beat or at least do as well as the index does, the fund may actually become an index fund—at actively managed prices.

A Slight Detour

It is here that I will introduce you, at least in a small way, to the idea of an index. I have mentioned indexes as a benchmark. I have slighted funds for comparing their performance to an index. But an index is a simple concept that is good in some circumstances and not so good in others. Indexers—folks who preach the epistle of John Bogle, the legendary investor from the Vanguard Group who is largely credited with the innovation that changed the way the average person could invest and diversify all in one broad brush stroke— believe that index funds are the be-all-and-end-all investment. These funds have low fees (we like that), low turnover (the composition of the index that they follow is adjusted only periodically or on the whim of the folks who pick the stocks in the index), and low expectations (that is what you get when you diversify too much).

Indexes can be as confusing as actively managed mutual funds, perhaps even more so. Take the S&P 500 index, a collection of 500 companies published by Standard & Poor's. This popular index is considered to be a gauge of how the largest companies in America are trading, but is not necessarily that at all. In fact, the S&P 500 has no set market capitalization parameter; instead, it uses leadership in an industry as its reason for including specific companies. The average company in this index has a market cap of $25 billion, give or take a few billion.

The index was created back in 1926, and the companies included in it change only occasionally. Mergers and acquisitions can alter its composition. Loss of leadership in a particular industry can force Standard & Poor's to make changes in the benchmark, which is used not only by institutional investors like mutual funds and pension funds that are trying to determine how well they are doing, but also by economists who are hoping to divine how investors feel or think. Generally, over a given year, the composition of the index will change by only about 5 percent.

The S&P also publishes several other market benchmarks for investors. The MidCap 400 index is split into growth and value sectors and measures businesses with an average market cap of about $2.5 billion. The two groups are divided based on price-to-book ratio, with the growth companies having the higher ratios and the value companies having the lower ratios.

What is price-to-book ratio?

The book value can be simply explained as the worth of a company should it close its doors right now. When you add up all of its assets (what it owns) and subtract all of its liabilities (what it owes), the book value of the company is what is left. This is a sort of snapshot, an accountant's version of a company's position frozen in time. It is a wholly different matter if the doors would actually close. The price part of the equation, as we discussed earlier, refers to the amount of stock the company has issued times the price at which it is trading at the moment. Value investors love the price-to-book ratio more than growth investors do. Growth investors look at the higher prices at which growth companies sell as a signal that all is well, even if the liabilities are higher.

A low price-to-book ratio, on the other hand, might signal a missed value. Investors who look for a lower ratio understand that there can be elements of a company that you cannot simply put a number on. Intellectual property and potential human capital are examples of things that a business might have that are not easily measured and therefore are often overlooked by growth investors. When Warren Buffett buys a company because he likes its management, he has tapped a value that investors might have missed.

Small-cap stocks are measured by the S&P's 600 SmallCap index. This index includes companies with an average capitalization of about $700 million, and, like the Midcap index, it is split into two groups, growth and value, with the division being done using price-to-book ratios.

Standard & Poor's indexes are actively managed. Because there is a human element involved, and because each stock is subjected to what Standard & Poor's calls a strict criterion, the list of stocks included in the index changes. While some companies determine their indexes using a sort of top-down approach (Russell begins with the whole marketplace or 3,000 companies and divides itself into smaller groups, the most popular being the Russell SmallCap 2000), the S&P indexes begin with subsets of stocks and add them together to create an index of 1,500 stocks called a Super Composite.

Standard & Poor's includes companies in its indexes based on certain parameters. To be included, a company must be a U.S. company. This generally means that it has its headquarters in the United States, trades on American exchanges, and employs U.S. generally accepted accounting principles (often called GAAP). Standard & Poor's sets market cap minimums ($4 billion for the S&P 500 index). Companies must have ongoing profitability, usually for four consecutive quarters. They must have a certain acceptable level of liquidity. We looked at liquidity earlier as a measure of risk. If the share price is too low, liquidity will be affected. The most important test for inclusion in the index is the float. This is the general availability of stock to trade. Having more than 50 percent of the company's stock out on the exchanges is considered good. Less than that number signals the possibility that a single entity may hold a greater position than the marketplace, excluding mutual funds. The index committee meets once a month and makes determinations on which companies will remain and which will be removed at that time. Significant changes in how a company operates or changes in the company's makeup after a recent merger or acquisition can lead the committee to make the decision to exclude that company.

And while we are off on this slight detour, we should look at some of the other indexes and how they operate before we move on to our profile of equity funds and how they operate. Indexes, by the way, are normally traded as exchange-traded funds (ETFs)—which, as much as I regret having to say again, we will get to further along.

I mentioned the Russell index as being a top-down index. It begins with a collection of stocks called the Russell 3000. These companies are ranked by size. In any given year, if a business is among the largest on the last Friday in June of that year, is registered in the United States, and is not a closed-end fund (which trade on the open exchange), a limited partnership, a royalty trust, or Berkshire Hathaway (an investment company), it will probably be in the 3000. The Russell Company divides all these companies into two groups, the Russell 1000 for large caps and the Russell 2000 for small caps. Russell also breaks these companies down into 21 different indexes, but for the sake of discussion and space, we will talk only about the two I just mentioned.

The Russell 1000 represents 92 percent of the investable market, divided into growth and value groups. The median capitalization of the businesses ranked is just under $5 billion.

Making up what is essentially the rest of the market is the Russell 2000 index of small-cap companies. Like the Russell 1000, the index is divided into growth and value groups, with about 70 percent of the index falling into one group or the other. The remaining companies fall somewhere in between.

The Russell indexes are used for comparison purposes, as no fund could possibly purchase all of the companies that are ranked. Some of the smallest companies have very little trading activity, making it difficult for all of the funds that want to post the same returns as the Russell 2000 to find shares.

Offering a look at the total marketplace is the co-branded Dow Jones Wilshire 5000 Composite Index. There are not necessarily 5,000 stocks in the index, as the number can shift for a variety of reasons, including bankruptcies and mergers. And to add to the confusion somewhat, the values of the stocks in the index are calculated in two different ways.

One, the full-cap calculation of the DJ Wilshire, uses market value to rank the companies in the index. The other provides a more curious look at the top 5,000 companies. The "float-adjusted" calculation subtracts the value of privately held shares, restricted stock, stock that other companies hold, and any other stock that for whatever reason is not available to the average investor. In many respects, the float-adjusted DJ Wilshire 5000 index is more representative of what can actually be bought or sold. If there is a large amount of stock *off market*, the share price may not actually be representative of the true price.

Morgan Stanley Capital International (MSCI) offers yet another look at indexing large groups of stocks to offer investors a comparison tool. MSCI covers almost all of the stocks that trade, although it has a long list of exclusions, such as real estate investment trusts (REITs) and mutual funds, to name a few. The index focuses on a stock's liquidity and how long it has been available for trade, and it takes free float adjustments into account in determining a company's market capitalization.

Index funds run the risk of being front-run every time they make an announcement of a rebalancing. Some investors use index changes as an opportunity to buy stocks ahead of the index fund managers and sell before they can do so. While there is nothing illegal about this activity, the costs can be high for investors in indexes. MSCI believe that it has created a method of deterring this type of activity. It has created buffer zones. Simply, these are areas where, because of market forces, a stock may be ranked as both a large cap and a mid cap.

Upside and Downside Buffer Zones for Market Capitalization Indices (Company Rank)				
	Large Cap	**Mid Cap**	**Small Cap**	**Micro Cap**
Market capitalization segment definition	1–300	301–750	751–2500	
Upside buffer zone		201–300	551–750	1851–2500
Downside buffer zone	301–450	751–1100	2501–3000	

The numbers represented in this chart are rankings. If a company loses capitalization, it can drift in the MSCI index between the two segments, allowing fund managers to make the decision before it is officially adjusted every six months.

Morningstar uses a wholly different approach to identifying the markets. Using what it refers to as "style boxes," it breaks the market down based on size and methodology and offers a closer glimpse at how the market breaks down.

For instance, its broad market style box, which includes 97 percent of the equity offerings traded, would look something like this : ▓

To accommodate the largest companies in this type of grid, its indication of large-cap funds, representing about 70 percent of the traded markets, would look like this : ▦

Mid-cap funds, including 20 percent of the markets, would appear on Morningstar as ▦

The remaining funds, which are listed as small caps and represent only 7 percent of the investment-worthy markets, are charted as ▦

Morningstar takes this several steps further and indicates value (▦), core (▦), and growth (▦) funds, making the identification of a fund's discipline somewhat easier. When Morningstar refers to value funds, it means funds that primarily invest in companies whose worth may not be realized by the markets because of their slower, more stable growth and therefore are likely to be "undervalued." Core simply represents funds that invest in a wider group of stocks that fit into a specific size category (large, mid, or small) and may contain both value and growth stocks depending on the fund manager's charter. Growth funds are often defined or characterized as those investing in actively engaged companies that may or may not pay a dividend, may or may not be finished expanding, and may or may not be considered risky.

Morningstar uses 10 variables to determine inclusion in each category, with each of these categories representing a third of the overall market that the company tracks.

Large-cap value funds would be stylized as ▦.

Large-cap core funds would look like: ▦.

Large-cap growth funds would be shown as ▦.

Mid-cap value funds would appear to users of the Morningstar system as ▦.

Mid-cap core funds would look like this: ▦.

Mid-cap growth funds would be shown as ▦.

Small-cap value funds would occupy the bottom rung of the style box and would look something like this: ▦.

Small-cap core funds would appear as ▦.

Small-cap growth funds would be shown like this: ▦.

Morningstar style boxes are very easy to use—just a glance at the graphics can provide you with a good deal of knowledge before you actually begin doing any more research.

Where the Fun Kids Are—Small Growth

Popularity is glory's small change.

Victor Hugo

Keep in mind that the more aggressive the fund, the greater the chance for reward. Of course, that risk can also bring greater losses. But investing in something that could some day be an outsized company worth hundreds of billions of dollars is too alluring for some investors to pass up.

Gone from these funds are the numerous currency problems that many other funds, from bond funds to international bond and stock funds and even some of the large-cap mutual funds, whose underlying investments might be affected by the worth of the dollar. The political risk that international funds offer is virtually nonexistent here. There are no uprisings; there are a lot of disgruntled citizens who become vocal when the economy is not humming along profitably in their favor, but for all intents and purposes, this country is a relatively calm place in which to invest. Instead of currency and political risk, the risk is borne by the marketplace.

And no corner of that marketplace has more risk than investing in companies that are trying to gain their footing.

Gaudenzio Ferrari painted the first picture of a violin in 1520. But the violin is widely believed to have made its debut in 1555 as a four-stringed instrument crafted by Andrea Amati. We are familiar with names such as Guarneri, Stradivari, and Gagliano, great craftsmen who magically combined wood and strings to create a sound that had never before been heard. The names of modern-day violinmakers, artists and architects, might not resonant as much with us as those of the classic craftsmen. But their invention, designed to eliminate some of the flaws, such as tonal control, uses five resonators to do the job. Once Johannsson, Eliasson, and Eggertsen develop the final product, all of the resonators will operate as a mechanical rather than an electrical instrument, the product that they hope will become the instrument of choice among violin players.

The difficulties of looking for the right companies to invest in when their track records are not very long and their products, if they have already been developed, are not very numerous make the reward of finding the right "next" thing that this group of funds looks for the most satisfying.

When it comes to the small-cap universe, things take a tumble. Fund managers move around more quickly, often not racking up a lot of tenure before moving on to bigger funds or to hedge funds, a largely unregulated world of investing that has been siphoning off the best of the mutual fund world. Turnover often skyrockets as fund managers, for any number of reasons, trade more often. But expenses should not need to climb, and this is one category in which you will not want to buy a fund with a load.

Wayne Collette has run the Columbia Small Cap Growth I Z (CMSCX) for just under three years at this writing. Like all of the funds in this category, this fund is built for speed. It does not throw around words like "capital preservation."

While the turnover number (113 percent for the category) seems higher than usual, the fund claims to trade among its holdings as opposed to actually eliminating positions and moving into new ones. The holdings of this fund tend to focus heavily on health care and industrial materials, two relatively stable sectors that are not too greatly affected by economic swings.

The fund offers a relatively decent expense ratio compared to its peer group (1.60 percent). More importantly, each dollar invested is put to work, not so much by the fund, which can hold a rather large cash position, as by the absence of loads.

Fund	Annual Return (over three years)	Expense Ratio/ Turnover
Columbia Small Cap Growth I Z CMSCX	17.98%*	1.15%/151%
iShares Russell 2000 Growth Index IWO	5.49%	0.25%†/45%
iShares S&P SmallCap 600 Growth IJT	5.88%	0.25%†/32%
S&P SmallCap 600/Barra Growth & S&P SmallCap 600/Citigroup Growth	26.41%	

* You will notice that the three-year returns we have been tracking do not beat the index over the same period. In real life, no fund purchases the entire index. To do so would push some thinly traded stocks higher simply because of an increased interest.
† ETFs, as we'll discover later, are different from mutual funds in numerous ways. These are funds that mimic the indexes they track based on performance before fees and expenses.

Between a Rock and a Hard Place

Within that often ignored and blurry netherworld of mid-cap investing lies a fund sector that may or may not need to exist. I have nothing against dividing the market into ever-smaller chunks. ETFs, as you will find, have done a better than adequate job of shredding the indexes that they often copy into what seems like a million little disciplines.

But what constitutes a mid-cap stock? Is it a small-cap stock that has breached the hypothetical barrier of $2 to $4 billion in worth, or is it a large-cap stock that has fallen from favor, dropping out of the top 500 into the MidCap 400? What mid-caps are, it turns out, are extremely important. They lack the bulk of their big company brethren, but because they are better researched, better analyzed, and better traded than small-cap stocks, they offer less risk and often better reward over short periods.

Devoting at least 10 percent of your portfolio to small-cap stocks in the name of diversification has almost always been considered a golden rule. Many investors have dealt with that diversification by looking at a small-cap index like the Russell 2000 and calling it good. But those doing so missed out on some better returns, which they would have achieved if they had looked at the mid-cap funds that ply their trade in these middle waters.

Mid-cap investing can be more difficult than the name implies. The parameters for mid-cap stocks can range from $2 to $4 billion up to $10 to $20 billion in market capitalization. Fund managers in this sector often drift more often than large- or small-cap fund managers do, slipping into the small-cap world to pick up some needed risk and potential reward that will make their fund stand out amongst its peers.

Some funds, like the Janus Orion fund (JORNX), which holds a core group of stocks numbering not much more than 30, have a charter that allows them to look overseas if need be. Because of the strong international market, this has paid off in diamonds for Janus Orion. John Eisinger, the fund's lead manager, holds two international companies among his top 10 holdings, many of which are well-known names like CVS Pharmacies and Research in Motion.

Because the core stocks are invested around, whether adding to or subtracting from current positions, the turnover is remarkably low when compared to the sector (113.42 percent). Expenses also make the fund an attractive pick.

Fund	Annual Return (over three years)	Expense Ratio/ Turnover
Janus Orion JORNX	17.98%	0.92%/24%
iShares Russell MidCap Growth Index IWP	7.59%	0.25%*/30%
PowerShares Dynamic Mid Cap Growth PWJ	12.70%	0.63%*/69%
S&P MidCap 400/Barra Growth & S&P MidCap 400/Citigroup Growth	27.80%	

*ETFs, as we'll discover later, are different from mutual funds in numerous ways. These are funds that mimic the indexes they track based on performance before fees and expenses.

At the Top of Their Game

Every company on the S&P 500 index of large caps had humble beginnings. Each had some root idea that grew to something much larger than perhaps the founders even hoped would happen.

 The next time you have the opportunity to see a horse run across an open field, whether courtesy of the Nature Channel or on a trip through Kentucky, think of its powerful stride, the forceful authority of its gallop, or even the pastoral quietness in its stillness as the reason you speak English. Archaeologists have now begun to accept the idea that languages from German to Kurdish, Hellenic to Iranian, Lithuanian to French and, yes, to English were all the result of this majestic creature. Without the horse, there would have been little wheeled transportation. Without the horse, the telling of poetry would never have spread as far across the planet as it did. The acceptance of one language over another in different regions is much more complicated. What can't be questioned is the equine influence in its spread.

As history tells it, there is more to the story of how a company becomes a large-cap than just a dollar denomination. The popularity of big companies comes from the perception that your investment in such a company is much safer. This is because of the perceived ability of multibillion-dollar companies to weather financial storms and roll with the changes in the economic landscape, and because the fact that their size has made them much more diversified implies that you are getting many more underlying businesses as a result.

History tells us that smaller companies have greater exposure to risk, lack access to capital, and will be the first to be crushed in a market downturn. Small-cap mutual funds have been relegated to the 10 percent category in most mutual fund portfolios, alongside bonds and international funds. Large-cap stocks, however, always have the biggest piece of the pie; they are the elite investment that is accepted because of its size and, well, its history.

I'll give you an idea of what I mean. Back in August 2007, Jonathan Burton wrote in the *Wall Street Journal* that asset allocation, or how you divvy up your portfolio based on how much risk you can tolerate, is done for one reason: risk control. He then went on to explain how to do it. "With a conservative allocation of 60% stocks, for example, give brand-name S&P 500 stocks 35% of the portfolio and small caps 5%. Then earmark 15% to an international index fund that holds companies of all sizes, plus another 5% to a geographically dispersed emerging-markets fund."

Growing Large

Once a company reaches a market capitalization of $10 billion, it is generally promoted into the large-cap group. Or as we learned in the discussion of the MSCI indexes, the company will enter a buffer zone somewhere between its former mid-cap self and its possible large-cap state.

I am reluctant to mention two funds from the same company in the same chapter. However, Janus is doing everything right, and its Twenty Fund has regained its footing. The fund, managed by Ron Sachs, actually can choose up to 30 stocks, and among those stocks, it may also pick a smattering of foreign companies, both debt and equity securities.

But the Twenty Fund looks at the idea of large-cap growth as a place where risk simply takes place on a grander scale. Major holdings include Research in Motion, Google, and Apple. The average portfolio in this category changes completely about once a year. The Twenty Fund shifts position less than a fifth

What difference will it make?

This is the fundamental question that you should ask yourself with every investment decision that you will make, have made, or have yet to even dream up. What difference will it make if you choose one mutual fund over another? What difference does asset allocation make if any particular allocation of x number of funds across a variety of sectors—growth and value, large and small, domestic and foreign—is not something that anyone can conclusively say is the best combination?

Consider this: suppose there are 153 large-cap funds, 38 fixed-income funds, 16 U.S. short-term fixed-income mutual funds, and finally 25 non-U.S. equity mutual funds. You get to pick one from each group. There are 2,325,600 (153 × 38 × 16 × 25) potential portfolios available.

The Financial Planners Association wondered as well. "Obviously, rational investors will attempt to conduct some level of fundamental mutual fund analysis to find funds with competitive performance, low expense ratios, appropriate fund size and sufficient management stability, rather than randomly choosing one of the 2.3 million options. But how important is fund selection at this point in the process?" The portfolio it was trying to construct consisted of the following allocations: 50 percent U.S. large-cap equity, 30 percent U.S. fixed income, 10 percent U.S. short-term fixed income, and 10 percent non-U.S. equity.

In their article for the *Journal of Financial Planning*, William E. O'Rielly, CFA, and James L. Chandler, Jr. challenged several studies on the topic. What they concluded still left the question more or less unanswered. In the short term, we apparently take more time, and perhaps that is the reason for better performance.

In the long term, however, the benchmark performance had some influence over the portfolio's performance, and it wasn't necessarily for the better. Oh, and lastly, investment income is 100 percent the result of asset allocation. What difference does it make?

as much, making some of its small number of stocks true long-term investments. Expenses for the fund remain well below the 1.36 percent that the category can average. No loads are charged.

Fund	Annual Return (over three years)	Expense Ratio/ Turnover
Janus Twenty JAVLX	19.16%	0.87%/20%
iShares Russell 1000 Growth Index IWF	6.11%	0.2%*/15%
iShares S&P 500 Growth Index IVW	4.77%	0.18%*/23%
S&P 500/Barra Growth & S&P 500/Citigroup Growth	13.32%	

*ETFs, as we'll discover later, are different from mutual funds in numerous ways. These are funds that mimic the indexes they track based on performance before fees and expenses.

The game has only three moves. And although there are rules governing the game and variations to it add some excitement, each move defeats another move. There are world championship tournaments. There is evidence that it may be a force of nature, a sort of balancing act that repeats itself over and over again. The game is so simple that it has been used to decide court cases and even disputes over works of art. Some scientists even suggest that the game may govern the equilibrium of the universe. Of course, I am talking about rock-paper-scissors.

Competitors face off, pump their arms, and reveal either a fist (rock), an outstretched hand (paper), or two fingers (scissors). The best of three wins, and world titles are awarded. If there was ever a place where rock-paper-scissors could rule, it would be in mutual fund selection.

At any given time, there is no right and no wrong choice; instead, there is a cycle of options that may offer the best reward. What mutual funds do best is keep the chances of winning more in the hands of the investor. By choosing a portfolio of mutual funds investing in stocks, bonds, or a combination of stocks, bonds, and anything else the fund's charter allows it to employ to get the best return relative to its designated benchmark, you have the advantage at any given moment over the investor who picks stocks for his own portfolio, in essence, building his own personal mutual fund. You throw rock. The markets throw paper. The economy throws scissors.

At any given moment, the tables may turn. Remember, you get three pumps of the arm, and according to the rules of the game, once your arm passes perpendicular to your body, your choice is made. Yes, even at rock-paper-scissors, people will cheat.

Growth funds offer us a look at companies that are on the move. They are normally growing, and in their quest to become bigger, small wants to become mid, mid wants to become large, and large wants to become mega-cap, a realm of $200 billion plus capitalization.

But some companies are simply overlooked among all the hype. They still have viable business models, even though their niche might be established, or even a little shopworn. Sometimes they even pay dividends, distributing to shareholders those profits that they cannot spend on growing their business because, well, they have grown about as much as they can. Or think they have. They have become value companies.

In the next section, we will look at domestic—although that word can be stretched to mean mostly domestic—equity mutual funds that invest in these overlooked companies. And although they seem like they might have been overlooked for a reason, they have proven time and again to outperform growth companies over long periods of time.

One more reminder before we move on. The numbers that I use to portray these funds are just snapshots of where a fund is at this particular moment in time. Any number of forces could change the performance of these funds. I offer you a peek at these particular funds not because I believe that you should buy them, but because you should be scanning them and others for similar details. Most of us will encounter funds in our 401(k) or as part of our retirement plan. We will need to be able to pick one over another. Profiling these funds as I have done is only a tool to make the decision: rock, paper, or scissors.

CHAPTER 13
Inside an Equity Fund—Value

◆◆

Gene Fama and Ken French developed a three-factor model to make their argument that small-cap value investing far outpaces any other kind of investing you can do. It beats large-cap value. It generally does better than growth. But is it actually a better investment?

To accept this argument, you have to believe in the efficient market theory (EMT). The EMT basically suggests that a stock is priced the way it is because investors have determined that this is what it's worth. High book-to-price ratios would suggest that the EMT may be a factor in determining whether a company is actually a good buy or undervalued for a reason.

Skepticism is the first step on the road to philosophy.

Denis Diderot

There is good reason to believe that the markets have not priced certain value companies correctly. Peter Lynch secured his place in history by buying stock in hundreds of small companies that he felt were good value. Because of the sheer size of the Magellan Fund and the relatively small percentage of the total portfolio that each of these value companies represented, he was able to hold them until the market realized what they were actually worth.

This would point a finger at some of the inefficiencies that the market at this level offers. Many of these companies are underanalyzed, and unless they make the evening news, they remain so until investors become aware of them.

Then they become large-cap stocks. Think about it: Microsoft, now worth $262 billion, once traded for $700 million. While it may have been categorized as a growth company, until it was recognized for what it was trying to do, it qualified as a value company.

Much of the unrealized value in these kinds of investments comes from the high cost of innovation at larger-capitalization companies. Simply acquiring an undervalued company can often save a larger company billions in research and

In the Real World...

No book on investing would be complete without some pearl from Warren Buffett. And because his expertise is in following the gospel of Benjamin Graham, investing in companies that have value that may not be readily recognized, here is an excerpt from a 1999 shareholders' meeting.

Shareholder: Recently, at Wharton, Mr. Buffett, you talked about the problems of compounding large sums of money. You were quoted in the local paper as saying that you're confident that if you were working with a small sum closer to $1 million, you could compound at a 50 percent rate. For those of us not saddled with a $100 million problem, could you talk about what types of investments you'd be looking at and where in today's market, you think significant inefficiencies exist?

Buffett: I may have been very slightly misquoted, but I certainly said something to that effect. I talked about how I polled this group of 60 or so people I get together with every couple of years as to what rate they think they can compound money at if they were investing small sums: $100,000, $1 million, $100 million, $1 billion, etc. And I pointed out how the return expectations of the members of this group go very rapidly down the slope.

But it's true. I could name half a dozen people that I think can compound $1 million at 50 percent per year—at least they'd have that return expectation—if they needed it. They'd have to give that $1 million their full attention. But they couldn't compound $100 million or $1 billion at anything remotely like that rate.

There are little tiny areas, as I said, in that Adam Smith interview a few years ago, where if you start with A and you go through and look at everything—and look for small securities in your area of competence where you can understand the business and occasionally find little arbitrage situations or little wrinkles here and there in the market—I think working with a very small sum, there is an opportunity to earn very high returns.

But that advantage disappears very rapidly as the money compounds. As the money goes from $1 million to $10 million, I'd say it would fall off dramatically in terms of the expected return—because you find very, very small things you're almost certain to make high returns on. But you don't find very big things in that category today.

development and even marketing costs (although larger companies usually have the marketing channels in place).

We rely on mutual fund managers in this category to do this sort of research for us. Few of them have mastered this space better than John Montgomery, the lead manager of the Bridgeway Small-Cap Value N fund (BRSVX) since 2003. The three-year returns that the fund has posted are all his doing.

Small-cap value funds do what all value funds do, only with riskier businesses from which to choose. They look for not only capital appreciation but also long-term growth of that capital. The Bridgeway fund focuses on companies that fall below the cutoff point for the 500 largest.

Generally, this makes the turnover for the category lower than that for growth funds, which trade more often. The category average is 83.07 percent, and Mr. Montgomery's fund turns over only once every year and a half.

Because of his buy-and-hold strategy, Mr. Montgomery's expenses are roughly half of the sector average of 1.51 percent. Because of his no-load status, low fees, and reasonable portfolio turnover, investing $1,000 would have cost the average investor about $27 over a three-year period.

Blended by Design—Both Growth and Value

What do you get when you throw a little risk together with a little potential, focus on the smallest ingredients possible, and shun income or dividends? You get a small-cap blend that is invested in companies, at least according to Morningstar's definition, worth less than $2 billion.

Fund	Annual Return (over three years)	Expense Ratio/ Turnover
Bridgeway Small-Cap Value N BRSVX	13.08%	0.88%/58%
iShares Russell 2000 Value Index IWN	3.91%	0.25%*/43%
iShares S&P SmallCap 600 Value IJS	4.76%	0.25%*/32%
S&P SmallCap 600/Barra Value & S&P SmallCap 600/Citigroup Value	27.80%	

* ETFs, as we'll discover later, are different from mutual funds in numerous ways. These are funds that mimic the indexes they track based on performance before fees and expenses.

It is difficult to pin down exactly what this blend actually is. Some funds look for growth stocks that are undervalued; some offer a mix of growth and blend; others blur the line between what is small cap and what is mid cap, leaning all the while toward the value end of the spectrum. Some funds invest in the funds available through their own fund families.

Although the fund we are looking at a little more closely here does not do this, it is worth mentioning now. Fidelity recently caught some negative investor feedback when conservative bond investors found that the fund they had purchased did not come close to matching the performance of the comparable index. Unbeknownst to these investors, the fund followed the practice of buying some of the fund family's more risky, less funded offerings in the hopes of buoying some struggling funds and adding a little more gain to what would otherwise be mediocre returns. In Fidelity's case, some of the funds that the main fund invested in did so poorly that they brought down the overall performance of the fund.

The First Focus Small Company Instl (FOSCX) does none of this. It does draw the small-cap line at $4 billion in market capitalization. Run by Mark Wynegar since 1999, the fund could almost be an index fund if it held more companies. Its turnover, compared to an average of 83.07 percent for the sector, is almost nonexistent. Low fees keep the fund competitive, with a three-year performance that bested the category average by about half a point.

Fund	Annual Return (over three years)	Expense Ratio/ Turnover
First Focus Small Company Instl (FOSCX)	16.68%	1.38%/31%
iShares Russell 2000 Index (IWM)	4.89%	0.2*/25%
iShares S&P SmallCap 600 (IJR)	5.09%	0.2*/16%
S&P SmallCap 600/Barra Value & S&P SmallCap 600/Citigroup Value	27.80%	

* ETFs, as we'll discover later, are different from mutual funds in numerous ways. These are funds that mimic the indexes they track based on performance before fees and expenses.

Finding Value Mid-Way

Numerous companies find themselves languishing between objectives. Some of them are victims of the sector they are in. One of the top holdings in the TIAA-CREF Instl Mid-Cap Value Retire (TRVRX) is the financial services company Principal Financial Group Inc. (PFG). Analysts have had a tough

According to TIAA-CREF, mid-cap value stocks must exhibit some basic qualities in order to be considered for investment. These companies must "trade at a discount to their underlying intrinsic value, possess financial flexibility and strength" and "contain catalysts for price appreciation."

The fund considers a company's potential for rising earnings using conservative assumptions. Too often, growth companies greatly exaggerate their estimates of future sales and growth in hopes of attracting investors. Value companies tend to account for what they are doing much more conservatively.

Share repurchases can signal an excess of cash on hand, a share price in the eyes of the company officials is somewhat depressed, and a stock that is not correctly priced. This can prompt a company to begin offering insider buying or other management incentives, which would help the company achieve some share price appreciation

Value can often manifest itself when a company is trying to raise capital for additional growth by spinning off redundant or underperforming businesses it may have acquired during a growth period. These kinds of asset sales signal underlying value.

Sometimes finding value is as simple as looking at industries that are consolidating. If this begins to happen, it is usually the larger players who look for smaller acquisitions. If a fund can find just such a jewel, everyone wins.

Additional signals that a company may have reached a point of stagnation are the desire to pay down debt and/or increase dividends. In the world of personal finance, paying down debt is considered good. In business, however, it signals an inability to grow.

Offering shareholders increased dividends may, on the surface, seem like a good thing, and those dividends are ultimately passed along to mutual fund shareholders, but once the dividend yield on a stock rises above 7 percent, trouble is on the horizon. The dividend yield on a stock is the dividend paid to shareholders divided by the share price. Too much yield means that the business has run its course and there is nothing the current management can do to make it grow.

The fund's charter usually dictates the fine line that the fund manager walks. In the case of this fund, if a company that it once considered a value loses 20 percent of its purchase price, it gets sold.

time getting behind the company, with most of them finding what it is doing and how it executes its plan to be mediocre at best. But that is the essence of value investing. Like Buffett, who would page through 20,000-page reports looking for one company that might prove to be overlooked and undervalued, mutual fund managers must make the call on companies like Principal every day.

Richard Cutler does that with his fund, holding expenses to half of what his peers charge and doing it without the added cost of loads on an investor's dollar. The turnover in his portfolio is slightly higher than that for the sector, but he still finds himself owning most of his stocks for a little over a year.

Mr. Cutler has some latitude with his investments. He may, if the opportunity presents itself, look to foreign investments for 20 percent of the portfolio's holdings. Funds may be simply acquiescing to the international flavor of the

Fund	Annual Return (over three years)	Expense Ratio/ Turnover
TIAA-CREF Instl Mid-Cap Value Retire TRVRX	14.74%	0.63%/90%
iShares Russell MidCap Value Index IWS	6.50%	0.25%*/25%
PowerShares Dynamic Mid Cap Value PWP	4.26%	0.63%*/43%
S&P MidCap 400/Barra Value & S&P MidCap 400/Citigroup Value	26.91%	

* ETFs, as we'll discover later, are different from mutual funds in numerous ways. These are funds that mimic the indexes they track based on performance before fees and expenses.

markets, understanding that companies, even though they made be based in the United States, do a good deal of business off of our shores.

Holding On . . . Too Long?

We have made a big deal about turnover, but what happens when a fund manager does not change his positions over the course of the year, trading so infrequently that the turnover ratio begins to look similar to that of an index fund? And worse, what happens when that fund, although seeming to perform well enough, does not make the benchmark return over a period of five years? What do you do if a fund that performs this way is a value fund, the very essence of which is to buy and hold?

We are often faced with choices, and some of them are based on good, solid knowledge. More often, however, they are riveted into our memories for no apparent reason. We heard something somewhere from someone we considered, at least at the time, to be an authority. It is similar to the debate between white meat and dark meat on a chicken or turkey. One has more iron, zinc, riboflavin, thiamine, and vitamins B_6 and B_{12}, along with being full of myoglobins that help muscles transport oxygen. That healthier meat isn't the white meat. Sure, white meat may be have slightly fewer calories (46 compared to 50 for a one-ounce boneless serving) and one less gram of fat (breast meat has 1 gram per ounce; thigh meat weighs in at 2 grams), but what makes so many people say that breast meat is better for you, in spite of all the evidence to the contrary?

When the evidence weighs against what we know, we still may not question our decision. While the Westport R fund (WPFRX) is not necessarily guilty of being something it shouldn't be, drifting from small-cap to mid-cap to foreign stocks in the hopes of propping up sagging returns, it has struggled, barely besting its own competition in three of the last five years.

Edmund H. Nicklin, Jr. runs the fund and has done so for almost a decade. He focuses his investors' money on capital appreciation, with dividend considerations being further down the list. While Mr. Nicklin is permitted to invest in value companies of any size, he realizes that his best prospects are in the small- and mid-cap range. In a category that sees its core holding change every year, the Westport R fund is more than likely to be holding the same companies in 2008 that it held in 2007. The fund's expense ratio is higher than the category average (1.38 percent) by a fraction. There may be some purchasing of foreign companies.

Fund	Annual Return (over three years)	Expense Ratio/ Turnover
Westport R WPFRX	11.61%	1.49%/9%
iShares S&P MidCap 400 Index IJH	7.01%	0.2%*/12%
iShares Russell MidCap Index IWR	7.32%	0.2%*/19%
S&P MidCap 400/Barra Value and S&P MidCap 400/Citigroup Value	26.91%	

* ETFs, as we'll discover later, are different from mutual funds in numerous ways. These are funds that mimic the indexes they track based on performance before fees and expenses.

What Price Success?

A fund's publicity department often sees managers who have excelled at the helm of their fund as being ad-worthy. It's like seeing a local restaurant featured on a national food network show. You may never have been to that restaurant, but if you had been, you would have felt good about your choice of cuisine, and because the restaurant was recognized, you by default would have felt better. Its success would make you feel smarter. The same thing goes for mutual funds. Nothing would be better than having a fund manager's name pop up during a conversation, perhaps while two men are fencing.

The first gentleman offers a feint, then as they parry, the aggressor offers the suggestion that his current financial success is because of—then a disengage, followed by a counterattack—a certain fund manager. Try it some time when you are getting the best of your opponent in a game of one-on-one basketball. Start talking finance during your jump shot, or perhaps as you administer a wicked backhand during tennis. Hey, doesn't everyone talk about the state of her investments during the heat of the moment? Everyone does it, right?

Funds do need to publicize their returns if they have returns that are worth publicizing. Not many do. When a fund ranks high on this list or that in relation to its peers, that information becomes part of the ad. Even the least savvy among us will look just a little further than the advertisement. And when we do, we will focus on the return on our investment.

In the ad copy, the ROI is generally given as a percentage, usually for a one-, five-, or ten-year period. It is the most widely considered piece of information about a fund when a new investor is making a decision about investing in this fund or that, or, in some cases, when a current investor is deciding whether this fund or that is still worth investing in. Therefore, that number can have significant and numerous meanings depending on how you read it and what you read into it. "How much would my $1,000 be worth if I had invested 10 years ago?" has little bearing on where the fund is now or where it will go in the future.

Sadly, no matter what they try, mutual funds will always have detractors, quick with the scalpel to dissect intent from perception, truth from fiction. And even though I like mutual funds, I will do my fair share of cutting as well.

In the Real World...

Most of us are amateur photographers. Some of us even consider what we do to be sort of artistic. Some people frame those shots and hang them on the wall for others to see and admire. But what if you could manipulate a picture in such a way as to make it seem different from what it was? Would you spend hours on programs like Photoshop, blurring the edges of a cityscape shot at night to give it the surreal effect of looking like a photo of a scale model? Tilt-shift photography, developed by Olivo Barbieri, has done just that. The equipment to process these scale model–like photos is extremely expensive, although cheap imitations can be found all over Flickr. But what if this kind of sleight-of-sight was done by a mutual fund?

The CGM Focus fund, whose manager is Ken Heebner, used a commercial showing two men fencing to attract new investors while giving the fund an air of sophistication. But Mr. Heebner's fund also presents a conundrum for investors. What do you do when the fund has been as successful as it has been for three, five, and ten years running—Mr. Heebner took over at the helm in 1997—but has done so with high fund turnover, above-average expenses, and a huge tax bill? And why would it do it as a large-cap fund with both growth and value companies in the portfolio?

Both of these questions are admittedly nuanced. But they open up an interesting topic that needs to be discussed. We brought up asset allocation earlier. We showed you some of the ways in which funds are rated and how some benchmarks are constructed. But what about tilt? If a fund manager has the opportunity to buy both growth and value companies, is the manager buying more of one than of the other at any particular moment?

You can count on one thing: mutual fund managers need a steady of stream of both new investors and reinvestments from existing shareholders. This keeps the flow of funds available to purchase additional positions in a company that they feel very good about today or to pursue a new offering. The latter choice usually requires enough available stock to purchase so as not to artificially drive the price up. Lack of liquidity, as we mentioned earlier, creates risk and, at the same time, makes a company less desirable to mutual funds.

Some funds close their doors to new investors. This usually happens when investing the amount of investable money becomes too cumbersome. The most common reason for a fund to close is that it is a victim of its own success.

I have written about how each fund has a charter, a set of focused strategies that shareholders buy into, hoping to achieve the goals that they have set and to complement the risks that they are willing to take. We have also learned that some fund managers are given quite a bit of latitude when searching for the best companies to buy. But when the focus of the fund is small or even medium-sized companies, the number of companies that are available to invest in (remember liquidity) can be small. Despite the sheer number of companies in some indexes, many of these companies do not have enough shares for a fund manager to purchase.

So a fund closes its doors to new investors. But that doesn't necessarily mean that the fund will perform better than it did when it was open to all investors. In fact, closures are a cure for a problem that already exists.

Some funds reopen to investors. The Fidelity Magellan Fund, one of the largest actively managed funds, was the fund where Peter Lynch made his name a legend. His fund, it should be noted, would have netted an investor over $16 million had that investor put $10,000 into Mr. Lynch's able hands when he opened its doors in 1963. Had you invested the same amount of money in an index fund, it would have grown to slightly more than $800,000 over the same period. So why would such a successful fund—which Mr. Lynch has long since retired from managing—reopen its doors?

Fidelity Magellan Fund has not done as well as it once did, and investors have headed for the doors. This forces a fund to raise cash to settle these exiting investors' accounts and takes money away from new investment opportunities. The bottom line was, the fund needed fresh money.

Full Tilt

It is often an innocent mistake. Attempting to achieve a blend of growth and value in equal proportions is, if you think about it, kind of silly. Such harsh divisions would be nearly impossible. So fund managers move between the two in an effort to boost returns. One year they may be mostly growth-oriented with the option of value investing, and the next year, the whole structure of the fund may have changed.

 What the Experts Say

Fragments came floating into his mind like bits of wood drifting down a stream, and he fished them out and fitted them together.

Elizabeth Gray Vining

Some data suggest that this happens far more frequently when you are investing in small-cap blended funds. According to Craig L. Israelson, an associate professor in the department of home and family living at Brigham Young University, the shift toward value rather than growth is more pronounced in large- and mid-cap blended funds. It is for that reason, Professor Israelsen believes, that the performance of these types of actively managed funds has been better than that of either value or growth funds as stand-alone funds. In other words, "higher risk does not always lead to higher return."

The CGM Focus Fund seems to be an exception to numerous rules and beliefs. It is a large-cap blended fund that has produced outsized capital gains (a less tax-efficient situation), above-average turnover (its peers generally turn over their portfolios about once every nine months, or 71.97 percent), and an expense ratio that is higher than that of the average fund in this group (1.11 percent).

Of the top 10 holdings in the fund (at least for the moment), four are foreign-based companies. Each offers some degree of yield. The fund focuses on companies that are worth at least $100 million, making almost the entire investment world available to Mr. Heebner. When the focus is on capital growth, with this fund, anything goes. En garde!

Fund	Annual Return (over three years)	Expense Ratio/ Turnover
CGM Focus CGMFX	33.15%	1.27%/384%
Vanguard Total Stock Market ETF VTI	6.36%	0.07%*/4%
iShares Russell 1000 Index IWB	6.04%	0.15%*/7%
S&P 500/Barra Value & S&P MidCap 400/Citigroup Value	21.91%	
S&P 500/Barra Growth & S&P 500/Citigroup Growth	13.32%	

* ETFs, as we'll discover later, are different from mutual funds in numerous ways. These are funds that mimic the indexes they track based on performance before fees and expenses.

What's Next ▷ In the late nineteenth century, Milton Bradley was painting portraits of Abraham Lincoln. Then Abe grew a beard. As a result, Mr. Bradley turned his attention to (it's hard to believe) board games. His first game, the Checkered Game of Life, came out in 1860 at a time in U.S. history when most of the country was taking the high moral ground. Using a spinner instead of dice, he mapped out a journey that began with infancy and moved throughout a fictional life. The goal was twofold: to avoid suicide (a sure way to end your play) and to reach what Bradley described as "Happy Old Age." Along the way, you learned lessons about how to live a moral life conducted in the proper manner. The game sold 45,000 copies in its first year, and Mr. Bradley also included it in a set of fireside games that could be sent to loved ones in the Civil War. Along with the Checkered Game of Life, he included backgammon, chess, checkers, and dominoes.

In the next chapter, we will look at the final group of funds. Like the game of life, they have a role somewhere between infancy and old age. Like the board game, the goal of investing is to land on the good spaces while avoiding the bad ones. But with markets being what they are, risky and volatile, investors needed something that they could hang onto, a fund that was everything to everyone who knew little about investing. The birth of the index fund created just such an opening.

In the remainder of this book, we will examine three separate types of index funds: those that track the markets using the popular indexes (we will also explore a few variations on those themes), exchange-traded funds (which are—at least until recently, when the first actively managed ETF was released—essentially indexes that are publicly traded), and sector funds (funds that may be actively managed but that focus directly on one type of industry, such as communications, financial, health, natural resources, precious metals, real estate, technology, or utilities. We will even take a look at funds that invest in bear markets.

CHAPTER 14

Inside an Equity Fund—Indexing

◆◆◆◆◆◆◆◆◆◆◆◆◆◆◆◆◆◆◆◆◆◆◆◆◆◆◆◆◆◆◆◆◆◆◆◆◆◆◆

"*When everyone is against you, it means that you are absolutely wrong— or absolutely right.*" Albert Guinon is credited with that observation, despite his having lived and died before the first indexed mutual fund ever made its debut. The comment even predates the Cowles Commission Index, which made its appearance shortly after its founder, Alfred Cowles, proclaimed that the markets were just too difficult for any one person to master. Could John Bogle have felt this way as well when he championed his thinking on the subject?

When was the first mutual fund created?

Back in the Wild West days of our stock markets, there were no laws governing how securities were traded. This freedom led to wide-open manipulation of the markets, as well as rampant speculation and a generous share of backroom dealings. Without any regulation, there was no one who could be trusted. Each rumor might be fact, and that meant that stocks could collapse on hearsay alone.

The first precursor of mutual funds was something called an investment trust. These were elegantly simple. Investors pooled their money, and they were issued shares based on their investment. Once an investor had those shares, he could trade them on the stock exchanges just as he could stocks. Immediately, shady traders began to capitalize on something called free float. It worked like this: an investment trust purchased stock in various companies on behalf of its shareholders. That stock, which was also traded, could be bought and sold for less than the value of the trust.

Suppose the trust was worth $100,000 in total stock. And suppose you owned 1/100 of that trust, with each share being worth $10. Suppose you wanted to sell all 100 of your shares on the open market, but a bigger shareholder in the trust began suggesting that some company or another inside the trust was in financial trouble. Whether or not the rumor was true, your shares would no longer be worth $10 and might trade well below that price.

Small investors were particularly vulnerable to this sort of manipulation. After the shares of the trust fell as the result of a rumor, bigger investors would swoop in and buy the discounted shares. There were numerous other reasons why these trusts gained a bad reputation, as will any enterprise that is allowed to operate without concern for all of its investors, big and small.

Mutual funds formally came into existence in 1924. Three things made these funds the vehicle of choice for millions of investors from that point on. Because these funds invested only in common stock of publicly traded companies, investors could accurately calculate what each share of the fund was worth. Investment trusts were able to borrow money, leveraging their positions in certain companies; mutual funds were not permitted to do this. The value of the fund was calculated at the end of each day, not during the trading session.

That first mutual fund still exists.

It was in the spirit of Cowles's statement that the idea for an index fund was kicked around for the next 50 years. Although the idea was sound, the costs and the level of sophistication that were required to operate such a fund were far too high to be worth the effort. This problem was eventually and simply solved by the invention of the computer.

In those early days, the cost of trading a stock was nonnegotiable. Brokers charged a minimum commission for their services. Once regulation of the cost of trading was removed, the overall cost of buying stocks for an index fund became much more financially appealing. Unfortunately, those changes took 50 years.

Today, a simple phone call or an e-mail can begin the purchasing process. Mutual funds have never in their 90-or-so-year history been more accessible to the investor. Until 1976, the primary place where mutual funds were available was from a stockbroker. Brokerage firms were paid 8 percent for the sale, adding to the high costs of creating an index fund.

The high cost of trading, the lack of computing power and, as if that wasn't enough, the inaccessibility of mutual funds made the idea of indexing just too hard to promote. And so the industry didn't promote it.

A Change of Heart

There are basically two ways to run an index fund: market-weighted and equal-weighted. There are numerous variations, but these two types were the true first attempts at indexing. *Equal-weighted investing* requires the fund to buy an equal amount of each company. Try this in the produce department some day. Buying two dollars' worth of everything it sells will help you begin to grasp the logistical nightmares involved in keeping up with an ever-shifting marketplace.

You end up with much more of things that are cheap (and probably for good reason) and not enough of the high-priced produce. In investing, the balance is important. Equal-weighted funds failed to achieve this, and it was evident that the costs of operation were too high.

The *market-weighted index* started out as a presentation at the Harvard Business School. Three years later, the fund began to sell shares. The idea of basing the number of shares bought on the size of the company was elegant in its simplicity. If one company was worth more than another, the percentage of the shares of each that the fund owned would attempt to mimic that difference.

ERISA sealed the deal. The 1976 Employee Retirement Income Security Act held pension managers accountable for poor performance. Until that moment, these fund managers were forced to purchase only actively managed mutual funds, and the cost of that was becoming increasingly prohibitive.

Along Came a Rebel

Bogle's reputation was based on a senior thesis suggesting that mutual funds should be able to say what their objective was in such a way that investors understood it; cut back on the cost of getting into the fund, called loads, and on the prohibitive layering of fees that management tacked on; and last, be humble. To this bastion of good old boys, this was heresy.

When Bogle had the chance to try out his low-cost, co-op-type investment company, the Vanguard Group was born. But Bogle's battle was far from over. He couldn't get brokers to sell the fund for a lower commission than they received for selling actively managed funds.

 What the Experts Say Revolutions are not about trifles, but spring from trifles.

Aristotle

Bogle made his next revolutionary move in February 1977. He sold his funds without brokers and without loads. Three years later, the Vanguard 500 Index Fund was officially named.

The result of Bogle's fighting this marketplace headwind was increased returns for his investors. Not even an index fund introduced some three years later could survive with a 1 percent fee, close to the average for an actively managed fund.

Bogle continued to open funds that tracked different parts of the market. He took his strategy to the bond market next (Bond Market), and then introduced the Extended Market Fund covering the rest of the equity markets.

Although the latter fund was indexed to the Wilshire 4500, an index that removes the top 500 companies in terms of market cap from the total, the fund did not purchase shares in all 4,500 of the remaining companies.

Bogle understood that at the lower end of that benchmark index, the smallest companies might be too thinly traded to be considered a prudent investment. So the fund generally holds the top 2,800 companies. The smallest companies in this group, around 800 or so, are bought based on a statistical sampling.

What is statistical sampling?

In statistical sampling, there are some specific rules about the size of the group and proportion of that group that will be surveyed. Statistical sampling measures probability and risk and actually falls into five separate categories: random, systematic, stratified, cluster, and convenience. While *random* sampling might work, it has too many pitfalls to succeed when it comes to picking companies for an index. The use of *systematic* sampling, a method that picks every fifth or tenth in a group, would fail to capture the companies that trade frequently and influence the marketplace. *Cluster* sampling, the most exhaustive type of survey and not always accurate when spread over a large group, considers all elements of each company that is traded. Government accounting uses methods like this when researching consumer habits. *Convenience* samples often miss key elements of each company, such as whether earnings or markets can be sustained over long periods. This type of sampling offers the greatest chance of bias. To get a good sample, *stratified* sampling separates large groups into smaller, more similar groups. To work properly, the group being surveyed must be large enough to be representative (in the case of Vanguard's approach to the Wilshire 4500, the bottom 2,500 companies were removed from consideration, leaving 2,000 stocks to choose for the index. From that group, 800 stocks were further culled, giving Vanguard a survey sample for its fund that was more representative of the group that was left) and proportionate (the groups' small size made them all similar. Dividing the group into different strata gave Vanguard a good cross-section of companies for the index, mostly free of bias and sampling error.

What Is an Index Fund?

Although you can see why Mr. Bogle is often spoken of in such reverent terms, his idea for indexing markets gave investors something that they had not had prior to the introduction of his fund philosophy. To be able look into a fund and see what was going on was unheard of. Being able to see what a fund manager is doing is often referred to as transparency.

People often make the mistake of confusing index funds with the market. They are not. In fact, index funds use indexes as benchmarks. The companies that publish benchmarks do so as a tracking device, a measure of performance.

Vanguard's 500 Index Fund and Extended Market Fund, for instance, track and index benchmarks published by Standard & Poor's and Wilshire. Its Bond Market Fund, which was the first index for this corner of the market, uses the Lehman Brothers Aggregate Bond Index.

And most importantly, not all indexes are created the same way. As you saw earlier when we compared the performance of those early attempts at indexing, indexing requires more than just throwing a dart at the stock pages. The increase in the level of sophistication has not stopped, as fund families, and the academics they often hire to help them, chart new areas to explore and new combinations to attempt, and, with any luck, produce better overall performance.

Even determining market capitalizations isn't easy. The simple way to determine market capitalization is to multiply the price of the shares times the number of shares issued. This makes the mistake of including shares of stock that are held inside the company and thus are not available for trading.

A company is only as good as the price of its shares. The larger the number of shares available to the marketplace, the better this yardstick becomes as a measure. Closely held shares that are literally "off the market" blur the overall picture.

By using a method called *free float*, the creators of an index can accurately determine what the true market value of a company is. The S&P 500 uses this method. Free float drops restricted shares, ownership holdings, and other blocks of stock that are not available to the public and considers only those shares that could be traded.

These broad indexes have had a reputation for long-term outperformance. Outperformance is a nice way of saying that they did better than actively managed funds, and for some very obvious reasons. The high cost of running an actively managed fund means that the actively managed fund must cover those costs through its performance *before* it can begin to post competitive returns.

To see how index funds are doing, you do the reverse of what actively managed funds do. You compare them to those that compare themselves. And that worked just fine up until about a decade ago.

Market Efficiency

The theory of market efficiency, if you will recall, suggests that the market prices each company at its fair value. But when things got scary during the stretch between 2000 and 2002, that thinking was challenged. Small-cap value funds were doing better than index funds. In fact, a lot of the value funds of all sizes began to perform very well. Some more actively managed funds, despite higher fees than the index funds, had some long runs of admirable returns. Index funds should have done better.

People began thinking that there must be another way to keep up with the savviest active managers. Perhaps the index needed to be rejiggered.

Jeremy Siegel, a finance professor at the University of Pennsylvania's Wharton School, conjured up a new way to calculate the performance of a segment of the market. His fundamentally weighted indexes looked at dividend payments as a measure of financial strength. (We will discuss this type of investing when we get to exchange traded funds in the next chapter. Mr. Siegel is the strategic advisor to the newly created Wisdom Tree Asset Management.)

The ever-quoted Dow Jones Industrial Average uses a price-weighted method to determine the value of the index. If we took that thinking back to the produce department, you would give a higher value to the rare fruit flown in from some far-off distant part of the globe because its price was higher. The lowly onion or potato, in spite of its high availability and popularity, would receive a far smaller percentage of the index because of its smaller price point. Although potatoes and onions are far more valuable based on their role in our diets, they would actually carry a smaller percentage of worth in a price-weighted index.

 In the Real World... Some of the highest-priced food in the world can be found in Japan. The Japanese loyalty to homegrown fruit and vegetables has pushed the prices of these commodities to levels that Americans hope they never experience. Peaches that cost $8 and melons that cost $50 are not uncommon at Japanese markets. One bargain: cabbage.

It is amazing that the DJIA is still considered relevant in today's market-place, on the evening news, and as a measure of how the broader markets are performing. Ask someone what the Russell 2000 did today, and she will look at you clueless. The same question about the performance of the Dow Industrials might get a response, especially if the news about the markets had changed for the worse or some new psychological number was about to be reached.

Benchmarks and Indexes

An index is only as good as the benchmark it follows. The Chartered Financial Analysts Institute (CFA Institute) holds the investment community to higher standards. Its mission statements reads: "Financial markets should be equitable, free, and efficient so that every investor has a chance to earn a fair return, the interests of the ultimate investor must take precedence over the interests of all other market participants," and "high ethical principles and self-regulatory standards are as important to market efficiency and fairness as rules and regulations."

This body of professionals has standardized conduct among index funds, and because of this code, index funds are used as benchmarks for the actively managed mutual funds we have just read about in the previous pages.

The CFA Institute felt that an index should have certain characteristics. Stability was extremely important, not only for controlling the fees that came from frequent trading, but also to maintain a passive voice. However, the index would occasionally need to be readjusted based on how it was "weighted." Stability in a benchmark/index allowed the average investor to try to mimic the portfolio. Okay, the average investor with a lot of money.

This replication is important. Market participants should be able do the same thing that the index/benchmark does. How a strategy performs should be something that can be measured over time.

The CFA Institute also believed that the index should be relevant. Relevance has to do more with understanding. Investors can grasp why you would want to invest in the top 500 companies, but not in an index of the top pillow makers. Rules about barriers were created for international funds.

Many of John Bogle's ideas were adopted as well. Low expenses were a must, and this was achieved by making them consistent. If costs were kept low and indexes agreed on some fees for trading-related costs, then the index could become *the* measuring stick. One of Mr. Bogle's other tenets was a clearly stated objective. The CFA Institute agreed.

Those Pesky Fees

What most people assume is that since an index is a benchmark is an index, the returns should be the same. If it weren't for those trading costs, this would be true. This difference is called the tracking error. This may be the best way to tell the difference between one index and another when both profess to invest using the same passive strategy.

We have talked at length throughout the book about the expense ratio. This is how much your direct costs for hiring a particular fund manager are. These fees can be extensive and can detract from your fund returns, as they are deducted from the total assets in the fund. The higher the fee, the less of your money is invested. Actually, it is the higher the fees, the less the return on invested money. But since numerous people utilize mutual funds for their retirement planning and countless others have those returns on their investments reinvested, it does end up being less money. (Index funds have extremely low expense ratios, but they are not without fees.)

Actively managed funds also assess investors for higher than average brokerage charges, research, mailings, and 12b–1 fees, to name just a few.

 What to Ask?

What is a 12b–1 fee?

The SEC describes 12b–1 fees as "fees paid by the fund out of fund assets to cover distribution expenses and sometimes shareholder service expenses. 12b–1 fees get their name from the SEC rule that authorizes a fund to pay them. Distribution fees include fees paid for marketing and selling fund shares, such as compensating brokers and others who sell fund shares, and paying for advertising, the printing and mailing of prospectuses to new investors, and the printing and mailing of sales literature." This type of fee is largely antiquated and in many cases unnecessary.

For more information, see http://www.sec.gov/answers/mffees.htm.

All these ever-so-slight fractions of a percentage point can add up over the long term and take away from your return. Many people use mutual funds for the most fundamental part of their financial life: retirement. These small nicks at the shell of what is often referred to as your nest egg are meaningful. They would be more so if you had paid attention to the way your fund's value was being eroded as each fee was deducted. Here's good news: not all fees are charged to the shareholder. Some are deducted from the value of the fund, of which, ironically, you happen to be a shareholder. This is much like what David Byrne and Brian Eno, Chris Frantz, Jerry Harrison, and Tina Weymouth, writing as Talking Heads, meant in "Once in a Lifetime" (*Remain in the Light*, Warner Brothers, 1980) when they wrote: "same as it ever was."

Some people will argue that even index funds have these expenses when they sell a stock or two that have fallen out of favor and been dropped from the index and replace it with a stock or two that have become worthy of inclusion. Actively traded mutual funds often take this to an extreme. Index funds, by their nature and because they trade infrequently, are unable to do so. Their brokerage costs tend to be very low.

But sometimes a fund changes course, and as a result, the cost of "turning over" a portfolio as a measure of a fund's performance becomes an inexact measure. Although we used this measure a great deal throughout the book, it can change, often dramatically, over the course of a year or two. New managers at the helm often adjust the fund's holdings, creating outsized trading numbers in the short term. Using a longer average and coupling it to the manager's tenure at the fund eliminates most of these excuses. Once a fund manager starts selling the entire portfolio more than once, she has probably reached the limit that I would consider tolerable. (Best-case scenario: look for funds that are adding to current positions with new money rather than selling their positions to buy new companies.)

But these were the only two fees that we actually talked about in any detail, and index funds are largely, but not entirely, immune to these costs. For the rest of this section, we will discuss some of the differences between an index fund and an actively managed fund, using fees as the criterion. Some of these fees do occur in index funds, and smart money will avoid these added-on costs.

But first, the charges.

Shareholder Charges

Sales Loads

We talked about the difference between front-load and closed-end funds earlier, but only briefly. These fees are largely unneeded. There are mutual fund families that offer funds that carry loads, sometimes both front-load and closed-end, and sell them right alongside the funds that have no loads. Beware this strategy. This type of sleight of hand often means that the fund is capturing those fees one way or another.

The reasoning behind sales loads is summed up in those brokerage costs I mentioned in the discussion of the turnover ratio. After all, funds do need brokers to sell their shares, and in a typical transaction, the brokers need to be compensated. But this load goes to the broker who sold you the fund. A sales load is a commission that investors pay when they purchase any type of security from a broker. However, even though some funds do not employ outside firms to sell their funds, they still charge sales loads.

You will be pleased to know that these fees have a ceiling. The agency that you might assume would regulate these issues for the shareholder, the SEC, does not limit the size of the sales load a fund may charge. The Financial Industry Regulatory Authority (FINRA), however, does put a limit on how much funds can charge, capping the maximum fee at 8.5 percent.

What is FINRA?

The Financial Industry Regulatory Authority is a nongovernmental agency that acts as a credibility and ethics check for brokers and mutual funds. This agency oversees many of the rules and regulations, offers mediation and arbitration, and offers numerous educational tools for brokers. If you want to find out more about how this agency conducts itself, you will find rulings and regulations that FINRA has been involved in at http://www.finra.org/RulesRegulation/IssueCenter/MutualFunds/index.htm.

The good news about sales charges, if you are inclined to pay them, is that they tend to be lower to offset other charges the fund may levy. And more good news: according to FINRA, most funds do not charge the maximum.

A front-end sales load forces investors to pay when they purchase fund shares. Before I show you an example of how this affects your returns over a period of time, I want to offer a disclaimer. No two funds trade the same way or have the same underlying portfolio makeup. And if they did, it is even more unlikely that they would reveal that information before you bought your shares.

In a perfect world, the funds used in this example would be exactly the same. If you are looking for a large blended mutual fund and you are having difficulty choosing, I offer this side-by-side comparison. Both funds charge 1.25 percent for management fees, still levy a 12b–1 fee of 0.25 percent on their shareholders, and have returned the same 10 percent for their investors for 20 years running. You have $10,000 to invest, and you do not plan on adding to the fund.

Year	Front-End Load Fund Account Value	No-Load Fund Account Value
1	$10,307	$10,875
5	$14,285	$15,211
10	$21,479	$23,136
20	$48,564	$53,528

The difference of $4,964 between the two ending values is a significant sum even without the standard reinvestment of dividends and gains and without any additional funds being added over the course of *that* 20 years. So why, then, do people buy funds with these fees? The best guess is the trust in their brokers that they may have built over the years or, if not blind faith, simply not knowing where to look for a better deal.

Often the advice investors receive about these purchases comes from their advisors, who as we have learned, often are in fact brokers rather than advisors. The less-than-savvy investor, in other words, would have no idea until after the fact.

Deferred Sales Charge (Load)

This fee catches you when you're going. After the party is over, funds with this fee will charge you for your stay. Many investors leave a fund when the fund does not perform as they expected, when a better opportunity comes along, or, worse, when they need to change the way their portfolios are allocated. *Allocation of your assets* in this instance may reflect a changing tolerance for risk

Funds come in different classes, many of which designate the kind of shareholder fees the fund might charge.

Class A shares typically impose a front-end sales load but have lower 12b–1 fees and often lower annual expenses. Your broker will tell you that of all of the classes, this is the best for the long-term investor. From the broker's point of view, two things validate this argument, the first being that the broker wants his money up front, not at the end of the investor's ownership of the fund, and the second being that if you do hold the fund for the long term, it's always possible that the fee will be forgotten.

Chances are, your broker will offer breakpoints on these Class A shares. This means that the front-end fee will be lowered if a larger amount is deposited. The fee may be waived altogether if the initial shareholder purchase reaches the million-dollar range.

Class B shares have a contingent deferred sales load and may have higher 12b–1 fees. Once the contingent period is satisfied, the Class B shares convert to Class A shares with the lower 12b–1 fee.

Class C shares sold in the same fund family offering other classes of shares are no-front-load shares but will generally have higher expenses. Often, these funds will have redemption fees that act like a back-end sales load for shareholders who redeem their money within a year.

The redemption fee for Class C shares tends to be lower than the back-end load charged for Class B shares. Class C shares always remain Class C shares and do not convert to another class. It is for this reason that you should pay particular attention to those higher fees. No-load funds should not penalize the investor for his investment.

and the attempt to protect some of your capital (invested money) from any potential loss. However, with a deferred sales load, the final loss is not assessed until you sell.

"Deferred Sales Charge (Load)" in the fee table in your prospectus refers to this charge that investors pay when they redeem shares in the fund. The actual transaction does not entail the selling of shares to another investor. It involves the sale of the shares back to the fund, which then makes those shares available to other investors.

Unlike with front-load funds, all of your money goes to work for you when you invest initially. If an investor were to invest the same $10,000 as in the previous example in a fund with a 5 percent back-end sales load, and if there are no other fees involved in the purchase of those shares, the entire $10,000 will be used to purchase fund shares.

Year	Back-End Load Fund Account Value	No-Load Fund Account Value
1	$10,875	$10,875
5	$15,211	$15,211
10	$23,136	$23,136
20	$53,528	$53,528

Just like front-end loads, the back-end load is a broker's fee and is turned over to the broker when the shares are redeemed. If the back-end load is 5 percent, this charge is assessed based on your original investment, not on the sum of the investment and returns over a 20-year period. If your fund's value has declined from its original investment value, then the deferred fee is levied on the lesser amount.

Most funds use a closed-end load that declines over a period of time. A contingent deferred sales load, also known as a CDSC or CDSL, is the most common type of back-end sales load. The charge can decrease to zero if the investor holds the fund long enough, typically more than five years. Each successive year will see a decline in the charge of about 1 percent. Eventually, the load goes away completely.

There is a one in four chance that in any given year, a fund that charges a load of any kind, held in comparison to a similar type fund, will outperform that fund.

Redemption Fee

This fee acts somewhat like a contingent deferred sales charge or back-end charge. It too is levied when an investor redeems shares. Unlike contingent deferred sales charges, however, this fee is paid to the fund (contingent fees are the cost of selling the shares back to the fund). It covers costs, other than sales costs, that are involved with a redemption and is primarily designed to keep investors from buying and selling funds too quickly. The fee is expressed as either a dollar amount or a percentage of the redemption price.

This fee tends to keep investors put for a certain amount of time, with the fee diminishing over a certain period. Each time a redemption takes place, a cash-short or fully invested fund will need to sell assets to cover the redemption. In a volatile fund, this can cost all shareholders.

Exchange Fee

This fee may be charged when an investor transfers money from one fund to another within the same fund family. This is an unnecessary fee unless the transfer is large, and then the fee is generally waived. It is also waived if the trading is done infrequently.

Purchase Fee

If you run into this type of fee when buying a fund, find another fund. A purchase fee is another type of fee that some funds charge their shareholders when the shareholders purchase their shares. While it does differ from a front-end sales load, this difference involves only who receives the money. Purchase fees are paid to the fund, whereas front-end load fees are paid to a broker (most of the time). The fund will tell you that the fee is to help offset some of the costs, but it is wholly unnecessary and is not found too often.

Annual Fund Operating Expenses

Management Fees

Management fees pay managers for the services that they provide to the fund. These fees are paid out of fund assets directly to the fund's investment advisor (or its affiliates) for its services in managing the fund's investment portfolio. The fund's performance needs to cover these fees, even if they are exorbitant (over 1.25 percent); if the fund manager can do that, she would be worth the few extra trinkets. But that would be a rare fund manager indeed. Keep those management fees low and you will have shareholders who are pleased with mediocre returns. The fees are often lumped with administrative fees payable to the investment advisor that do not find their way into the "Other Expenses" category.

Other Expenses

This can be a financial black hole for mutual fund fees and should be watched closely. It does not include the "Management Fees" or "Distribution [and/or Service] (12b–1) Fees," which are listed separately, but it does include such costly tidbits as custodial expenses, legal expenses, accounting expenses, transfer agent expenses, and other administrative expenses.

Total Annual Fund Operating Expenses

Then add it all up. This line on the fee table is the total of a fund's annual operating expenses, expressed as a percentage of the fund's average net assets. In the following example, we compare the costs of three mutual funds using a 10 percent return over 20 years.

One of the funds we profiled earlier in the book, the Janus Twenty, is a no-load fund, as is the Alger Capital Appreciation Institutional Fund. The difference in return is due to the smaller fees that Janus charges (0.87 percent versus. 1.23 percent) and its much smaller turnover (20 percent vs. 232 percent). The John Hancock fund has a front-end load fee of 5 percent.

Class A shares often have smaller expenses to offset the front-end load. The Janus fund still trumps on both counts, expense ratio (0.87 percent vs. 1.14 percent) and turnover (20 percent vs. 40 percent), and although both are lower than their peers, the following table will illustrate what these subtle difference can do to a return over 20 years.

	Janus Twenty Fund	John Hancock Large Cap Equity Fund Class A	Alger Capital Appreciation Institutional Fund Class I
Ticker symbol	JAVLX	TAGRX	ALARX
Investment amount	$10,000.00	$10,000.00	$10,000.00
Fund value after 20 years	$56,462.53	$50,049.86	$52,684.06
Profit/loss:	$46,462.53	$40,049.86	$42,684.06
Total fees	$4,703.56	$5,966.53	$6,280.56
Total sales charges	$0.00	$500.00	$0.00
Total fees & sales charges	$4,703.56	$6,466.53	$6,280.56

If you would like to run the funds in your portfolio through a similar test, FINRA has set up a calculator at the following address: http://apps.finra.org/investor_Information/ea/1/mfetf.aspx.

Scientists have recently begun a census of all the living organisms in the ocean. From the smallest fungi to the largest plants and animals, everything will need to be counted. This will help answer the question of what is out there in those vast biodiverse systems under the surface. Ultimately, by 2010, the scientists will begin asking what all of these elements of the system do.

As we move to the next chapter, we will begin looking at how the mutual fund industry has continued to diversify, carving out smaller and more detailed corners of the investment world. While this dissection and cross sectioning began in sector funds, they saw their true flourishing in the exchange-traded funds.

We will begin this discussion by talking about the difficulties that even indexes have in hitting their benchmarks and whether the index is the best measurement tool for investors. We will also consider the best place to use these funds, with a nod to your retirement portfolio.

Because sector funds and ETFs are not considered the best place for retirement dollars, what they are and how they operate can add some interesting diversification for the average investor.

CHAPTER 15
Exchange-Traded Funds

W hen Roger Lowenstein wrote, "It's a good time to be a financial dis- aster writer," we had not yet experienced what happened at the end of 2007 and through 2008. We hadn't seen the credit markets falter worldwide, average people lose their homes to foreclosure, or the economy stumble. Mr. Lowenstein wrote those words in June of 2005, and the gist of his article in the *New York Times Magazine*, "See a Bubble?" was a much more poignant question: "Is all the anxiety warranted, or even productive?"

Investors are looking for ever-smaller corners of the markets that will allow them to gain the slightest edge. This entails taking ever-greater risks, and if those bets fail, the flip side of reward is loss. What makes investors even more nervous is what they may be missing when they build a wall around their portfolios.

In early Renaissance paintings, a garden setting was imbued with religious meaning. The inner wall surrounded the peaceful setting, with floral violets and reds decorating a lawn or mead. The area beyond the outer wall was por- trayed as a pagan place, full of uncertainty and less than angelic pursuits. This area beyond the outer wall, where realism is pushed to the edges, is where the risk is.

The question is, is crossing into that place worth the effort? Does more mean better? Not necessarily. And especially not for index funds. Mr. Lowenstein fin- ishes with the following piece of wishful thinking: "Perhaps," he writes, "if there were fewer traders dulling their anxiety with financial Zoloft and fewer invest- ment options available to the rest of us, we would make better decisions—and sleep more soundly."

When Index Funds Miss

Surprisingly, some index funds miss the benchmark that they are attempting to mimic. Perhaps not so surprisingly, the reason is fees. If an index fund invests a hundred dollars, and the benchmark it tracks returns $7^1/_2$ percent, in a perfect world, the fund balance would increase by $7.50, to $107.50. But then some costs much be extracted—even the biggest and the best fund managers, as we have come to find out, are not performing this service for free.

So why do some index funds miss these benchmarks, while others achieve a near hit time and again, year after year? Some index funds use investment research and roll the cost of that service into their trading commissions. Actively managed funds willingly pay for this service, which can offer insights into a company's performance that are usually based on visits to the business, exploration of financial records, and predictions based on any number of indicators that will foretell future performance.

But index funds do not need this kind of information. They are attempting to track a preselected group of stocks or bonds, and improvement in their performance comes from getting the cheapest deal on trades.

 What the Experts Say

Industry is fortune's right hand, and frugality its left.

John Ray

The index funds that do the best job do so because they excel at penny-pinching, and do so with more than just a smattering of skill. They must maintain the underlying portfolio, making moves seemingly in an instant each time the index is rebalanced (and doing so before the rest of the traders increase the price of the stock that was added and deflate the price of the stock that is being sold out of the index).

Any difference between the index's benchmark and the underlying portfolio is considered a *tracking error*. These tracking errors are particularly pronounced during an unsettled market. Index fund managers may have enormous amounts of cash sitting idly on the sidelines as the markets adjust to news.

They would like to invest this cash but, much like the rest of us, they are gripped by the fear that wherever they put their money, it will be the wrong place. Unsure of the merits of beefing up one position at the expense of another, they allow the money to languish, largely uninvested, while the benchmark moves ahead in most instances, completely unfazed by these issues.

Measuring These Errors

Just when you thought that all you had to do was buy an index and forget about it, along comes this paradox. But how do you determine how much of an error is acceptable? The simple answer is, choose the fund whose return is closest to the benchmark. Of course, in the real world, that fund may not be accessible to you (perhaps it is too costly to buy into, or perhaps your retirement plan at work doesn't offer it). In that case, use this measure.

If over the course of a year (not a quarter or half a year), your index fund's return is more than 5 basis points lower than the return posted by the benchmark, you should consider moving your money.

What is a basis point?

A basis point is 1/100 of 1 percent. You will hear this term used more frequently when the discussion is about bonds and bond funds. These investments reflect much more fully the impact of the slightest change in interest rates or returns. Equity investors take individual basis points in stride, like so many pennies in your pocket. And in some ways, this is the best way to describe how they are calculated.

One hundred basis points, like a single dollar, is expressed as 1.00 percent. When I mentioned 5 basis points as a measure of whether a fund should be considered to be underperforming, this is 0.05 percent deducted from the whole. The difference is significant when numbers (in dollars) are used. At 5 basis points less, a $100 investment is now worth only $99.95.

The most common use of basis points is with interest rates and bond yields. When the Federal Reserve, acting as the central bank, raises the rate on short-term overnight loans to its biggest customers, namely other banks, it expresses the increase (or decrease) in basis points. An increase of 25 basis points would be expressed as 0.25 percent.

Bond yields are expressed as percentages, and when these yields change, the change is expressed as a change of a given number of basis points. Suppose a bond was offering a 5 percent yield that dropped to a 4.65 percent yield. This would be expressed as a 35-basis-point drop.

Considering moving your money does not mean that you should necessarily do so. Instead, this is the first warning sign of what could turn into a long-range problem. Compare the fund to its peers as well. If they all tracked as low, then make a note of this and check them again in a year. If more than half of your fund's peer group did better than your fund, consider selling it.

Because most people keep index funds for the long term and use actively managed funds as an asset allocation tool, shifting them among different investment strategies, these little differences in returns can be meaningful.

The following table gives the performance of the S&P 500. From 1997 to the end of 2007, the index returned just shy of 10 percent. A five-year return would have netted the index investor 19.16 percent.

Year Ending	Price Close	Price Change	Percent Change	Total Return Percent Change	Dividend Component	Dividend Component of Total Return
12/31/07	1468.36	50.06	3.53%	5.49%	1.96%	35.72%
12/29/06	1418.30	170.01	13.62%	15.79%	2.17%	13.77%
12/31/05	1248.29	36.37	3.00%	4.91%	1.91%	38.89%
12/31/04	1211.92	100.00	8.99%	10.88%	1.89%	17.34%
12/31/03	1111.92	232.10	26.38%	28.69%	2.30%	8.03%
12/31/02	879.82	−268.26	−23.37%	−22.10%	1.27%	−5.73%
12/31/01	1148.08	−172.20	−13.04%	−11.89%	1.15%	−9.69%
12/29/00	1320.28	−148.97	−10.14%	−9.10%	1.04%	−11.42%
12/31/99	1469.25	240.02	19.53%	21.04%	1.51%	7.20%
12/31/98	1229.23	258.80	26.67%	28.58%	1.91%	6.69%
12/31/97	970.43	229.69	31.01%	33.36%	2.35%	7.05%
12/31/96	740.74	124.81	20.26%	22.96%	2.70%	11.74%
12/29/95	615.93	156.66	34.11%	37.58%	3.47%	9.23%
12/30/94	459.27	−7.18	−1.54%	1.32%	2.86%	216.61%
12/31/93	466.45	30.74	7.06%	10.08%	3.02%	30.01%
12/31/92	435.71	18.62	4.46%	7.62%	3.16%	41.41%
12/31/91	417.09	86.87	26.31%	30.47%	4.16%	13.66%
12/31/90	330.22	−23.18	−6.56%	−3.10%	3.46%	−111.59%
12/29/89	353.40	75.68	27.25%	31.69%	4.44%	14.01%
12/30/88	277.72	277.72	12.40%	16.61%	4.21%	25.35%

Here is a list of the top large growth, actively managed funds for the same five-year period. You will notice that several of these funds are sector funds, tracking an individual corner of the market and investing in a specific number of companies.

Top Performers—Five-Year (out of 1,314)		
Fund Name	**Symbol**	**Annual Return**
CGM Focus	CGMFX	37.00%
Janus Contrarian	JSVAX	25.61%
ING Janus Contrarian S	IJCSX	23.45%
ING Janus Contrarian S2	IJCTX	23.26%
Leuthold Select Industries	LSLTX	21.56%
Fidelity Advisor Industrials I	FCLIX	21.20%
Vice Fund	VICEX	20.95%
Fidelity Select Industrials	FCYIX	20.94%
Fidelity Advisor Industrials A	FCLAX	20.87%
Fidelity Advisor Industrials T	FCLTX	20.58%

Using the Vanguard 500 Index as a further illustration of these differences, here's how it performed over five years. (Just as a little side note, the mutual fund industry could not have been happier when mid-2007 arrived. For the first time in five years, it no longer needed to average in any of those dismal years between 2000 and 2002. Many funds, index funds included, posted some terrible losses during that period, and when those were averaged with the total returns of the following years, they made the recovered returns seem paltry by comparison.) We won't add ETF comparisons to the mix just yet. Because of the relative infancy of the industry, records dating back far enough to compare accurately are not often found.

	VFINX	**S&P 500**	**Error**	**Fund/Peers**
2007	5.39%	5.49%	−0.10	0.15%/1.11%
2006	15.64	15.79	−0.15	
2005	4.77	4.91	−0.14	
2004	10.74	10.88	−0.18	
2003	28.50	28.69	−0.18	

Cap Rules

Both mutual funds and ETFs are taxed by the Internal Revenue Service and regulated by the Securities and Exchange Commission under the Investment Company Act of 1940. These restrictions are designed to protect shareholders and to make sure that any gains are properly taxed and, conversely, any losses are properly accounted for.

These rules not only limit the funds to a certain number of holdings of more than 5 percent, but also limit the amount of interest that a fund can have in any one stock to 25 percent. When index funds and ETFs get more specific, the limits on how much of one company can be held in the portfolio become doubly difficult for the fund manager.

While exchange-traded funds warrant a book of their own, giving a short description of this growing sector becomes more difficult with each passing day.

If a fund manager registers with the SEC, following clear and established procedures, and declares how he plans to operate the fund, an exchange-traded fund is created—almost. From this point on, it gets complicated. For a big mutual fund company that is already running enormous index funds, this is basically what it does. But for newer funds that track less visible sections of the marketplace, other rules begin to apply.

A market maker is needed before the ETF can officially begin. This middleman of sorts creates the marketplace by purchasing stock (from you, an investor, for instance) even if there is no immediate buyer and setting a firm ask price (the lowest price that the stock will be sold for) and bid price (the highest price that someone might pay); the difference between the two prices is called the spread.

The market maker then assembles the stocks for the fund. These "baskets," which can be quite large, represent the ETF and can contain as many as 50,000 shares. A custodial bank checks these shares (with each share representing a portion of the index, which represents a basket of stocks) and forwards them to what is known as an authorized participant. This in-kind trade, so called because there is no gain or loss involved in the transfer, places the stock in the custodial bank's hands, giving the fund manager the right to monitor it. Although there are oversight functions that the manager must take care of, there is little for the fund manager to do until capital gains or dividends are received.

Once all this has been done, the ETF is free to trade on the open market. The fund manager receives a fee for his services based on the assets of the fund (this can be found in the prospectus). Some investors lend the fund stocks for the portfolio and receive a small fee for doing so. The fund manager pays the custodial bank from his portion of the fees.

ETFs are especially transparent. At any given moment, all of these layers must be readily visible to the investor. Doing otherwise would leave the door open for fraud. Investors need to have faith that should they decide to exit, they can do so at a fair price. The market maker may not make as much money (fees) as it would like to have made, but its presence keeps the open-market price of the ETF close to the net asset value. This, as you may recall, is the underlying worth of the stocks in the portfolio.

Tax Advantages

Index funds are extremely tax-efficient. Because they trade so infrequently, any capital gains that they may receive come mainly from dividend payments. For this reason, index funds should be kept on the outside of your tax-deferred retirement plans [401(k)s or traditional IRAs].

Should you use an index fund such as Vanguard's 500 Index Fund in your retirement plan?

Yes and no. Yes, if your choices are limited. Many company-sponsored plans are relatively small, offering a small basket of funds that give the employee a broad choice. At the other extreme, some companies offer so many funds that the S&P 500–type funds become the default choice of those who do not know any better.

In these types of plans, the main objective is to grow money and pay the taxes later. We have learned that the increased risk that can be found in actively managed mutual funds comes with increased tax consequences. Capital gains taxes may have to be paid each time a stock is sold at a profit. Because index funds trade so infrequently (only during the rebalancing periods), they incur very little in the way of capital gains taxes. They do receive dividends, which are taxed as capital gains, and although dividends amounted to a full third of the S&P 500 index's returns in 2007, index funds are still more efficient taxwise than actively managed funds.

But ETFs are even more tax-efficient than index funds. They compare well to mutual funds that manage their portfolios to minimize taxes, and they far outperform actively managed funds. Index funds are forced to distribute any capital gains or dividends on a periodic basis.

ETFs, on the other hand, can store those gains, reinvesting them and giving the investor the option of receiving them at the end of the year. In the meantime, those reinvested capital gains and dividends have been growing, whereas in an index fund or a regular mutual fund, taxes would have been paid on them. Mutual funds must sell stock on the open market, and if there are gains, they must be accounted for or realized. ETFs use the *in-kind* trade with the custodial bank, and so no shares are sold.

On the Flip Side

ETFs do have some downsides and can achieve some lesser-than-index-type returns as a result. Commissions are a consideration, but not in the fund. Because the fund uses those in-kind trading techniques, the commissions will be paid by you to your broker. You will need to have a brokerage account that allows you to trade ETFs, and each trade you make, however large or small, will have a cost. And the cost is not only for the purchase of the security. Just as with stocks, you will pay when you sell an ETF as well.

Now would be a good time to talk about brokers again, but only briefly. The low trading costs that the online brokers spend millions of dollars advertising are often only for clients with larger-than-average portfolios and/or for clients that trade frequently. These are the clients that will be the most profitable for the firm. Smaller investors pay a much higher cost per trade and often fail to factor that into their trading strategy.

Here's a short example. An investor buys 50 shares of stock at $10 a share. She ponies up not only the $500, but also a $15 commission on the transaction. The investor should also include the selling costs as well at this time ($15 to buy; $15 to sell). To break even, taking into account both the initial investment and the costs of the trade, the stock would need to rise at least 6 percent ($30/$500 = 0.06 or 6 percent).

One of the most prominent ETFs is the SPDR (Standard & Poor's Depository Receipts, ticker SPY). Focused on the S&P 500, this ETF traded on the

Friday I wrote this for $138.00. With the benchmark returning 5.49 percent for 2007 and this fund returning 5.39 percent during the same period, you might consider this a way to play this index. Low fees like those on an index fund make it attractive enough. It is tax-efficient. It has low turnover. Perfect.

But once you purchase the SPDR and calculate the cost of that trade, the share price will have to climb to $146.28 (a gain of $8.28) to cover that cost. And as I write this, the ETF is down 9.44 percent year to date.

The NAV in an ETF

I mentioned that ETFs need to trade as close to their net asset value (NAV) as possible. There are several reasons for this. An investor who senses that what the ETF is holding is worth more than the current trading price could theoretically purchase an enormous block of the ETF. This savvy investor could then take possession of that stock and sell it at a profit.

Because the ETF is traded on the stock exchange, an equally savvy investor, seeing that the underlying shares of the ETF were worth less than the price, could short the ETF. This is not as complicated at it seems, but it is not a strategy for the inexperienced.

What happens when an investor shorts a stock or an ETF?

The decision to short a stock or an ETF is based on the belief that the stock or ETF's value is too high. You also believe that the market will eventually correct this mistake. So you approach the market maker and ask to borrow the stock. For the sake of the example, suppose that the ETF is worth $10—which, because it is an ETF, represents the net asset value of the stocks that the fund is holding. You ask to "borrow" 50 shares, making the total amount of the transaction $500. You immediately sell those shares.

If you are right and either the underlying value of the assets in the ETF or the stock is incorrectly valued, the share prices will fall. At this point, you the savvy investor will buy back the stock, all 50 shares, at the newly reduced price and pay off your debt to the market maker. It gets the stock back, and you make a tidy profit.

Slipping . . .

Gaps occur not only through tracking errors in both index funds and ETFs and brokerage costs for ETFs, but through the bid-ask spread. Because ETFs are traded throughout the day, they are prone to something called slippage. This often surfaces as a hidden charge that acts almost the way a closed-end fund would, imposing a slight fee as you exit or sell your ETF shares.

Like index funds, ETFs hold a basket of stocks that attempts to mimic the benchmark. And we have learned that as the index gets narrower (or in the case of small- and mid-cap indexes and their numerous variants, as the number of companies grows while the ability to purchase them get smaller), it becomes more difficult for the fund to get the right mix or even compare its performance to the correct benchmark.

. . . And Sliding

The funds that are most likely to be closest to the indexes they track are those run by the largest fund families. This doesn't make them better, just more efficient. Index funds generally hold almost 40 percent more stocks in their portfolios than do ETFs. And as we have learned, any sort of tracking error can cost you dearly. But the smaller number of total holdings can widen that gap considerably.

Why, then, are investors attracted to ETFs?

There are tax advantages and expense considerations. There is the off-chance that the ETF might actually beat the index that it tracks. And ETFs allow a more nimble presence in a particular sector than index funds do. Speculative investors have done very well with guesses on gold, oil, and natural resources. ETFs cater to that marketplace. ETFs also can generate additional cash revenue by lending stocks to hedge funds that, in turn, short the stock. The fund gets the shares back with a small fee for the service. Some mutual funds do this as well, but it is primarily something that ETFs do to create an extra edge.

The high cost of trading internationally, as we have learned, is due to insta-bility in those markets, currency valuations, and liquidity. This is where you will have the most difficulty with ETFs, if only in terms of keeping your costs low while matching the benchmark. For example, the MSCI Emerging Markets Index includes 927 companies. Because of those higher costs, ETFs focused on international investing are generally unable to buy enough stocks to accurately mimic the benchmark.

And if they attempt to reduce the tracking error, they end up paying the price in commissions and increased risk, both of which add to the tracking error. However, if you have an affinity for stocks from a country such as Germany or a region such as Asia, there is an ETF for you.

Be aware that not all ETFs are what they seem. As more of these funds come to market, focusing on more treacherous corners of the investment world, investors need to be cautious. In many instances, an ETF may no longer act as a fund at all, holding notes or other complicated investment structures instead of stocks.

We are all familiar with the fable of the wolf in sheep's clothing. The wolf dresses as a sheep, throwing fleece over its shoulders in an attempt to deceive the shepherd. But the hungry shepherd chooses the disguised wolf for slaughter. The fable teaches us about fraud and the high cost for those who use it. So why tell this tale during a conversation about ETFs?

When ETFs begin to invest in currencies, commodities, and commodity futures, they are no longer buying stocks; instead, they are buying contracts. This activity falls outside the Investment Company Act of 1940, which regulates funds. So these ETFs come under a different regulatory agency with different organizational rules.

These funds—or, more accurately, these products—do not have independent boards like their mutual fund and stock ETF counterparts. They register with the SEC, but they answer to the Commodity Futures Trading Commission. There is often a blurry tax treatment. This means that although some of the products might suggest that the lower capital gains tax would be applied, the IRS may, at any given time, treat this situation differently.

The streetTRACKS Gold Shares (GLD) is a good example of how this type of situation works. Investors actually own a portion of a quantity of actual gold. Each shareholder reaps any profits from the commodities price after the expenses are deducted. The profits on this "fund" are distributed as income at the end of the year and are taxed at your marginal rate.

The performance of this instrument over the last three years has been truly amazing, with returns of 28.29 percent. That's not typical, but it's definitely worth mentioning.

. . . And Selling

One final note before we move on: it is unfortunate that ETFs are available only through brokers. It doesn't matter whether you are using a full-service or a discount broker; the fact remains that ETFs must be sold. And so many of these types of funds have been created that the choices are staggering.

For this reason, ETFs are probably not the right investments for a full 75 percent of the investing public. If your trading costs are low because you have so much in your account or you trade so much that you get the advertised big discounts, ETFs offer a certain amount of adventure that simply cannot be had with index funds.

If you reason that your costs will be lower the longer you hold on to an ETF, you will probably find a few holes in that theory as well. Numerous fund families have cut the expenses on their index funds, and many will continue to do so. While the changes in expense ratios might be low, each nick at the shell of your nest egg, each hand in your investment pocket can be subtracted—in real dollars—from your fund's worth.

Investors who tend to invest lump sums will do better in ETFs. If they hold the ETF for the long-term, they may do slightly better than break even. And if the index you pick does well, your ETF will seem like a wise investment. For some investors who are managing a windfall or an inheritance, ETFs may be an ideal place to keep the money until further decisions can be made. (ETFs invested in this manner should not be considered savings. Fully insured institutions are a better place to put your money if your intent is preserving capital. So are money market accounts and certificates of deposit. ETFs are traded in the open market and have no guarantees of growth or capital appreciation.)

In 2007, about three dozen ETFs beat the benchmark. This is called a positive tracking error, and although you might think that this is a good thing, you would be mistaken.

The goal is to meet the benchmark, not beat it. If an ETF, with all of its costs and charges, does better than the benchmark it tracks, there is a reason. Keep in mind that any fees that the ETF can generate from lending securities are split between the ETF and the management company.

Common sense is calculation applied to life.

Henri Frédéric Amiel

Investors who use a more common approach to investing, either trickling money into an investment in small increments or using dollar cost averaging, will not get the same advantages. Index funds may charge an annual fee if the balance is below a certain amount. ETFs do not. If for some reason you have ETFs as an option in your tax-deferred company-sponsored account, ask what the commission costs are before you consider using them.

Who Issues ETFs?

There is definitely a fortune to be made from ETFs, and numerous companies have issued these funds since they were created by the American Stock Exchange in 1993.

ETF Sponsor	ETF	Category
State Street Global Advisors	Diamonds Trust Series I SPDRS	Dow Jones Industrial Av Numerous sectors
Merrill Lynch	HOLDRs	Narrow industry groups (20 stocks)
Barclays Global Investors	iShares	Wide number of indexes
ProShares	QUBEs	Nasdaq-100 (QQQQ)
Vanguard Group	VIPERS	Wide number of indexes

Exchange Traded Fund Screener: http://www/amex.com/?href=/etf/EtMain.jsp

New Faces

With so many new ETFs becoming available to investors each day, there are bound to be challenges. In 2007 alone, 260 new ETFs were created. Not all of them fared well, however, as competitors released similar funds. Among the

650 available ETFs, 10 of the largest ETFs control almost half of the market-place's potential investments.

It requires is a certain amount of interest coupled with an aggressive sales pitch to allow an ETF to reach the $1 billion invested mark. Few of them do so. But this information has not stemmed the steady increase in the number of ETFs. In 2007, numerous bond ETFs came to market, with municipal bond funds arriving as I write this.

But size remains a nagging issue. Some of these small funds will find themselves in the red from an operational standpoint, often leaving investors wondering just where their money is. Like many failed mutual funds, some of these ETFs will be consumed by other ETFs. This creates diversification, allocation, and sometimes tax issues for the investor.

Actively Managed ETFs

There is increased concern that as this part of the investment world grows, there will be some broken promises, some of them broken knowingly and with a shrug. ETFs are creating their own indexes and then pinning their charters to those benchmarks. Many of these benchmarks have no history, but even though they are not the best indicator of future performance, they are better than no measure at all.

Investors who have been in the markets for more than five or ten years understand that history is not how you predict the future, it is how you hope the future will act. If a fund has shown great restraint and is guided by a management team that you can trust not to put your money at risk for a simple short-term reward, that sort of history is a relatively good guide to how the fund's performance will weather the next year.

Only those who will risk going too far can possibly find out how far one can go.

T. S. Eliot

How each fund achieves its goals, especially as ETFs become more specialized, depends largely on what you, the investor, bring to the table. Because ETFs buy stocks, the area of focus may not translate well into the companies that service the sector.

Consider the First Trust Dow Jones Internet Index Fund (FDN). This ETF, which follows the Dow Jones Internet Composite Index, tracks only 40 companies, all of them considered blue-chip businesses. These are companies that generate their revenues from Internet-based activities.

Company	Ticker	Weighting in the Fund	Index Weight
Akamai Technologies, Inc.	AKAM	5.83	5.95
Amazon.com, Inc.	AMZN	8.07	10.13
BEA Systems, Inc.	BEAS	7.58	Not indexed
Check Point Software Technologies	CHKP	3.92	4.06
eBay Inc.	EBAY	8.96	10.84
Google Inc.	GOOG	7.61	12.72
IAC/InterActiveCorp	IACI	3.92	3.99
TD Ameritrade Holding	AMTD	4.41	4.15
VeriSign, Inc.	VRSN	7.68	8.04
Yahoo! Inc.	YHOO	13.12	9.34

The fund may invest no less than 90 percent of its assets in these companies. However, there is one caveat: to be considered an Internet company, at least by this ETF's standards, only 50 percent of the company's revenue needs to be generated online.

Actively managed ETFs (at least, ones that admit to being so) have begun to make their appearance in 2008. These ETF products may, depending on how they are taxed, be somewhat more efficient than their actively traded mutual fund counterparts.

Although it remains to be seen—these funds are still very much in their infancy and have no track record whatsoever—these products could have a lower internal portfolio turnover. If they can do this while keeping their expense ratios lower than those of mutual funds, this could be a bonus for investors.

Active ETFs will have to overcome the stigma of indexing. Also, with the additional portfolio exposure in ETFs, the risk of revealing strategies to competitors would be higher. Since these products try not to be indexes, they will need some benchmark to compare their performance to, and their proximity to what they strive not to be may confuse some investors. And they have no proven performance track record.

The newly available actively managed ETFs are:

PowerShares Active Low Duration Fund (PLK). As this fund grows, it will add corporate debt to the portfolio, but until then, this ETF will seek to outdo the Lehman Bros. 1–3 Year U.S. Treasury Index.

PowerShares Active Mega Cap Fund (PMA). By using earnings momentum, price trends, management action, and relative value, this ETF hopes to do what many large-cap actively managed funds have failed to do: beat the index. In this case, the fund will attempt to outdo the Russell Top 200.

PowerShares Active Alpha Q Fund (PQY). This fund holds the top 50 of the largest 100 Nasdaq stocks with positive cash flows.

PowerShares Active Alpha Multi-Cap Fund (PQZ). This product is dropping the bottom 10 percent of the S&P 500 and focusing on stocks with P/E ratios of 17 or less.

Birds, it is now widely assumed, sense the earth's magnetic field and use it to move from one nesting area to another, often over large distances. The part of a bird's brain that becomes the most active during this process receives richly oxygenated blood. This blood is also rich in magnetism. So by simply resetting its compasses at sunset, a bird needs only to open its eyes to know where it is going.

If only it were that simple for people. In the next chapter, we will discuss not only what sector funds are, but how they might provide some added oomph! to your portfolio. Some of the newer funds available to you seek to do much of the heavy lifting: the rebalancing and allocating that you are often told need to be done periodically. We will discuss this and the necessity for tweaking your portfolio, even if just a little bit. And as we close out the book with some strategies for using mutual funds, we will look at how they can fit your beliefs and socially conscious attitudes.

CHAPTER 16

Sectors, Targets, and Special Funds

◆▬▬▬▬▬▬▬▬▬▬▬▬▬▬▬▬▬▬▬▬▬▬▬▬▬▬▬▬▬▬◆

I f you are an animal, remaining a little on the dumb side can give you a natural advantage. This doesn't mean that animals can't learn; some do, and with great success. What scientists are finding, however, is that in order for a species to be successful, learning needs to reach an equilibrium. If you are too smart, you risk overspecializing, bringing more to the game of survival than was intended. With that in mind—and humans expend fully 20 percent of their energy fueling that noggin—we move on to the next chapter of the book.

We have a covered a great deal in the previous chapters, explaining as we went how many of the funds fit into the way you approach investing. Mutual funds play an integral role in all of our investment lives. Metaphorically speaking, a mutual fund is the car on the retirement road.

Mutual funds provide so many benefits to both the average and the experienced investor that they are often overlooked and almost taken for granted. People spend enormous amounts of time and effort creating nuanced and detailed portfolio of individual stocks—in essence, creating their own mini-mutual funds. And they compare their performance to that of mutual funds as a way to measure their own investment prowess and success.

And as complicated as mutual funds are (and with any luck, they're not so complicated for you any longer), they offer a much more economical way to stay invested, spread the risk of investing, and still have time for the important things in life.

I have purposely saved this chapter until last because of what it offers. It may, for some of you, give you a chance to exercise that inner mental maniac

I mentioned earlier—the one that wants to trade dangerously. And while there is nothing wrong with this, it has a time and a place in your portfolio.

Strategies

Mutual funds can be grouped together in such a way that they will provide the perfect protection from a future that is insufficiently financed, help to see a loved one get to college, and keep what we have gained through years of hard work. But those strategies rely on several key contributions from you.

In *Retirement Planning for the Utterly Confused*, I took a bold step away from some of the most standard pieces of advice. Believing, as I firmly do, that retirement is not going to be what our parents experienced—and given what you already know, most of you can't argue with that assessment—why then, I reasoned, do we still see ourselves constructing our retirement portfolio the same way?

 If you think dogs can't count, try putting three dog biscuits in your pocket and then giving Fido only two of them.

Phil Pastoret

Investing in a mix of stocks and bonds is sage advice, except when neither provides adequate cover from a faltering economy. Moving to a mix of stocks and bonds as we grow older and closer to retirement age (an age that is becoming much more a numerical target than anything else) is thought to be the best way to preserve our capital after a career during which we have worked well and saved diligently. But many of the people I speak to have started saving far later in life, so that this strategy is not only somewhat foolish but dangerous as well.

There are numerous mutual funds available that take conservative approaches to investing without loading the portfolio with fixed income. These are places where money can be considered actively invested without too much market volatility.

For the late-to-the-game investor (which is anyone who is over 40 years old and has all of the generally assumed responsibilities of house, kids, cars, and possibly parents) who has saved little for the future, building a conservative portfolio may mean that you will have to work another 20 to 30 years before (even thinking of) retirement. Slowing down the growth of your portfolio by taking on bond funds at the exact moment when you are trying to grow that portfolio just doesn't seem to fit.

Three Approaches

There are basically three types of working portfolios. These are baskets of mutual funds that will provide you with the needed exposure to growing your money for a retired future.

While indexing is great, and a portfolio of index funds can be built with all the basic tenets we look for—good management, low expenses, and proven returns over time—index funds fall short of giving us some of the potential we could have earned had we ventured just outside their all-encompassing reach.

The perfect indexed portfolio would hold exposure to the top 500 companies, a fund that covers the remaining businesses, and an index with a total bond market exposure. An S&P 500 index fund provides a nice mix of growth and value, but because so many of the companies in that large-cap index pay dividends, which provide capital appreciation of a different kind, they are more value than growth.

An index that tracks the rest of the market, like the Wilshire 4500, provides growth and, because it spreads so widely, diversity as well. There are no dividend payers in this group. These companies are seeking to become larger and better positioned, and, with any luck, to graduate to the big-cap world of the top 500. These companies plow their capital back into the business and bother little with increasing shareholder loyalty through offers to share outsized profit gains by sending those shareholders a check.

Bond funds and indexes that cover this market have a purpose. However, these quiet corners of the investment world also have their share of volatility. As all mutual fund managers attempt to do, bond fund managers seek new investors by growing their returns. In doing that, as we have seen, even in the brief peek we took inside these funds, they take on more risk than we may have thought they could—or, in some cases, should.

If You Are Under 40 Years Old

I will give you two possible scenarios for each of the three strategies. One will focus on the use of index funds to get to the goals I suggest; the other will use actively managed mutual funds that have a certain type of mission.

If you are under 40 years old, you should be focused on growing your money. No matter how timid you might be or how risk-intolerant you think you are, this is no time for bonds. Instead, your portfolio should be made up of 70 percent growth funds and 30 percent core funds.

Those growth funds can cover the territory from an emerging-markets or international fund (both can be indexed) to a small-cap or mid-cap index fund (or a representative growth fund servicing those areas). This part of your portfolio should include at least three different funds to achieve this. The only caution I offer (in addition to all the ones we have discussed thus far) is to be sure you avoid investment overlap.

Core funds can be a simple S&P 500 index fund. (*Core* is an investment style that uses the following criteria to classify a fund: "average price-to-earnings ratio, price-to-book ratio, and three-year earnings growth figure, compared to the U.S. diversified large-cap funds universe average." Lipper, like Morningstar, offers a way to categorize mutual funds. Morningstar calls the same type of fund "blend." In both cases, these funds have a great deal of latitude when investing for their shareholders.)

This type of index fund includes both large-cap growth and large-cap value companies and provides a good baseline, without the added bonds that often turn up in traditional core or blended funds. But an index fund, while it is the least expensive answer, is not necessarily the best one. Also avoid funds with the word "balanced" or "income" in their title. These funds use bond holdings or cash to balance the risk. You do not want to balance the risk. You want to embrace it.

When you are looking for funds of this type, use the criteria that I suggested earlier: long-term manager, low expenses relative to the fund's peers, modest turnover (although growth funds do tend to change their portfolios more frequently), and better than average returns over three to five years.

If You Are Over 40 but Not Yet 60

This is the most critical part of your investment years. You want risk, but not too much. You want to protect what you have accumulated, but not to such a

Only on the rarest of occasions do the top performers stay at the top for any length of time. Statistics have proved this ever since the first investigation of this a phenomenon took place in the 1970s. Burton Malkiel (*A Random Walk Down Wall Street*, 7th rev. ed., W. W. Norton & Company, June 2000) first pointed this out when he charted the returns of the top 20 large-cap funds in the 1970s and compared their performance 10 years later. No one is quite sure why the top dogs fail shortly after they make the list. Some people have suggested that the sudden influx of money that comes when a fund has had a stellar year or quarter simply overwhelms whatever strategy the manager was using. Some have suggested that a fund's success is nothing more than luck, with the fund being in the right place at the right time by chance. No matter how many people like me have warned people like you, the mistake is made time and again.

degree that you smother any future earning potential. These are the middle earning years. Even though you will be focused on investing for your retirement, now is the time to create portfolios outside of those retirement savings, and using mutual funds is by far the best way to do that.

Much of what you would call core funds should be outside of your retirement portfolio. Once again, an S&P 500 index fund serves this purpose nicely. Until 2010, and possibly beyond, the capital gains taxes you pay on this tax-efficient type of fund will be lower, so you can pay them as you build the fund. Within your retirement account, you should use an international index fund to supply the core holdings.

I have suggested that people in this age group still stay away from bonds. Unless you have amassed a serious nest egg (and I'd be willing to bet that you haven't), bonds simply do not make any sense while you are still employed. As we have seen, the economic strife that waylaid the markets at the end of 2007 and well into 2008 took its toll on bonds as well as on equity offerings.

For that reason, plan on creating a portfolio that is 60 percent growth (preferably with some exposure to small-cap and mid-cap funds), 30 percent value (this can be a large-cap fund, but if you are holding an S&P 500 index fund, the overlap might be too great—stick to a mid-cap value fund instead), and 10 percent core.

Could you load up these percentages with index funds? Sure. Would you do just as well as if you picked the funds yourself? Depends. Talk to most Wall

Street types and they will all blurt out the same thing, which is pretty much a standard statistic: 80 percent of the actively managed mutual funds do not beat the benchmark. But 20 percent do.

If You Are 60 or Older

This is a tough time. If your portfolio has grown sufficiently and you have made all of the calculations (and if you didn't work another day and lived another 30 years, would you be confident that you would not run out of money?), and you have decided that you are sitting pretty good, you may be looking at some of the more standard offerings that do balance your holding between stocks and bonds. But I disagree with that thinking.

You still want capital appreciation. Bonds and balanced funds provide capital preservation. But you want to seriously temper the risk. By using core funds for the majority of your portfolio (around 70 percent) and placing the remainder in value funds (around 30 percent), you will have good exposure to some growth without jeopardizing your future earnings. You will be thinking about drawing down your holdings when you retire, and investing like this will allow your remaining holdings to continue to grow, pay dividends, and appreciate.

The Lure of Preservation

Before we move on to some of the other products that take the shape of mutual funds, we should face the fact that you will worry. You will worry about protecting your assets, and that will lead you to wonder whether you should preserve some of that money in a conservative location. As Jonathan Clements of the *Wall Street Journal* once suggested, the greatest threat to your portfolio is staring back at you in the mirror.

There is always the chance that you will get a larger-than-average payout at the end of your working career, and because you are at the end of your employment, you will want to preserve as much of that money as possible. Bond funds can help with this worry.

They can give you the much-needed laddering effect (buying securities with varying maturity dates), good pricing (few individual investors will get the same price that institutions will), and, in some instances, protection against inflation. Using a total bond market fund may be the best way to achieve this goal.

Social Responsibility

When I was helping my daughter with her investment goals, she was quite specific that none of the funds she invested in be invested in companies that support tobacco, guns, or war, had a record of poor environmental policies, or had socially repugnant attitudes toward its workers. And I'll admit that these were not even considerations in my investment choices. Did that make me less of an investor because I was focused on the ability of the company and the funds that invest in them to turn a profit? Possibly so.

 Only after the last tree has been cut down . . . the last river has been poisoned . . . the last fish caught, only then will you find that money cannot be eaten.

Cree Indian Prophesy

Socially responsible investing is not new. Socially irresponsible companies who have turned a blind eye to the consequences of their business practices are usually screened carefully by these kinds of mutual funds. Researching an individual company and its business practices, while not always easy, does prove much less difficult than delving deep inside a mutual fund to find a company that might discriminate against its workers, damage the environment, or otherwise subscribe to business practices, whether moral, religious, or based on the principles that you use to guide your own life, that some folks might find repulsive. Using a fund that has done the heavy lifting for you gives investors much easier access to funds that share similar beliefs.

What investors using these funds are looking for is "the double bottom line." Socially responsible investors are looking for profits, just as all investors are, but are willing to sacrifice some of those profits if their investments are leaving a socially acceptable and green footprint in the process. But how do you marry the two while satisfying your conscience?

 Originally called Il Grillo Parlante in Carlo Collodi's classic novel *Pinocchio*, Jiminy Cricket acted as the puppet's conscience. Appointed by the Blue Fairy to accompany Pinocchio on his travels, Jiminy (previously unnamed) was given the name by Walt Disney, becoming Pinocchio's world-wise partner and voice in his ear.

Here is a list of the biggest players in this field:

Calvert Group: The mutual fund family offers 14 equity funds, 9 bond funds, and 3 money market accounts with $30 billion under management. They have benefited from the focus on green investing of late, raising their profile considerably. (http://www.calvertgroup.com)

Domini Social Investments: The Domini Funds promote a philosophy that values human dignity as well as environmentally friendly standards. Its flagship fund, The Domini Social Equity Fund (DSEFX), was launched in 1991 and now has $837 million under management. (http://www.domini.com)

Parnassus Investments: Established in 1984, this group of six mutual funds uses social screens that filter out companies that manufacture alcohol or tobacco products, are involved with gambling, the manufacture of weapons, or generate electricity from nuclear power. (http://www.parnassus.com)

Pax World: Credited with giving birth to this industry, Pax's founders Luther Tyson and Jack Corbett, according to their Web site, "had worked on peace, housing, and employment issues for the United Methodist Church, and wanted to make it possible for people to invest in keeping with their values. At the same time, they wanted to challenge corporations to establish and live up to specific standards of social and environmental responsibility. It has been in operation since 1971." (http://www.paxfund.com)

This field is still rather small, with only 53 funds representing a variety of socially conscious values. The industry has over $1.2 trillion invested in these types of funds and is growing quickly as "green" capitalism takes hold.

Slicing and Dicing the Mutual Fund Market

Barry Schwartz, the author of *Paradox of Choice* (Harper Perennial, 2004), suggested that because of our wants, choices have emerged at such a rapid rate that we have difficulty deciding among them. This ever-growing number of choices often causes more anxiety than it solves, leading us to make trade-offs or, worse, to fail to take action. Mr. Schwartz was not the first to tackle this topic. Daniel Kahneman and Amos Tversky suggested that we rely on "rule of thumb" measures rather than actual proof. Economist Richard Thaler calls this *sunk cost*, a term that refers to the satisfaction we get from selling something, even if the value was not what we had hoped for, but what we received was good enough.

Mr. Schwartz did uncover an interesting tidbit in his research: the happier we are, the more likely we are to consider other choices. The mutual fund industry has dissected itself to cater to every conceivable option or type of investing. Not all of these offerings are what they seem, and some of them are so arcane that they should generally be avoided by all but the most savvy investors.

Commodity Funds

Remember, funds buy stocks issued by companies. They do not hold actual commodities, a reference to actual tangible items like oil, gold, corn, or pork bellies. These funds look at companies that are doing business in a particular area and invest in those that could benefit from changes in the price, or, as good old Economics 101 teaches us, the difference between demand and supply.

Quantitative Funds

This is sort of a reinvention of the index wheel. Stocks in a quantitative (quant) fund are often the leaders of a certain group based on specific criteria—dividend growth, past stock performance, potential price-to-earnings appreciation. And with the help of ever-greater and less-expensive computers, each company can be run through the mill, so to speak, leaving a basket of stocks that fit whatever algorithm the fund uses.

That's right, a computer does all of the work and removes the investor emotion that even the best fund managers bring to the table. Think Hal in *2001: A Space Odyssey*. The advantages of this kind of investing are numerous. Computers can scan many more stocks than their human counterparts. But analysis is only as good as the input.

And in many quant funds, the human factor remains. Some funds allow the management team to make the ultimate decisions; others are giving the computer newer modeling options. There is, however, higher turnover when the computer is left in charge, and this can not only increase expenses but also affect the overall tax efficiency of the fund.

Investors who are looking at quant funds are often chasing performance. Because these types of funds are focused on beating the benchmark, they often do not outperform funds in the same arena.

130/30 Funds

Do you yearn to act the way the rich do? Do you want to invest the way they do as well? Hedge funds, which are small, mostly unregulated funds that cater to the wealthy and institutional investors, have given the average investor a bad case of envy. While some expensive cars are within the average person's reach (with some clever financing in most cases), the way the rich invest has been a relatively closed world.

We read about the enormous paydays that hedge fund managers receive, and because of those enormous windfalls, even if things don't always go right, some of the brightest mutual fund minds have defected to this cloistered sector. The latitude that hedge funds offer these managers can be alluring as well.

Many of us sit on the sidelines, unable to fathom how any one person can earn what some hedge fund managers do. John Paulson earned $3.7 billion in 2007. When *Alpha* magazine began tracking the pay of these elite investors in 2002, its inaugural list showed *George Soros* at the top with a $700 million paycheck. In 2007, that would have placed him in the number nine spot on the list. To make the list, now at 50 individuals, the minimum paycheck would be $210 million.

These managers are typically paid on a 2 and 20 pay scale. The "2" represents a percentage of assets under management (2 percent of $1 billion is $20 million). The "20" is a percentage of the profit the fund generates, both realized and as-yet-to-be-realized gains in the fund. Some funds charge as much as 40 percent of the fund's profits.

Investors who use hedge funds often believe that if they are making money, the cost of management is well worth the price.

A 130/30 fund uses a strategy that many hedge funds employ. There is speculation that the creation of this type of fund may be a way to prevent gifted managers from taking flight. The concept is simple enough, but the possibilities for investor confusion are high.

The fund uses a long and short strategy in buying stocks for the fund. The fund will buy $100 worth of stock. This is considered a long purchase. A short strategy, as we have learned, basically involves borrowing stock that the fund manager considers overvalued, selling it, and then repurchasing the stock after it declines to return the borrowed stock. The difference is the profit. The "30" part of the fund is shorted stock. So the fund actually purchases $130 worth of long-positioned stock and shorts $30 worth of equities.

There are several downsides to this type of fund. First, it is a relatively new type of offering in the mutual fund universe. Second, many of the fund managers running this type of investment also run a long-positioned mutual fund as well. Third, many of those who are running a 130/30 fund are new to the idea of short-ing stocks and make many of the errors that individual investors make—but with your money.

And lastly, there is a great deal of potential for overlap. Your fund may be long a certain company, but another 130/30 fund in the same family may see it as overvalued and short the stock. Who would be right?

While 130/30 funds are the first to be introduced, several fund families are looking to offer 110/10 and even 150/50 funds in the near future. Investors should be wary of these funds, as they have yet to have a discernible track record and there may be few benchmarks for comparison. The best thing that could happen to funds of this type rests with a decision the SEC has not, as yet, made. If it raises the income requirements and initial investment levels for hedge fund investors, those who are left out of that world will seek these types of funds.

Sector Funds

I have mentioned this numerous times over the years. Some speculation is dri-ven by human nature. Investors, deep down, want the outsized gains that come from picking the right stock or the right mutual fund. And not just the right one, but also the one that was propelled to the top of the best performers' list. While I warn people about picking their next investment from a short-term best of list, most of us want to be in that stock or fund *before* it made the list.

Benjamin Graham, the often quoted and well-respected investor who took folks like Warren Buffett under his wing, understood this hidden nature. He devised a solution: the mad money account, a place separate from your serious investments where you can put unneeded investment dollars to appease the speculator in all of us.

This account would, according to Mr. Graham, be funded only once. If you lost it all, take the lesson to heart, but never refund it. If you gained from the experience, revel in it, enjoy it, and celebrate the good fortune that your luck has brought you. But Mr. Graham also believed that investors who were unable to "master their emotions are ill-suited to profit from the investment process."

Investors who use sector funds already hold a diversified portfolio and are looking to sector funds to either hedge some of their growth positions or "speculate" on potential growth. These investors have, for lack of a better phrase, "mastered their investment universe" and fully understand the risks involved in this type of investment.

As we begin our look at sector funds, it is important to remember three principles: this type of investment could easily be called "speculator funds"; these funds invest in companies, not commodities; and stocks aren't always a clear reflection of the company they represent. Many of these companies have not reached a level of maturity that would be considered worth the risk for the average investor.

Sector funds are classified in two ways by two separate agencies. The Global Industry Classification Standard (GICS) is published by Standard & Poor's and MSCI Barra and tracks over 50,000 companies in both developed and emerging markets. To be listed as an active company—about two-thirds of the businesses that the GICS tracks are considered to be such—revenues, earnings, and market perception must be significant.

The GICS breaks down its classifications into 10 sectors, 24 industry groups, 67 industries, and 147 subindustries. This allows investors to take a global view of what could be a specific market trend.

One-upping the GICS is the newer standard for this type of investing, published by Dow Jones and FTSE (an independent company jointly owned by the *Financial Times* and the London Stock Exchange). The Industry Classification Benchmark (ICB) offers an wider sweep of companies (60,000) and securities (65,000) than the GICS does. It uses a similar structure, breaking its benchmark down into 10 industries, 19 supersectors, 41 sectors, and 114 subsectors.

The difference between the two standards is nuanced. The ICB might classify coal as a component of the mining industry, whereas the GICS lists companies that focus on that resource as consumable energy.

Since sector funds are relegated to such a small part of your portfolio, the methods for investing in them can be hard to develop. Larger, more speculative investors usually—but not always—use one of three strategies to achieve some measure of risk protection while remaining nimble enough to flee (or jump into) any sudden changes that a specific sector might suddenly experience.

I want to devote 10 percent of my portfolio to sector funds. How should I do this?

The simplest and most efficient (least risky) way is to purchase a broad index fund such as the S&P GSCI index.

This particular index uses a world production weighting. This means that as it tracks commodities, it also monitors their general availability. Because commodities are so different from securities, which are generally measured by their market capitalization, consideration of price risk, consumption, and production is vital. This index currently contains 24 commodities from all commodity sectors: six energy products, five industrial metals, eight agricultural products, three livestock products, and two precious metals. Once this type of index is owned, an investor might focus her attention on one particular sector that she feels will outperform and invest in that as a separate sector index. Other broad indexes include the S&P/Barra Growth Index (SGX) or the S&P/Barra Value Index (SVX).

More savvy investors in these funds will look at owning funds that focus more directly on an area where they have experience and knowledge, choosing to avoid an index in favor of a more specific approach. One could own funds in all of the top sectors or just eight to ten. Because they are mutual funds (ETFs have also created a major footprint in this area and may, because of the ease of trading them, be better for some more skittish investors who are unsure), sector funds are diversified within each fund. The following is a list of Fidelity's current offerings. There are other fund families, such as ProFunds and Rydex Funds, that also offer a wide variety of sector funds. ETFs that focus on sectors can be found as Select Sector SPDRs, iShares, and Sector HOLDRS. (Be aware that the funds listed here are only for illustrative purposes; I do not own any of these funds.)

Fidelity Utilities Fund (FIUIX)	Utilities
Select Air Transportation Portfolio (FSAIX)	Cyclicals
Select Automotive Portfolio (FSAVX)	Cyclicals
Select Banking Portfolio (FSRBX)	Financials
Select Biotechnology Portfolio (FBIOX)	Health Care
Select Brokerage and Investment Management Portfolio (FSLBX)	Financials
Select Chemicals Portfolio (FSCHX)	Cyclicals
Select Communications Equipment Portfolio (FSDCX)	Technology
Select Computers Portfolio (FDCPX)	Technology
Select Construction and Housing Portfolio (FSHOX)	Cyclicals
Select Consumer Discretionary Portfolio (FSCPX)	Consumer
Select Consumer Staples Portfolio (FDFAX)	Consumer
Select Defense and Aerospace Portfolio (FSDAX)	Cyclicals
Select Electronics Portfolio (FSELX)	Technology
Select Energy Portfolio (FSENX)	Natural Resources
Select Energy Service Portfolio (FSESX)	Natural Resources
Select Environmental Portfolio (FSLEX)	Cyclicals
Select Financial Services Portfolio (FIDSX)	Financials
Select Gold Portfolio (FSAGX)	Natural Resources
Select Health Care Portfolio (FSPHX)	Health Care
Select Home Finance Portfolio (FSVLX)	Financials
Select IT Services Portfolio (FBSOX)	Technology
Select Industrial Equipment Portfolio (FSCGX)	Cyclicals
Select Industrials Portfolio (FCYIX)	Cyclicals
Select Insurance Portfolio (FSPCX)	Financials
Select Leisure Portfolio (FDLSX)	Consumer
Select Materials Portfolio (FSDPX)	Cyclicals
Select Medical Delivery Portfolio (FSHCX)	Health Care
Select Medical Equipment and Systems Portfolio (FSMEX)	Health Care
Select Money Market Portfolio (FSLXX)	Money Market
Select Multimedia Portfolio (FBMPX)	Consumer
Select Natural Gas Portfolio (FSNGX)	Natural Resources

Select Natural Resources Portfolio (FNARX)	Natural Resources
Select Networking and Infrastructure Portfolio (FNINX)	Technology
Select Paper and Forest Products Portfolio (FSPFX)	Natural Resources
Select Pharmaceuticals Portfolio (FPHAX)	Health Care
Select Retailing Portfolio (FSRPX)	Consumer
Select Software and Computer Services Portfolio (FSCSX)	Technology
Select Technology Portfolio (FSPTX)	Technology
Select Telecommunications Portfolio (FSTCX)	Utilities
Select Transportation Portfolio (FSRFX)	Cyclicals
Select Utilities Growth Portfolio (FSUTX)	Utilities
Select Wireless Portfolio (FWRLX)	Utilities

Target-Dated Funds

 What the Experts Say If you're forecasting something, don't promise a specific date. That way, if the date passes, you're not wrong. This has been great advice for me.

Abby Joseph Cohen

We love convenience. And when target-dated funds were first introduced in defined-contribution plans, they were seen as a way to invest without needing to know all the terminology, without having to do the research, and without having to balance and reallocate and diversify. All you needed to do was pick a year when you would like to retire, and all of the heavy lifting—the research, the balancing and allocating and diversification—would be done for you. For instance, if you were 30 and you wanted to retire in 30 years, you would simply find a fund that correlated with that time span and set your contribution, and you were, at least in theory, done. Mutual fund investing in your retirement plan on autopilot.

Sound too good to be true? Unfortunately, it is. In fact, target-dated mutual funds, or, as they are sometimes called, lifestyle funds, may actually require a bit more homework up front than the other funds in your portfolio.

As we have learned, mutual funds are governed, albeit self-governed, by a charter that allows you to see what they plan to do with your money and why. This kind of transparency is key to all the portfolio-building exercises we have been doing. But with target-dated funds, all you have to go on is the promise that your fund manager will make the right moves at the right time and will do so based on some formula for adjusting the balance within the fund.

These funds, however, have not perfected the technique. Granted, there is a learning curve. These fund managers do not have it as easy as you might think, and that is where most of the problems begin.

The technique involves a curious balance, not between how many stocks or bonds to hold at any one given time—although the idea is to rebalance the portfolio as time moves on—but between past returns and attracting future investors with little more than a date based on some far-off future event. This might even be too difficult for any one fund to do.

Yet the Department of Labor has approved this type of fund as the "default" investment for those who fail to choose a fund for their defined-contribution plan.

Recently, Uncle Sam has stepped in to ensure that everyone is saving something for retirement, even if it means picking the fund for you and suggesting that your employer, instead of giving you pay raises, put the money into your retirement plan for you. This is a result of the fact that far too many working Americans who had access to 401(k)-type plans where they worked failed to enroll or, if they did enroll, failed to choose a plan, but instead took the default option, which in too many instances was a poorly performing money market account.

The Pension Protection Act of 2006 gave employers two clearer fiduciary options: use automatic enrollment, making certain contributions mandatory for employees or giving them the opportunity to opt out. This allows the employees to participate or to receive their full compensation rather than contributing a fixed portion of it to the plan.

Since 2001, when the first target-dated funds were introduced, participation in them has climbed dramatically, from just over $12 billion invested to almost $200 billion by the end of 2008.

But the managers of these funds are faced with the same pressures to perform as their untargeted cohorts. When the charter suggests an increasingly conservative approach, moving from stocks to bonds, how do you keep an investor's interest piqued? What is beginning to turn up with alarming frequency as these types of funds are scrutinized more closely is more stocks than bonds and, worse, more risky stocks than you would expect the funds to choose.

The worry is not so much that a fund manager's appetite for risk is based on a risk tolerance that is generally assumed (younger investors, more risk; older investor, less risk), it is the appearance of fad chasing. Increasingly, these types of funds have considerable exposure to overseas markets, and some portfolios carry almost their entire investment in equities.

Another scenario that has arisen with the advent of this type of investing is market timing. This is the opposite of what most sage investors subscribe to. Some think tanks, such as the Compass Institute, a subscription-based retirement strategy group, believe that these target-dated funds should be moving into bonds and cash when the markets go down and changing their allocations back to primarily stocks when they recover. This could cause an unnecessary increase in turnover, which, as you have found, increases the cost to you. Those

Retirement investors are the primary users of target-dated funds. These are not often the most savvy investors, and despite constant prodding from Washington and Wall Street, they still make some basic mistakes, faux pas that will cost them dearly down the road. There are only two ways to increase your retirement wealth: save more or retire later. Increasing risk, as some target-dated funds do, is not a wise decision. Yet some mutual fund families have split their offerings, allowing investors to choose between a more aggressive approach and a more conservative one. Both are risky business.

With a risky portfolio, we are not always sure what the fund manager means when he suggests a riskier approach, and you could find yourself with too little at retirement as your fund manager chases opportunities around the globe. Keep in mind the success rate of actively managed mutual funds. Will your fund manager's aggressive investment style land the fund in the 20 percent that beat the benchmark?

Too conservative an approach will take your money out of some good opportunities for growth as the capital you put in is preserved rather than appreciated. Even these funds, because of their newness, cannot guarantee a minimum return. And while no fund can make such claims, the expectation that investors who use these funds have is that they will meet or beat the market over the long term.

increased fees may go largely unnoticed by the investor who has chosen the fund and, for lack of a better phrase, simply forgotten about it.

Dow Jones has recently published a list of indexes that can be used as a benchmark for this type of fund. The company will create a new index each five years.

Promising to focus on inflation, the beginning index portfolio is focused on "equities, commodities and real estate investments. To reduce the volatility of this relatively aggressive index portfolio," the company says, "some less-risky assets, such as TIPS [Treasury Inflation Protected Securities] and bonds, are included." While this mix may not be the best for the 25-year-old investor, its allocation to equities is around 90 percent. After that, "a mix of assets integrated to represent accumulation during the first 25 years and then increasingly reflects asset preservation later in the investment/time horizon" allows the investor to determine where the fund is headed.

Dow Jones Real Return Today Index	DJRRTO
Dow Jones Real Return 2005 Index	DJRR05
Dow Jones Real Return 2010 Index	DJRR10
Dow Jones Real Return 2015 Index	DJRR15
Dow Jones Real Return 2020 Index	DJRR20
Dow Jones Real Return 2025 Index	DJRR25
Dow Jones Real Return 2030 Index	DJRR30
Dow Jones Real Return 2035 Index	DJRR35
Dow Jones Real Return 2040 Index	DJRR40
Dow Jones Real Return 2045 Index	DJRR45
Dow Jones Real Return 40+ Index	DJRR4P

What is the difference between balanced funds and target-dated funds?

Balanced funds generally maintain one level of investment allocation throughout the years, changing what is included within the percentages, but never changing the 60 percent stocks/40 percent fixed income allocation. Target-dated funds start with a 90/10 mix and gradually change the mix to a 40/60 allocation.

Generally, the sales pitch for these funds points to a "glide path" based on past history and modeling from 1960 to 2007. But the only available comparison is with a balanced fund, making the side-by-side analysis somewhat skewed. Craig Israelson, who made the argument for target-dated funds, suggests that the balanced fund performed at a 9.26 percent rate over the 48-year period, while a modeled lifestyle fund that gradually shifted its market position would have returned the investor 9.59 percent.

(Coincidentally, the S&P 500 index fund, which was created during the same time frame, returned 10.83 percent. It should be noted that if you had invested $1,000 in the index, the worth of that investment would be greater than $170,000. Also worthy of note: of the original 500 stocks in the index, only 88 remain, but had you held on to those original companies, Professor Jeremy Siegel of the Wharton School of the University of Pennsylvania's true buy-and-hold strategy, your portfolio would have risen 11.71 percent.)

Dr. Israelson, who is an associate professor at Brigham Young University and the principal at Target Date Analytics, a company specializing in the field of lifestyle funds, suggests that you should expect "middle-of-the-road returns compared with core individual assets in an accumulation portfolio." He continues to say, "Bland is good."

So the question remains: should you buy these funds? Yes and no. If you are expecting a pension when you retire, then you *could* look at the more aggressive target-dated funds as a way of supplementing that monthly payment. Once again, the fee structure of these funds might not be as good as buying several broad market indexes.

The fee structure may include the purchase of other funds within the fund. These fund-of-fund holdings can run up the costs very quickly. Some fund families, seeing an opportunity to boost the participation in a lagging or out-of-favor growth or value fund, force these types of funds to buy in.

If your plan at work is limited to a handful of these types of funds, and using them is the only option, consider this strategy. The idea behind these target-dated funds is to keep timid investors and those who are less savvy in stocks over a longer period than they might normally have done so. And taking into consideration how I feel your retirement portfolio should be structured (all in stocks, with gradual reduction in risk over time), you could target a lifestyle fund for 20 years beyond your actual target. For instance, if you expect to retire in 20 years, pick a lifestyle fund with a target date that is 40 years out. This gives you maximum stock exposure during the initial years while tempering your risk as you head toward retirement, but not as dramatically as would have happened with a much shorter-dated fund.

 There are two classes of forecasters: those who don't know, and those who don't know they don't know.

John Kenneth Galbraith

And because these funds still lack transparency, many of the past models projecting forward will not accurately capture the changes in what has become a global economy, and many are fee-prohibitive (as compared to a similar portfolio of indexes covering both broad stock market and fixed-income exposure).

These funds are not no-work investments. The vast majority of us already have some sort of investment in mutual funds, if not in stocks and bonds. There is a chance that you could throw whatever allocation system you had in place out of whack. Turnover is higher than I would like, with the sector currently averaging 27 percent. This average does not show how much turnover any of the underlying funds are likely to have. Vanguard does an excellent job with its expense and turnover ratios.

The growing number of choices will also leave many potential investors stymied. The industry, being what it is, will continue to introduce new ways to make this market work for every type of investor. Not all of these ideas will be successful, and many funds may fail well before you retire.

Which brings me to my final worry about target-dated funds. It is the set-and-forget idea. No matter what investment you own, never tending to it can make for some interesting surprises down the road. Good investors reevaluate where they are periodically, even if they rarely make any changes.

Managed Payout Funds

Managed payout funds are the newest kid on the mutual fund block. Unlike annuities, a hybrid mutual fund/insurance product that guarantees a steady stream of income (albeit at a very high cost), managed payout funds offer a steady stream of income and the opportunity to continue to keep your money invested, often for a very low cost.

The idea behind these funds is to provide the retiree with a steady stream of income based on historical information about performance and on a fixed payout percentage over a set course of years. These funds, many of which are still quite small in terms of assets under management, do not promise more than the market will permit. Their payouts may change should the markets change.

Fund families like Fidelity do as much as possible to protect your funds from any market fluctuation by investing within their own fund family. The top 10 holdings in the Fidelity Income Replacement Fund 2038 (FIRVX) allocate 10.76 percent of the portfolio to cash and 25.12 percent to bonds, with stocks making up 60.54 percent. The remaining investments are simply listed as "other."

Here's a look at how the portfolio is structured:

Fidelity Total Bond	15.89%
Fidelity Advisor Intl Discovery I	12.65
Fidelity Broad Market Opportunities	10.04
Fidelity Large Cap Core Enhanced Index	9.97
Fidelity 100 Index	7.40
Fidelity Equity-Income	6.30
Fidelity Disciplined Equity	6.24
Fidelity Advisor Mid Cap II I	6.15
Fidelity Strategic Real Return	5.51
Fidelity Government Income	5.37

What's Next ▷ Just a recap of what we have covered. We have learned that mutual funds are an important part of every investor's portfolio. They can provide diversification and more than enough risk for those who are seeking to "push the envelope." They can provide stability and in many cases transparency. Mutual funds are an unavoidable fact of retirement planning, and with any luck, they are also used outside of those plans to increase personal wealth.

But what about us? This question has been the focus of investment surveys, studies, academic papers, and speculation for decades. There are more than 8,000 mutual funds that offer us every conceivable type of investment for every possible whim we might conjure up. The only thing that has not been identified is our antagonistic investment gene.

When scientists mapped the human genome, they expected to find up to 140,000 genes that were coded to some protein. Instead, they found only

30,000. Discoveries related to that have turned up a curiosity that many of us were not expecting: we may wish that we were better looking, but something inside that complex code suggests that we are better off with less-than-perfect mates. Katharina Foerster at the University of Edinburgh found this oddity while studying red deer in Scotland.

Based on her research, which determined that the best-looking bucks often produce fewer offspring than their less desirable counterparts, I have developed a theory for an as-yet-to-be-discovered gene that complicates our investment decisions. But I have some suggestions that may allow you to overcome the powerful pull that this gene may unwittingly be having on your portfolio.

As much as I hate to say so, indexing is the best form of investing for the vast majority of us. It does not provide glamour or speculation, nor does it provide the kind of returns that some actively managed funds may post, but its ugliness is what makes it the top long-term choice. Indexers call any other form of investment gambling, and if you ever have an opportunity to speak to someone who believes this mantra, you will find that they are resolute in their thinking.

Indexers offer some convincing arguments for why their form of investment is superior to any other. Low costs are one that can hardly be denied. Vanguard recently ran an ad featuring two glasses, one with several drops in it alongside one that was nearly full. The point of the advertisement was to illustrate the effect that fees (of which Vanguard's are the lowest, 0.20 percent compared to an industry average of 1.22 percent) can have on a long-term investment. The ad suggests that on a $10,000 a year investment with an average return of 8 percent (before expenses), using Vanguard would save you $58,000 in fees over a 20-year period.

And if, having read this book, you choose the path of the index, it is probably because of the often subliminal facts I have presented that point toward its ease of management, its low cost and often low-risk style, and its general simplicity and overall availability. Such a choice will let you sleep well at night. And if I were to give you five things to take with you, this would be the first on the list.

Investments need tending, but not a lot. If you devote one hour a month and perhaps an extra hour each quarter to your investments, you will have spent less time managing your future than some folks spend staring at a charcoal grill. While no investment is a set-and-go, indexes provide the best "set-and-sleep" option. While no investment can be worry-free, indexes provide the least amount of worry per investment dollar.

The second lesson should be embracing your ABCs: age, balance, and continuity. Your age takes into account how much risk you might be willing to take at any given time. Unfortunately, we all begin investing at different points in our financial life, and no one set rule will apply to everyone.

What is certain is how we feel as we age. We become more protective and more conservative. That's not to say that we turn into less adventurous or more timid individuals, but our ability to recognize cause and effect is heightened, especially when we add recovery time to the equation. Mistakes tend to be magnified as we get older, and that makes the field of choices just a little more narrow.

This type of change in thinking will apply to the way you regard your portfolio as well. There is no set formula. Here are some strong suggestions, but only you can decide whether they are worth considering. I say stay in stocks, albeit with a gradual switch over time from aggressive growth when you are in your twenties and thirties to a much more conservative approach when you are in your fifties and sixties. Indexes won't do that for you, and target-dated funds may not provide enough of the right investment at the right time.

Balance can be a little more difficult, but not impossible. While balancing is often referred to as a way of keeping your investment mix in the right place at the right stage in your life, I prefer to think of balance as a lifestyle. Getting your financial house in order will keep your investments growing. Once you begin to eye your savings or your 401(k) or other retirement savings as a potential source of cash for your everyday expenses, you need to reevaluate the way you are handling your personal business.

Most of us will use mutual funds for our retirement, and it is important that we keep them where they belong for the long term. Fix whatever is out of balance in your life, even if it means making some drastic changes. Getting your balance, a mix between saving, investing, spending, and living comfortably, aligned correctly gives you the greatest opportunity to achieve some sort of financial success.

Continuity is especially important for two reasons. First, compounding creates wealth without work (or at least without a lot of work), and second, it provides you with the knowledge that whatever you are saving for—retirement, college, or something else—you can do so without pain.

Defined-contribution plans do this without any effort. Be sure to contribute at least your employer's matching contribution or, if you need a minimum baseline, at least 5 percent of pretax income. Make continuity really work for you by increasing those percentages with each pay raise or adding your bonus to the plan.

If you are using an IRA or other self-directed plan, have the money deducted from your checking account; if you get a tax refund, send it along each year as well. (Your tax refund should be as close to zero as possible, with the additional money that appears in each paycheck being added to that monthly deduction.) In this instance, no pain means more savings and, by default, more sleep.

The third piece of advice is how to allocate that one hour a month. You will not need to tweak your investments each and every month, and possibly not even every quarter. You are just reviewing how things are going. But each time you sit down with your financial life in front of you, look at it in total. You will not need a financial professional to do that, and I do not believe that many of us do.

If your life is so busy that you can't manage an hour a month, you probably can afford the 1 percent of your assets ($1 for every $100 invested; $1,000 of a $100,000 portfolio!) it will cost you to have a professional manage your portfolio. But few financial professionals look at what you already have and try to make it work. Instead, many will offer their products as an alternative to yours and suggest changes in where and how your money is allocated.

Investments are lumpy. They can be inconsistent and erratic. Actively managed funds may not beat their benchmarks year over year, but they may do so in the long run. Financial professionals, without any disrespect for these learned individuals, are focused on their own bottom line as much as on yours. Few of them are willing to be transparent, laying their financial lives bare for your scrutiny. In other words, they mostly subscribe to "do as I say, not as I do" thinking that could cost you unnecessary fees in addition to the fees the investments charge.

(Should you choose to use a financial professional, do it on a recommendation and use a person who is employed at a reputable brokerage house, such as Charles Schwab or Morgan Stanley. If at all possible, avoid storefront financial supermarkets that have a laundry list of products. You can get good insurance on your own. Mortgages are more complicated financially, but when it comes right down to it, it is the math of disaster: can I afford the mortgage if I lose my job? But investments and taxes, and protecting one from the other, sometimes require a professional, especially when you are dealing with large sums such as windfalls or pension and insurance payouts. Still, most of us will do just fine.)

The fourth idea has to do with that mental maniac I've mentioned in this book and others I have written. This person in your head wants to do all the wrong things at the wrong time. This may be the primary outward manifestation of that antagonistic investment gene.

On-air advisors will say, "Move to cash if you are nervous about the markets" or "Buy on the upward momentum." Both of these thoughts fly in the face of what good advice was meant to be. If you are nervous, moving to cash, a protectionist move designed to protect your gains from any further downtrend, might be good advice *if*, and that's a really big *if*, you can determine exactly when to move back in.

Let your mutual fund manager decide when to move to cash. Let her make the moves that will allow you to worry less. Her success is based on investor retention and the inflow of new money. I only wish that everyone, after having done the research before the purchase, would allow the fund manager to perform over a longer period of time rather than fleeing for the exits as soon as she hits a bump in the road. If you must move, move to an index fund, not out of the market altogether.

That maniac wants to buy on the upside and sell on the downside. Both can be accomplished with consistency—see lesson number two.

And the last piece of investment advice: take care of you. Save to enjoy, not to pay unnecessary medical bills. Using mutual funds will allow you to partition your various needs into several baskets. One might be used for medical costs that have yet to be determined, one might be for housing and related costs, and one might be for needed income. The success of your investment future lies in your ability to save more than your parents ever dreamed of and to adjust your expectations throughout your life. You may encounter a disappointment or two, a setback, or even a roadblock along the way. But if you follow these five simple rules, what's next will be something that you will be looking forward to, not regretting.

APPENDIX
Indexes and Funds

◆◆

Major Indexes

INDU	Dow Jones Industrial Average
SPX	S&P 500 Large Cap Index
OEX	S&P 100 Index
NDX	Nasdaq 100 Index
COMPQ	Nasdaq Composite
NYA	NYSE Composite Index
MID	S&P 400 MidCap Index
SML	S&P 600 SmallCap Index
RUI	Russell 1000 Index
RUT	Russell 2000 Index
RUA	Russell 3000 Index
TRAN	Dow Jones Transportation Average
UTIL	Dow Jones Utility Average
VLE	Value Line Arithmetic Index
XVG	Value Line Geometric Index

WLSH	Wilshire 5000 Index
WSX	Wilshire Small Cap Index
XAX	AMEX Composite
DJA	Dow Jones Composite Average
DJUS	Dow Jones US Broad Market Index
DJULTC	Dow Jones US Large Cap Technology Index
DJUSLW	Dow Jones US Low Cap Index
DJUSM	Dow Jones US Mid Cap Index
DJUSS	Dow Jones US Small Cap Index
DJUSTP	Dow Jones US Top Cap Index
GTX	GSCI Total Return
GTC	GSTI Composite Index
RLG	Russell 1000 Growth Index
RLV	Russell 1000 Value Index
RUO	Russell 2000 Growth Index
RUJ	Russell 2000 Value Index
RAG	Russell 3000 Growth Index
RAV	Russell 3000 Value Index
SGX	S&P/Barra Growth Index
SVX	S&P/Barra Value Index

Mutual Fund Families

AARP Mutual Funds, http://aarp.org

ABN AMRO Funds, http://www.abnamrofunds-usa.com

Accessor Funds, http://www.accessor.com

AGF Group of Funds, http://www.agf.com

AIM Funds, http://aim_funds.htm

Alger Funds, http://public.alger.com/Algerpub/content/show

Alliance Bernstein Funds, http://www.alliancebernstein.com/

Alpha Analytics Funds, http://www.alphaanalytics.com

Alpine Funds, http://www.alpinefunds.com

Amana Funds, http://www.amanafunds.com

American Century Funds, http://www.americancentury.com/funds/index.jsp

American Express—IDS Funds, http://finance.americanexpress.com

American Funds, http://american.htm

AMF Funds, http://www.shayassets.com/

AmSouth Funds, http://www.amsouthfunds.com

Aquila Funds, http://www.aquilafunds.com

Ariel Mutual Funds, http://www.arielmutualfunds.com

Armada Funds, http://www.armadafunds.com/Funds/default.asp

Artisan Funds, http://www.artisanfunds.com

AXA Rosenberg Funds, http://www.brmf.com

Badgley Funds, http://www.badgleyfunds.com

Baron Funds, http://www.baronfunds.com/default.asp?P=26437

Berkshire Funds, http://www.berkshirefunds.com

True Bishop Street Funds, http://www.bishopstreetfunds.com

BlackRock Funds, http://www1.blackrock.com

Bramwell Funds, http://www.bramwellfunds.com

Brandywine Funds, http://www.bfunds.com

Burgundy Funds (Canadian), http://www.burgundy-asset.com

Burnham Funds, http://www.burnhamfunds.com

California Investment Trust Funds, http://www.caltrust.com

Calvert Funds, http://www.calvertgroup.com/funds.html

CGM Funds, http://cgmfunds.com

Columbia Funds, http://www.columbiafunds.com

Credit Suisse Warburg Pincus Funds, http://www.warburgpincus.com

Delaware Investments, http://www.delawarefunds.com/Corporate/index.html

Dimensional Fund Advisors, http://www.dfafunds.com

Direxion Funds, http://www.direxionfunds.com

Dodge & Cox Funds, http://dodgeandcox.com/funds/index.html

Dreyfus Funds, http://www.dreyfus.com

Eclipse Funds, http://www.eclipsefund.com

Enterprise Group of Funds, http://www.enterprisefunds.com

Federated Investors, http://www.federatedinvestors.com/ffw/funds/default.asp

Fidelity Funds, http://fidelity.htm

59 Wall Street Funds, http://www.bbh.com/products/ws_overview.html

First Eagle Funds, http://www.mfea.com/AboutMFEA/AboutThisSite.asp

First Focus Funds, http://www.firstfocusfunds.com

First Investors Funds, http://www.firstinvestors.com

Firstar Funds, http://www.firstarfunds.com

Firsthand Funds, http://www.firsthandfunds.com/index.cfm?fuseaction=
funds. main

Forester Funds, http://www.forestervalue.com

Franklin Templeton, http://www.franklintempleton.com

Fremont Funds, http://www.fremontfunds.com

Gabelli Funds, http://www.gabelli.com/funds/fndlist.html

Goldman Sachs Mutual Funds, http://www.gs.com/client_services/asset_management/mutual_funds/u_s_funds.html

Green Century Funds, http://www.greencentury.com

Guardian Group of Funds, http://www.ggof.com/Content/FundFamilies/p_FundFamilyList.asp

Harbor Funds, http://www.harborfund.com/fundContent/fundHome.page

Hennessy Funds, http://www.hennessy-funds.com

Heritage Funds, http://www.heritagefunds.com

HighMark Funds, http://www.highmarkfunds.com

Huntington Funds, http://www.huntingtonfunds.com/investors/default.asp

ICAP Funds, http://www.nylim.com/mainstayfunds/0,2058,20_12008756,00.html

ICON Funds, http://www.iconfunds.com

IDEX Funds, http://www.idexfunds.com

Invesco Funds, http://www.invescofunds.com

J&B Funds, http://www.jbfunds.com

Jamestown Funds, http://www.jamestownfunds.com

Janus Funds, http://www.janus.com

John Hancock Mutual Funds, http://www.jhfunds.com

Jundt Funds, http://www.jundt.com

Kinetics Funds, http://www.kineticsfunds.com

Kobren Funds, http://www.kobren.com/funds

Legg Mason Funds, http://www.leggmasonfunds.com/index.asp

Liberty Funds, http://liberty.acornfunds.com

Mainstay Funds, http://www.nylim.com/mainstayfunds

Managers Funds, http://www.managersfunds.com

Marshall Funds, http://www.mibank.com

Masters' Select Funds, http://mastersfunds.com

Merrill Lynch Mutual Funds, http://www.mlim.ml.com/Template.asp?id=
AN4&fl=LN1&sl=LN1_1

MFS Funds, http://www.mfs.com

Monetta Mutual Funds, http://www.monetta.com

Northern Funds, http://www.northernfunds.com

NorthTrack Funds, http://www.northtrackfunds.com/funds.html

Nuveen Funds, http://www.nuveen.com/mutual_funds/mf/web/mutual_fund_
home.asp

Oakmark Family of Funds, http://www.oakmark.com

Oppenheimer Funds, http://www.oppenheimerfunds.com

Parnassus Funds, http://www.parnassus.com/index.php

PBHG Funds, http://www.pbhgfunds.com

Perritt Funds, http://www.perrittcap.com/funds/4/mutual-funds

Pioneer Funds, http://www.pioneerfunds.com

Principal Funds, http://www.principal.com/funds/index.htm

ProFunds, http://www.profunds.com/ProFundsInfo/default.fs

ProShares, http://www.proshares.com/funds

Prudential Mutual Funds, http://www.prudential.com/investments/
prumutualfunds

Putnam Funds, http://www.putnaminvestments.com/individual/index.html

Regions Funds, http://www.regions.com/personal_banking/mutual_funds.rf

Reserve Funds, http://www.reservefunds.com/ps/ps_mmf.shtml

RiverSource Funds, http://www.riversource.com/rvsc/investments/individual-investors/funds-performance/default.asp

Rockland Funds, http://www.rocklandfunds.com

Roulston Funds, http://www.roulstonfunds.com

Royal Mutual Funds, http://www.royalbank.com/rmf

RS Investments Funds, http://www.rsinvestments.com/funds/fundoverview.html

Rushmore Funds, http://www.rushmorefunds.com

Rydex Series Trust Funds, http://www.rydexfunds.com

Safeco Funds, http://www.safecofunds.com

Schwab Funds, http://www.schwabfunds.com/fundDetails.asp

Scudder Funds, http://funds.scudder.com/t/index.jhtml

Selected Funds, http://www.selectedfunds.com/snavs.html

Seligman Funds, http://www.seligman.com/individual/individual.htm

Sierra Club Funds, http://www.sierraclubfunds.com

Smith Barney Funds, http://www.salomonsmithbarney.com/products_services/mutual_funds

State Farm Funds, http://www.statefarm.com/mutual/funds.htm

Stratton Funds, http://www.strattonfunds.com/smf/smf_aboutus.shtml

Strong Funds, http://www.estrong.com/strongweb/strong/jsp/funds/index.jsp

SunAmerica Funds, http://www.sunamericafunds.com/sun/equityandincome.htm

TCW Galileo Funds, http://www.tcw.com

TD Mutual Funds (Canadian), http://www.tdefunds.com/eng/index_static. html

Third Avenue Funds, http://www.thirdavenuefunds.com/taf/mutual-funds.html

TIAA-CREF, http://www.tiaa-cref.org/products/mutual/index.html

T. Rowe Price, http://www.troweprice.com/common/index3/0,3011,lnp%
253D10094%2526cg%253D910%2526pgid%253D7155,00.html

USAA Funds, http://"https://ww3.usaa.com/gas_corp/CpStaticPages?PAGEID=
cp_prodsvcs

U.S. Global Investors, http://www.usfunds.com

Value Line, http://www.valueline.com

Van Wagoner Funds, http://www.vanwagoner.com/funds

Vanguard Funds, http://"/cs/fundfamilies/p/vanguard.htm

Victory Funds, http://www.victoryfunds.com

Vintage Funds, http://www.vintagefunds.com

Vontobel Funds, http://www.vusa.com/Mutual%20Funds

Waddell and Reed Funds, http://www.waddell.com/jsp/index.jsp?top=
1&side=2&inner=1&subinner=0&supersub=0&pagetitle=
Mutual+Funds&wdrid=waddell

Wells Fargo Funds, http://www.wellsfargo.com/per/investing/prod_svcs/
wf_fund/wf_fund.jhtml

Westcore Funds, http://www.westcore.com

William Blair Funds, http://www.wmblair.com/pages/wbfunds_home.asp

WisdomTree Funds, http:/wisdom_tree.htm

Exchange-Traded Fund Families

Bank of New York: BLDRs (http://www.bldrsfunds.com)

Barclays Global Investors: iShares ETFs (http://www.ishares.com)

Claymore Securities: Claymore ETFs (http://www.claymore.com/etf/public/etf/
etfhome.aspx)

First Trust Advisors: First Trust ETFs (http://www.ftadvisors.com/retail/Pages/
products/etflist.aspx)

Invesco PowerShares Capital Management: PowerShares ETFs (http://www.powershares.com)

Merrill Lynch: HOLDRs (http://www.holdrs.com/holdrs/main/index.asp)

ProFunds Group: ProShares ETFs (http://www.proshares.com)

Rydex Investments: Rydex ETFs (http://www.rydexfunds.com)

State Street Global Advisors: SPDRs, streetTRACKS (http://www.streettracks.com)

Van Eck Global: Market Vectors ETFs (http://www.vaneck.com/etf/index.cfm?cat=3000)

Vanguard: Vanguard ETFs (http://flagship2.vanguard.com/VGApp/hnw/FundsVIPER?gh_sec=n")

Wisdom Tree Investments: Wisdom Tree ETFs (http://www.wisdomtree.com)

XShares Advisors: HealthShares ETFs (http://www.healthsharesinc.com)

Glossary of Investment Terms

Aggressive Growth—An investment strategy that accepts higher risk and volatility, investing in stocks that offer rapid growth potential or employing risky trading strategies.

Appreciation—An increase in the value of a fund or other asset from the time of purchase.

Asset—Anything of value owned by a business or individual.

Asset Allocation—An investment strategy that seeks to achieve both income and capital appreciation. To do this, the fund uses a combination of stocks, bonds, and cash to achieve the best overall return. Asset allocation funds are not tied to a specific asset ratio. A balanced fund (fixed allocation) differs because it maintains a fixed percentage of stocks to bonds.

Balanced Fund—A mutual fund that strives for stability by maintaining a constant ratio of equity to debt securities, usually 60 percent/40 percent. Also called *fixed allocation*.

Bear Market—A market that is generally experiencing negative investor sentiment. The result of such thinking is to depress the prices in that market.

Beta—A portfolio's or a stock's relationship to how the market is doing as a whole. A *zero beta* means that the investment is independent of the market's moves. A *positive beta* (above zero) illustrates the ability of the investment to move with the market, whether the market moves up or down. A *negative beta* (below zero) suggests that investment will fall even if the market rises.

Bid or Sell Price—The current net asset value of a fund when the shares are bought back by the fund (redeemed).

Blue Chip—The common stock of a large company with a record of stable growth and earnings over an extended period.

Bond—An agreement between a borrower (company, municipality, or government agency) and a lender (the bond investor). In exchange for the debt security, the issuer promises to repay the loan amount on a specified maturity date and, in most instances, makes periodic interest payments to the bondholder over the life of the loan.

Breakpoint—The dollar value at which the sales charge percentage changes in a schedule of load fees. Typically, a sales charge schedule contains five or six breakpoints, with the commission declining as the number of dollars invested rises.

Broker/Dealer (or Dealer)—A professional company that is licensed to buy and sell securities, acting as a market go-between for investors. These companies sell a wide variety of securities, including mutual funds.

Bull Market—A market that is generally experiencing positive investor sentiment. This good feeling often pushes the prices in a particular market higher in a sustainable fashion.

Capital—What a business or investor is worth. It includes the material assets of a business, including plant and equipment, inventories, cash, receivables, and so on.

Capital Gains—The profits realized from the sale of securities (stocks, bonds, mutual funds, and so on) that have appreciated while they were held by the investor. *Long-term capital gains* are from securities held for more than one year; *short-term capital gains* are from securities held for one year or less.

Capital Gains Distribution—Payment to investment company shareholders of realized capital gains on shares held. If the fund sells some of its underlying securities during the course of a quarter or trading year, and if those securities gained in value from the original investment, a capital gain is realized. Many mutual funds distribute those gains (creating a taxable situation on taxable funds). Shareholders can opt to reinvest those gains.

Capital Gains Tax Rates—The rates at which capital gains are taxed. Under present law, all short-term capital gains are taxed as ordinary income. For long-term capital gains, the maximum tax rate for individuals, estates, and trusts is guaranteed by law not to exceed 15 percent through 2010; if that law expires, these rates can be as high as 39.6 percent, the tax rate on ordinary income. *See* Capital Gains.

Capital Growth—The increase in the market value of securities.

Certificate of Deposit—A bank or thrift note guaranteeing that a sum of money will be held by the bank for a fixed period of time and will earn a prearranged interest rate.

Check-Writing Privilege—The ability to write a check and have the money drawn from an investment account, such as a money market fund. The holdings will continue to earn dividends until the checks are cleared.

Closed-End Fund—A fund that has a fixed number of shares to offer to the public and, because of this, trades based on supply and investor interest. These funds are managed but do not redeem shares.

Closed-End Investment Company—An investment company that trades on the open market and holds a fixed number of shares in the form of investments as stated in its objective. The market value of the closed-end fund will usually differ from the value of its holdings.

Closed-Up Fund—An open-end investment company that trades actively but does not accept deposits from new investors. It may continue to invest the money of current shareholders and allow those shareholders to reinvest. The reasons for closing a fund are numerous, but the most common is that investor interest in the fund (deposits) has outpaced investment opportunities.

Commission—A fee paid by an investor to a broker or other sales agent for investment advice and/or assistance.

Common Stock—A type of stock that represents partial ownership of a corporation. Each share comes with voting rights. Owners of common stock rank below the company's creditors (bond and debt holders) and holders of preferred stock in the event of bankruptcy or sale.

Common Stock Fund—An investment fund that maintains a portfolio consisting primarily of common stocks.

Compounding—The payment of interest on an investment. When interest is reinvested, each subsequent interest payment is based on the principal (the original investment) and the interest earned in all previous years. Over time, compounding can produce significant growth in the value of an investment.

Contingent Deferred Sales Charge (CDSC)—A fee that is payable when shares are redeemed. Also called *trailers* or *redemption fee. See* Load Fee.

Contractual Plan—A type of accumulation plan in which the total intended investment amount and the periodic payments required to reach that amount are specified at the time of purchase. The sales charge is based on the total amount to be invested, and usually is deducted from the initial payments.

Contrarians—Investors who move against major market trends at any given time, hoping, by so doing, to uncover undiscovered opportunities.

Controlled Affiliate—A company in which 25 percent or more of the outstanding voting securities are controlled by one source, as stipulated in the Investment Company Act of 1940.

Conversion Privilege—*See* Exchange Privilege.

Conversion Ratio—The specified rate of exchange from preferred stocks or bonds into common stock, as determined when a convertible security is issued.

Convertible Securities—Preferred stocks or bonds that give the investor the right to exchange them into given amounts of common stock before a specified date. Investors are paid a premium for these securities.

Corporate (Master or Prototype) Retirement Plan—A corporate or trust agreement that qualifies for special tax treatment because the company is investing for the benefit of its employees. Prototype plans typically take the form of pension or profit-sharing plans; 401(k) plans are also offered.

Credit Risk—A grade given to the issuer of a debt security based on the possibility that the issuer may not be able to pay the interest and/or repay its debt.

Current Liabilities—Obligations due within one year or less.

Custodian—A bank or trust company that holds all the securities and cash owned by an investment company. In some cases, the custodian acts as transfer agent and dividend disbursing agent, although it has no supervisory function with regard to portfolio policies. *Custodian* can also refer to an adult representative for a minor owner of a particular portfolio or fund.

Cyclical Stock—A type of stock that is tied closely to the current state of the economy. Stocks of companies in some industries suffer more than others during economic downtrends and benefit more from upswings in the economy. Air travel and large household goods often swing during a cyclical market.

Death Benefit—The amount guaranteed to the survivors or beneficiaries of a contract if the annuitant dies before the annuitization date; it is contingent upon several factors.

Defined-Benefit Pension Plan—*See* Pension Plan.

Defined-Contribution Plan—A self-directed company-sponsored retirement plan under which the employee directs the size and the amount of his or her contributions. These plans are referred to by the section of the tax code in which they are discussed: 401(k), 403(b), or 457.

Depreciation—A decrease in the value of a security or other asset since its purchase.

Discount Rate—The rate at which the Federal Reserve lends money to banks, which, in turn, guides commercial banks in establishing their loan rates for customers. .

Diversification—Using a number of different security issues to insulate a portfolio (spread the risk) from a painful drop in one market area. This is a risk-reducing strategy based on the wisdom of not "keeping all of your eggs in one basket."

Diversified Investment Company—A fund that has *not* invested more than 5 percent of its total assets in any single company and does *not* hold more than 10 percent of the outstanding voting securities of any company, as stipulated in the Investment Company Act of 1940.

Dividend—A distribution of income to holders of common or preferred stock. In a mutual fund, dividends are often reinvested, but they can create a taxable situation in some funds.

Dollar Cost Averaging—A method of accumulating capital by investing equal amounts of money at regular intervals. This is an attempt to dodge the ups and downs in the markets and the feeling that you, as an investor, should react. The purchase of more shares when the trading price is low and fewer shares when the price rises has the net effect of creating an account in which the collective shares are bought at an average price rather than at a particular moment. This helps the investor avoid trades when the market could be skewed, and in the process reduces the need to time the market correctly.

Dual-Purpose Fund—A type of closed-end investment company, originally developed in England and introduced in the United States in 1967, designed to serve the needs of two distinct types of investors: (1) those who are interested only in income, and (2) those who are interested only in capital growth. Two separate classes of shares are issued.

Duration—A gauge of price sensitivity to interest rates, expressed in years. Duration shows the weighted average time required for an investor to realize the currently stated yield.

Earnings Per Share (EPS)—Profits divided by the number of outstanding shares of stock.

Emerging Markets—Developing nations, usually defined by gross domestic product and various economic measures. Most of these new markets are in Latin America, Eastern Europe, and Asia (excluding Japan). Funds that invest in emerging markets can be high risk.

Equity—Stock holdings.

Equity-Income—An investment strategy that involves seeking income through investments in dividend-producing stock. These funds tend to be more conservative in nature, investing in older dividend-paying companies.

Equity Security—Technically, any security conferring an ownership interest, although the term is often used to describe common stocks as a stand-alone investment. It may even be used to describe preferred stocks that behave like common stocks.

Exchange Privilege—The right to exchange shares of one open-end fund for shares of another within the same family of funds without incurring new sales charges. This is important for investors, since it means that if their objectives change, they can switch funds without cost.

Expense Ratio—Total annual operating expenses as a percentage of net assets.

Face-Amount Certificate (Face Value)—A promise by the issuer of a security to pay the certificate (bond) holder a stated amount at a future date. The security may be purchased through periodic payments (installment type) or a single payment (fully paid).

Fair Value—A term that can mean a variety of things. It can refer to the esti-mated value of all the assets and liabilities of an acquired company. Account-ing for these values allows the purchasing company to consolidate the financial statements of the two companies. It can refer to a futures market event, where the fair value is the equilibrium price for a futures contract. On television, the "fair value" is a measure of possible investor sentiment. It monitors the rela-tionship between the futures contract on a market index and the actual value of that index. If the futures are above fair value, then traders are betting that the market index will go higher. If the futures are below fair value, it indicates the possibility of a down day in the markets. Finally, fair value can be a value determined by the board of directors for those securities and assets that do not have a market quotation readily available, as stipulated in the Investment Company Act of 1940.

Federal Funds Rate—The rate that Federal Reserve member banks charge each other for overnight loans needed to meet reserve requirements.

Fiduciary—A person or entity who has custody of the assets of another. This responsibility can fall on your employer, your retirement account administra-tor, or the financial professional that you hire.

Fixed-Income Security—A debt security or preferred stock that has a stated percentage or dollar income return.

Forward Pricing—Pricing mutual fund shares for sale, repurchase, or redemp-tion at the price computed after the receipt of an order. Pricing is usually done once or twice a day.

401(k) Plan—An employer-sponsored retirement plan that enables employ-ees to make tax-deferred contributions from their salaries to the plan.

403(b) Plan—An employer-sponsored retirement plan that enables employ-ees of universities, public schools, and nonprofit organizations to make tax-deferred contributions from their salaries to the plan.

457 Plan—An employer-sponsored retirement plan that enables employees of state and local governments and other tax-exempt employers to make tax-deferred contributions from their salaries to the plan.

Free Partial Withdrawal—The percentage of the investor's account values, earnings, premiums, or the greatest of some or all of these three that investors are allowed to withdraw free of surrender charges during a specific period of time.

Fully Managed Fund—A fund without restrictions on the securities that may be held, giving the portfolio manager maximum discretion with regard to all investments.

Fund of Funds—An investment company that invests in other investment companies.

Government Agency Issues—Debt securities issued by government-sponsored enterprises, federal agencies, and international institutions. These securities are not direct obligations of the Treasury but involve government sponsorship or guarantees, such as those on GNMA (Ginnie Mae) or FNMA (Fannie Mae) securities.

Growth Stock—A stock that has had better-than-average growth in earnings and is expected to continue to grow. Companies of this type keep investors interested by discovering additional resources, developing new products, or expanding their current exposure in the markets.

Hedge—A method used to offset a potential gain or loss by using a security that has offsetting qualities. For example, an inflation hedge would rise in value as inflation rises, counterbalancing the erosion in value normally expected as a result of inflation.

Hedge Fund—An investment company that, as a regular policy, hedges its market commitments. It does this by holding securities that it believes are likely to increase in value and at the same time shorting securities that it believes are likely to decrease in value. This is an aggressive approach to capital appreciation, and the number of investors in the fund is limited. This type of trading is done outside of hedge funds in 130/30 funds.

Incentive Compensation—A performance-based fee paid to an investment company advisor. If the fund's performance improves relative to specified market indexes, the fee is paid to the advisor. It is also sometimes called a *fulcrum fee*.

Income—Money earned through dividends or interest (but not capital gains). Gross income is the total amount of money earned, while net income is the gross income minus expenses, fixed charges, and taxes. Also referred to as *net investment income*. The word suggests a more conservative investment strategy that focuses its efforts on capital preservation rather than on appreciation.

Income Fund—A fund whose primary objective is generating income.

Incubator Fund—A private, closed fund used by an investment company to introduce a new trading style or method before offering shares to the public. An incubator fund is generally used during the period before a hedge fund is launched, in order to prove to investors that a particular strategy works.

Individual Retirement Account (IRA)—A tax-deferred retirement program for individuals, established under the Employee Retirement Income Security Act of 1974. The limit on contributions to an IRA in 2008 is $5,000 per individual, $6,000 for an investor over 50. In the following years, increases in the contribution limits will be indexed to inflation. IRAs do not fall into the category of defined-contribution plans.

There are, however, numerous other types of contribution rules for people using traditional IRAs, all of which can be found at the IRS Web site (http://www.irs.gov/publications/p590/ar01.html#d0e124).

Inflation—An upward movement in the price level of goods and services that results in a decline in the purchasing power of money. Such increases decrease spending power, slowing the economy. Inflation also acts as a negative force on your investments, decreasing their value.

Insured Redemption Value Plan—An insurance program designed to protect investors against loss in long-term mutual fund investments.

Investment Advisor—*See* Investment Management Company.

Investment Category—The stated purpose or goal of an investment company. It is often readily identifiable in the fund's name. I often refer to it in the book as the charter.

Investment Company—A corporation or trust through which investors pool their money to obtain supervision and diversification of their investments. This is a mutual fund.

Investment Company Act of 1940—A federal statute enacted by Congress in 1940 for the registration and regulation of investment companies.

Investment Management Company—An organization employed by an investment company to advise and supervise the assets of the investment company (also called *investment advisor*).

Investment Trust—*See* Investment Company.

Issuer—With reference to investment company securities, the company itself.

Keogh Plan—A tax-saving retirement program for self-employed persons and their employees. Also known as an H.R. 10 plan or a self-employed retirement plan, the Keogh plan comes in two types. The defined-benefit plan requires the participant to determine how much she or he would like to withdraw upon retirement. Those numbers are crunched (an actuarial formula is used to calculate the percentage of contributions based on the life expectancy of the plan participant, the amount the participant desires, and the number of years left to contribute before retirement), and the company or the employee makes the needed deposit.

The other kind of Keogh plan uses a defined-contribution format, also using two separate contribution methods: a profit-sharing plan and a money purchase plan. The contribution to the profit-sharing plan depends on the profits of the business. During lean years, this allows the owners to skip a payment to the plan. With the money purchase plan, a set percentage is contributed every year without fail, with no allowance for a company's profits or losses. The maximum deduction limit is 25 percent.

Large Cap—Stocks with an average market capitalization greater than $5 billion. This category includes any company in the S&P 500 index. Many of these stocks are considered blue chips.

Leverage—Borrowing money to invest in hopes of achieving greater returns on the new securities. This simultaneously adds debt and builds assets.

Leverage Stock—A junior security of a multiple-capital-structure company; generally common stock, but the term may also apply to a warrant or to a preferred stock established with loans.

Liquid—Assets that are easily convertible into cash or exchangeable for other values. Lack of liquidity adds to the risk of an investment. The term also refers to the financial ability of a company to raise money for growth or acquisitions.

Living Trust—A trust instrument made effective during the lifetime of the creator, in contrast to a testamentary trust, which is created under a will.

Load Fee—A sales charge. *Front-end load* is a sales charge imposed at the time of purchase. *Back-end load* refers to a sales charge imposed at the time of redemption. *Level load* refers to a single front- or back-end sales charge without breakpoints or a 12b–1 fee greater than 1.25 percent imposed annually. *No load* means that a fund does not charge the investor any front, back, or level sales charges.

Management Fee—The fee paid by an investment company to a management company for portfolio supervision and advisory services. *See also* Incentive Compensation.

Market Capitalization—The market value of a fund or stock, basically calculated by multiplying the market value of each share by the number of shares outstanding, although there are other factors that enter into the equation. It is used to determine the financial size of a company and how it fits into a particular category (or index).

Market Price—The price at which an investor is willing to buy or sell a security on the open market. This is the offer (bid/ask) price for closed-end funds.

Maturity—The date on which a debt obligation will pay its face value.

Maturity, Average—The average time until all of the securities held by a fund fully mature.

Micro Cap—Stocks with an average market capitalization of less than $500 million. These stocks are often thinly traded and are considered a high-risk investment.

Mid Cap Stocks with between $1 billion and $5 billion market capitalization. Some indexes understand that the difference between large-cap and mid-cap stocks (and between mid-cap and small-cap stocks) can often be blurred as a result of market changes.

Modern Portfolio Theory—A statistical method of analyzing investments by comparing their return and risk characteristics to each other rather than looking at the possible risk and return of a single stock. This helps the investor to diversify and to establish benchmarks. Diversification lowers the overall risk in a portfolio by using offsetting investments, one risky and the other not so risky.

Money Market Fund—A mutual fund that invests exclusively in short-term debt securities with the intent of maximizing liquidity, preserving capital, and producing current income. These funds typically maintain a stable net asset value of $1.

Multisector Bond—A type of fund that uses investors' money to purchase a wide variety of bonds, foreign or domestic, government or corporate, investment grade or high yield.

Mutual Fund—*See* Investment Company.

National Association of Securities Dealers (NASD)—A self-regulatory organization of brokers and dealers that regulates over-the-counter securities markets to prevent fraud and to protect investors.

Net Assets—The dollar amount of all resources at market value less current liabilities.

Net Asset Value (NAV)—The market price of an open-end mutual fund. The NAV is the value of all assets divided by the number of outstanding shares. For open-end funds, this is the daily price at which an investor can buy or sell shares. It is set at the close of each trading day and posted by 4 p.m. EST.

Net Cash Inflow/Outflow—The change in the amount of money entering or leaving a fund during a specific time period. It is the difference between what comes into the fund (inflow) and what leaves the fund as investors withdraw or sell their investments (outflow). It is a good indicator of a fund's popularity with investors.

No-Load Fund—A fund that does not have sales charges. *See* Load Fee.

Nondiversified Investment Company—*See* Diversified Investment Company.

Nonqualified Plans—Retirement plans that, under a tax ruling by the IRS, do not meet the requirements of the Self-Employed Individuals Tax Retirement Act or the Internal Revenue Code Section 401(a), 403(a), or 403(b).

Nontaxable Dividend—A dividend generally disbursed by tax-exempt bonds such as municipal bonds, or other tax-exempt investments such as general obligation (GO) bonds, revenue bonds, and industrial revenue bonds.

Objective—A clearly stated (in the case of the individual investor), widely published (in the case of a fund manager) goal that describes how the investor or manager seeks to grow capital, enhance current income, control the stability of invested capital, or any combination of these.

Odd Lot—A number of shares that is not a round lot (normally 100 shares) and therefore may incur higher exchange costs than a round lots. Not applicable to open-end investment companies.

Open Account—An account in which shareholders have reinvestment privileges along with the right to make additional purchases without a formal accumulation plan.

Open-End Investment Company—An investment company whose shares are redeemable at any time at approximate asset value. In most cases, new shares are offered for sale continuously.

Optional Distribution—An arrangement that gives a shareholder the choice of receiving distributions (capital gains or dividends) in cash or having them reinvested to purchase more shares. A cash distribution creates a taxable event, while reinvestment postpones it.

Par Value—The amount that the issuer of a fixed-income security promises to pay upon maturity. While price and yield may fluctuate, par value is what the underlying security is worth. Also known as the *face value* or *maturity value*.

Payroll Deduction Plan—An arrangement between a fund, an employer, and an employee to deduct a specified amount of money from the employee's salary to purchase shares in a fund.

Pension Plan—A program established by an employer, union, or other member-based organization to pay benefits to an employee/member upon retirement. This type of program has its roots in loyalty. An employee who leaves the company cannot take the pension with him or her. This type of program is also called a *defined-benefit plan,* as it gives the employee a fixed retirement payment based on number of years worked and wages earned.

Pension Portability—An arrangement allowing an employee to sever ties with the company before retirement by giving him or her the ability to move accumulated assets from a pension plan to an individual retirement account or other qualified retirement plan.

Pension Rollover—The opportunity to take distributions from a qualified pension or profit-sharing plan and, within 60 days of the distribution, reinvest them in an individual retirement account. Under current law, investors who do not transfer distributions to a qualified account within 60 days will be assessed a 20 percent withholding tax plus a 10 percent penalty for early withdrawal. By rolling over distributions, employees can defer taxes on the pension to a later date and adjust the amount of money (distribution) needed in retirement.

Portfolio—The collection of securities owned by an individual investor or an institution (such as a mutual fund); it may include stocks, bonds, and money market securities.

Portfolio Manager—A specialist employed by a mutual fund's advisor to invest the fund's assets in accordance with predetermined investment objectives.

Portfolio Turnover—A measure of the trading activity in a fund's investment portfolio that monitors how often securities are bought and sold by a fund. It is expressed as a percentage. A 100 percent turnover suggests that all of the stocks in the portfolio were traded over the course of a year. A 150 percent turnover suggests that all of the investments were traded during a 6-month period. A 50 percent turnover suggests that the fund held the underlying stocks for 18 months.

Preferred Stock—An equity security that generally carries a fixed dividend and whose claim to earnings and assets ranks ahead of common stock but behind bonds. Preferred stock is more common in older, established companies.

Premium—The amount above asset value at which shares of a stock or closed-end fund sell (often expressed as a percentage), or the percentage above conversion value at which a convertible preferred stock or bond sells. In closed-end funds, it is the difference between the market price and the portfolio value.

Prepayment Risk—The possibility that a bond owner will receive his or her principal investment back from the issuer prior to the bond's maturity date. This can create a reinvestment event that the fixed-income investor had not planned for.

Price/Book Ratio—The market price divided by stockholders' equity (assets minus liabilities). The ratio shows how much investors are willing to pay for each dollar of the company's net assets.

Price/Earnings Ratio—The market price divided by profit. It shows how much investors are willing to pay for each dollar of the company's earnings.

Principal—*See* Par Value.

Profit-Sharing Retirement Plan—A retirement program in which a company contributes a percentage of its annual gross profit to participating employees. In a Keogh plan, the earnings of the self-employed individual are substituted for gross profit.

Prospectus—An official document that describes investment policy, fees, risks, management, and other pertinent fund information as directed by the Securities and Exchange Commission. A prospectus must accompany any new offer to sell securities and should be read carefully. These are generally available electronically and are getting simpler to read and better organized.

Proxy Statement—An agreement transferring the voting rights of an investment to another person (with mutual funds, usually the fund) if the stockholder will not attend the stockholders' meeting.

Prudent Man Rule—As stated by Judge Samuel Putnum in 1830: "Those with responsibility to invest money for others should act with prudence, discretion, intelligence, and regard for the safety of capital as well as income." This law limits the investments in a fiduciary account to those that a "prudent" investor managing his own affairs would make, thus limiting the power of the trustee.

Qualified Plans—Retirement plans that meet the requirements of Section 401(a), 403(a), or 403(b) of the Internal Revenue Code or the Self-Employed Individuals Tax Retirement Act. For instance, holding a Roth IRA more than five years until it is qualified allows you to take a distribution under a rule that amended the Taxpayer Relief Act of 1997 and is referred to as TTCA–98.

R^2—A measure of diversification that indicates how closely a particular fund's performance parallels that of an appropriate market benchmark over a period. The market is understood to have an R^2 of 100 percent. Therefore, a fund with an R^2 of 85 percent contains 85 percent of the market's diversification and risk. The remaining 15 percent is the result of the fund manager's actions.

Realized—The appreciation or depreciation of a security between the time when it is bought and the time when it is redeemed. If a stock price increases from $50 to $100 and the shares are sold, the appreciation is realized and the investor receives his or her money. If the shares are not sold, the appreciation is *unrealized* because it exists only on paper. A security that loses value is said to have depreciated, and the loss may be realized or unrealized in the same manner.

Record Date—The date by which a shareholder must be registered on an investment company's books in order to receive a dividend.

Redeem—To sell shares in a fund back to the fund. This can be done on any business day, and the price you receive for the sale reflects the current share price (net asset value) less any redemption fees and deferred sales charges.

Redemption in Kind—The redemption of investment company shares for something other than cash, such as other securities. This is permissible in many mutual funds and tax-free exchange funds.

Redemption Price—The price at which an investor sells securities, i.e., redeems securities for cash. *See* Bid Price as applicable to open-end investment companies.

Registered Investment Company—An investment company that has filed a registration statement with the Securities and Exchange Commission under the requirements of the Investment Company Act of 1940.

Registrar—Generally a banking institution that maintains the list of the shareholders and the number of shares they hold.

Regulated Investment Company—An investment company that has elected to qualify for the special tax treatment provided by Subchapter M of the Internal Revenue Code; not to be confused with registration under the Investment Company Act of 1940.

Reinvestment Privilege—The ability to automatically reinvest distributions into additional full and fractional shares. This service is offered by most mutual funds and some closed-end investment companies.

Repurchase Agreement—The temporary transfer of a security to another person, with the understanding that ownership will revert at a future time and price. This "renting" of a debt security fixes the yield while it is held by the purchaser and insulates the return from market fluctuations during the temporary ownership.

Repurchases—In closed-end companies, the company's voluntary open-market purchases of its own securities. For open-end companies, the stock taken back at approximate asset value.

Restricted Security—A portfolio security that is not available to the public at large, as securities must be registered with the Securities and Exchange

Commission before they may be sold publicly; frequently referred to as a *private placement* or *letter stock.*

Risk—A complicated and personal evaluation of market tolerance that is used to determine how much the investor is willing to "gamble" on a certain set of existing information. Often, risk is the determining factor in how much (or little) reward will come from a particular investment or event.

Rollover—An important tax event that must be done in a timely manner. When moving funds from one qualified retirement investment to another, the investor can avoid tax liabilities. Once the investor receives money in hand, he or she must move it to another qualified account within 60 days or be assessed a 20 percent withholding tax plus a 10 percent penalty for early withdrawal. If the investor does not touch the money but has it moved from custodian to custodian, it is called a direct transfer. *See* Pension Rollover.

Round Lot—A fixed unit of trading (usually 100 shares) that forms the basis for prevailing commission rates on a securities exchange.

Sales Charge—*See* Load Fee.

Securities and Exchange Commission (SEC)—An independent agency of the U.S. government that administers securities transaction laws. For a full description of what this agency does, visit its Web site at http://www.sec.gov.

Selling Charge or Sales Commission—A fee paid at the time of purchase to a broker or financial advisor for the service of selling the fund, generally stated as a percentage of the offering price. *See* Load Fee.

Senior Capital—*See* Senior Securities.

Senior Securities—Securities (notes, bonds, debentures, or preferred stock) that have a claim on earnings and assets ranking ahead of that of common stock. Should a company liquidate, the claims of the holders of senior securities rank above those of the holders of junior securities because the company's creditors receive compensation before its owners.

Separate Account—An account that is completely separated from the general account of an insurance company, since its assets are generally invested in common stocks.

Shareholder Experience—A measure of the investment returns on a mutual fund, usually expressed in terms of a hypothetical $10,000 investment and including sales charges that a potential investment might face.

Sharpe Ratio—A measure of the portfolio returns compared to total risk. A higher value indicates a greater return per unit of risk. Risk in this calculation is provided by the portfolio's standard deviation. Sharpe ratios cannot stand alone, and can be effective only when used in comparison to other portfolios or securities.

Short Sale—The sale of a security that is not owned in the hope that the price will go down and it can be repurchased at a profit. The person making a short sale borrows stock in order to make delivery to the buyer, and must eventually repurchase the stock in order to return it to the lender.

Small Cap—Stocks with an average market capitalization between $500 million and $1 billion. These are considered high-risk investments because of their unpredictable growth, lack of liquidity, or thin trading. Some indexes provide for overlap between mid-cap and small-cap stocks and between small-cap and micro-cap stocks based on market valuations at any one moment.

Special Situation—An investment in distressed or undervalued securities, including restructurings, venture capital, mergers, reorganizations, and so on.

Specialty or Specialized Fund—Investment company offerings that are usually concentrated in a specific industry group, such as technology, natural resources, or gold. Also referred to as *sector funds*.

Split Funding—An arrangement that combines an investment in mutual fund shares and the purchase of life insurance contracts, such as under an individual Keogh plan.

Standard Deviation—A statistical measure of the month-to-month volatility of a fund's returns. When a fund has a high standard deviation, this usually indicates a greater variation from a benchmark. For example, if the standard deviations for Fund A and Fund B are 6.0 and 3.0, respectively, then Fund A will have a variation from its benchmark that is twice that of Fund B. Money market funds, which have stable asset values and low risk, have standard deviations of near zero.

Standardized Return—Return net of all fees, calculated according to Form N–4 as required by SEC rule 482.

Statement of Additional Information (SAI)—A supplementary document to a prospectus that contains more detailed information about a mutual fund that some investors find useful. The prospectus usually contains all of the needed information, but this statement, also known as "Part B" of the prospectus, can shed additional light on the fund's operation. This must be provided free of charge if you request it.

Subchapter M—The section of the Internal Revenue Code that provides special tax treatment for regulated investment companies.

Surrender Charge—Expressed as a percentage of assets, the charge that an insurance company assesses clients when they surrender all or part of their contract; similar to a contingent deferred sales charge.

Swap Fund—*See* Tax-Free Exchange Fund.

Tax-Free Exchange Fund—An investment company that permits investors with securities that have appreciated to exchange them for shares of the fund while avoiding capital gains taxes.

Total Return—An investment strategy that strives for both capital appreciation and current income and is generally considered to be more conservative than growth-oriented. The performance of a total return fund is calculated assuming reinvestment of all income and capital gains distributions.

Trustee—A party with the responsibility to delegate and administer assets for the benefit of others.

Turnover Ratio—A measure of the change in portfolio holdings; the extent to which an investment company's portfolio changes during a year. A rough calculation can be made by dividing the lesser of portfolio purchases or sales by average assets. This is done to eliminate the effects of net sales or redemption of fund shares.

12b–1 Fee—A fee covering marketing and distribution costs, named after the 1980 Securities and Exchange Commission rule that permits it.

Uncertified Shares—The ownership of fund shares credited to a shareholder's account without the issuance of actual stock certificates.

Unit Trust—An investment company or contractual plan that has a fixed portfolio, as opposed to the changeable portfolio available in open-end or closed-end funds.

Valuation Date—The day on which the value of a separate account is determined.

Value Investing—The strategy of buying securities that are believed to have a market price below their actual or potential worth. Warren Buffett and Benjamin Graham are among the most famous investors using this method.

Volatility—The price fluctuation of a security. This can be measured in various ways, most commonly by standard deviation and beta.

Voluntary—An accumulation plan without any stated duration or specific requirements as to the total amount to be invested, although conditions may be set on the minimum amount invested on each occasion. Sales charges are applicable to each purchase made.

Warrant—An option to buy a specified number of shares of the issuing company's stock at a specified price, often in the form of put or call options. Warrants become tradable securities with values determined by the performance of the underlying security.

Withdrawal—For a shareholder in an open-end fund, the option of receiving periodic payments from his or her account. These payments may be more or less than investment income during that time period and therefore may imply the selling of shares.

Yield—For stocks, the percentage income return, derived by comparing dividends to market price and capital gains. For bonds, the interest rate. In bond investments, the yield moves in the opposite direction from the price.

Yield to Maturity—The rate of return on a debt security that is held to maturity, including both appreciation and interest.

Index

About the Author

~~~

Paul Petillo is founder and managing editor of BlueCollarDollar.com. He is the author of *Building Wealth in a Paycheck-to-Paycheck World, Investing for the Utterly Confused,* and *Retirement Planning for the Utterly Confused.*